TIME OF THE BELLS

TIMB

Volume Two of a Planned Series on the
Historic Birthplace of California

THE HISTORY OF SAN DIEGO

OF THE BELLS

Written By
RICHARD F. POURADE

EDITOR EMERITUS, THE SAN DIEGO UNION

Commissioned By
JAMES S. COPLEY

CHAIRMAN OF THE CORPORATION, THE COPLEY PRESS, INC.

Published By The Union-Tribune Publishing Company

FIRST PRINTING NOVEMBER 1961

SECOND PRINTING FEBRUARY 1964

FIRST VOLUME, THE HISTORY OF SAN DIEGO. *"THE EXPLORERS"* WRITTEN BY RICHARD
F. POURADE COMMISSIONED BY JAMES S. COPLEY PUBLISHED, 1960, BY THE UNION-
TRIBUNE PUBLISHING CO. SAN DIEGO, CALIFORNIA

CONTENTS

LIST OF ILLUSTRATIONS

DEDICATION

The story of the Missions in California vividly recalls lines from the poem, "El Camino Real" by Thomas Shelley Sutton:

> *From a Day that is gone,*
> *To a goal that is deathless and fair.*
> *'Tis a vision of vanishing sorrow,*
> *Of Faith that is stranger to Fear.*
> *'Tis the Road of a Greater Tomorrow.*

From history we get a continuity of faith, beliefs and culture. But unless we understand the heritages of history, they mean nothing and cannot help or influence us in the making of a better tomorrow.

It is my hope that the pages of this book will bring inspiration from our past to shape our lives in a Faith that "is stranger to Fear" for the realization of man's greatest dream . . . a world free from want and a lasting peace.

JAMES S. COPLEY

THE BACKGROUND

"Time of the Bells" is the second book in a series on the history of the Southwest as it unfolded from San Diego, the gateway to California for Spain and Mexico and, in time, the United States. Each volume will be complete in itself.

The first book, "The Explorers," began the unfolding of the story, telling in words and illustrations of the discoveries and explorations, from Hernán Cortés to Juan Bautista de Anza, which opened the way to the first settlement of California. "Time of the Bells" is about the mission period, or the years of the Franciscan domination of California, from 1769 to 1835. Subsequent books will deal with successive historic periods.

The series originated with James S. Copley, Chairman of the Corporation, The Copley Press, Inc., who felt that too many of us were growing away from our past. Much of the story as possible is being told in the words of those who wrote it, as taken from their journals, diaries and correspondence, and thus the past comes alive with the freshness of personal experience.

The store of knowledge about the Spanish and Mexican days of California and the Southwest is growing, largely through the continuing work of The Bancroft Library of the University of California in the National Archives of Mexico, Mexico City, and in the General Archives of the Indies, in Seville, Spain.

We are indebted to The Bancroft Library for considerable new material being published for the first time. In fact, some of it was discovered in the National Archives of Mexico only this past summer, 1961, and made available to the Union-Tribune Publishing Company for this book by the library through Dr. George P. Hammond, director, and Dr. John Barr Tompkins, head of Public Services.

No history of San Diego, or of California, or the Southwest, could be written without drawing heavily on the work of the great historian Hubert Howe Bancroft, who fortunately made copies, or abstracts, of literally thousands of original California documents and correspondence which later were lost in the San Francisco earthquake and fire of 1906.

Any understanding of the mission period must start with Fr. Zephyrin Engelhardt, and his voluminous work on "The Missions and Missionaries of California," and with Fr. Maynard J. Geiger's detailed study of "The Life and Times of Junípero Serra."

Samuel Eliot Morison's research into the maritime history of Massachusetts, and of the early New England trade with California, and Adele Ogden's research into the pioneer otter fur trade between the Pacific Coast and the Orient, were invaluable in the preparation of this book.

The Henry E. Huntington Library and Art Gallery at San Marino made available its wealth of material, maps and art. The California Historical Society was a source of much original material and translations of Spanish and French documents and books. Other museums, societies and groups offering assistance and cooperation were the Peabody Museum, Salem, Mass.; the Massachusetts Historical Society, Boston, Mass.; the John Carter Brown Library of Brown University, Providence, R.I.; the Academy of American Franciscan History, Washington, D.C.; the California State Library, Sacramento; the California Room of the San Diego Public Library; the Junípero Serra Museum, San Diego; the Catholic Diocese of San Diego; the San Diego State College Library, and the San Diego Historical Society.

Dr. Abraham P. Nasatir, professor of history at San Diego State College, gave of his time and his knowledge in reading the manuscript during its preparation. He made many suggestions and criticisms which immeasurably contributed to the goal of thoroughness and accuracy. Jerry MacMullen, director of the Serra Museum, aided in checking local events and descriptions.

Richard F. Pourade

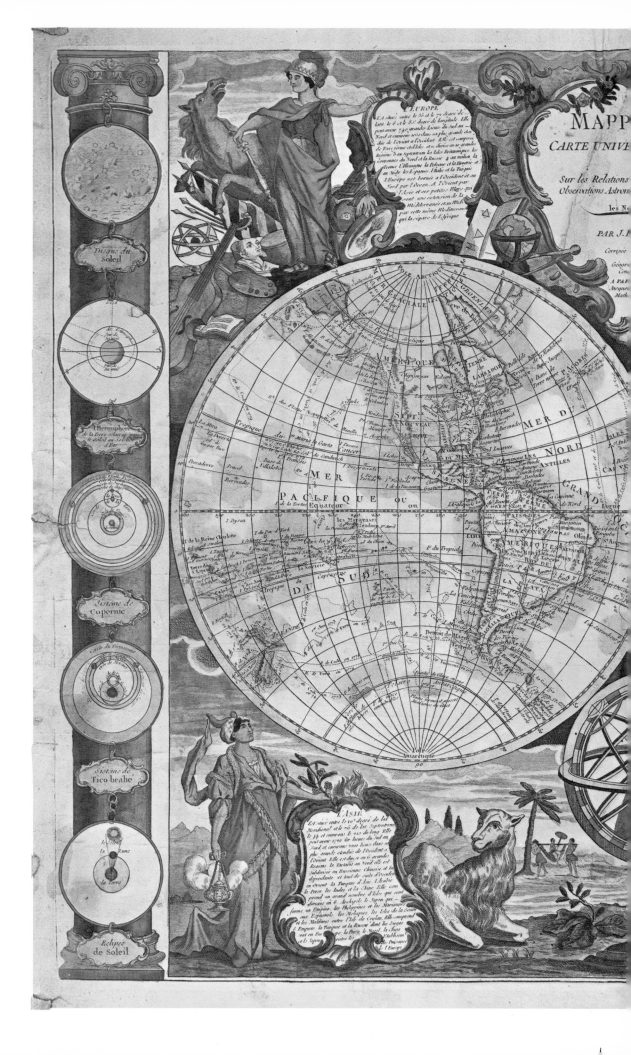

MAPP
CARTE UNIVE

Sur les Relations
Observations Astron

les N

PAR J. F.

Corrigée

Géogra
Con

A PAF
Jacques
Math

Disque du
Soleil

Hemisphere
de la Terre eclairée
le soleil au Solstice
d'Eté

Sistème de
Copernic

Sistème de
Tico brahe

Eclipse
de Soleil

L'EUROPE

L'ASIE

MER DU NORD

MER

PACIFIQUE OU

DU SUD

GRAND

Equateur

Tropique du Cancer

Tropique du Capricorne

Antarctique

What say the Bells of San Blas

To the ships that southward pass

    From the harbor of Mazatlan?

To them it is nothing more

Than the sound of surf on the shore,—

    Nothing more to master or man.

The chapel that once looked down

On the little seaport town

    Has crumpled into the dust;

And on oaken beams below

The bells swing to and fro

    And are green with mould and rust.

Henry W. Longfellow.

From the Bells of San Blas,
By Henry Wadsworth Longfellow.

PROLOGUE

The history of Western Civilization on the Pacific Coast of the United States begins on a little hill overlooking the Bay of San Diego. It is known as Presidio Hill. Here is the site of the first Christian mission and of the first military garrison of Royal Spain in California. The old adobe walls and buildings have sunk back into the ground, and green grass and black asphalt now hide all traces of the graves of forgotton soldiers and settlers who died in a lonely and at times unfriendly land.

The navigator Juan Rodríguez Cabrillo discovered California and claimed it for Spain, in 1542. But 227 years passed before a small band of Christian missionaries and soldiers arrived, by sea and by land, in 1769, to occupy and settle an almost legendary territory locked in by sea, mountains and deserts.

To the missionaries, California and the Pacific Coast was a land wealthy in pagans to be converted to Christianity. To the soldiers, assignment to California was a duty to be borne with fortitude. To the King of Spain and his commanders, California was to be a shield against the aggressions of foreign powers, in particular the Russians, who were creeping down from Alaska, and the English, whose fleets were sweeping the seas and who believed that occupation was a more effective claim to territory than mere discovery and explorations.

THE OCEANS HAD BEEN CROSSED and continents outlined by the time the first white settlement was established in California. But much of America was still an unknown land and the fire of adventure still burned in the world.

On the American Continent in the middle period of the 18th Century, England had a line of colonies along the eastern seaboard and controlled an area from the Hudson Bay to the Gulf of Mexico; France had lost an empire in the St. Lawrence and Mississippi Valleys, and New Spain's northern border curved in a weak, undefined line from western Louisiana through Texas, New Mexico and Arizona to somewhere in Northern California.

The story of California and much of the Southwest unfolds from Presidio Hill. The Franciscan missionary domination of California lasted 66 years. The birth, life and death of the Mother Mission, at San Diego, and of the King of the Missions, at San Luis Rey, in northern San Diego County, is the drama of all the missions on the frontiers of New Spain.

From Presidio Hill the story reaches east, to the Colorado River, with all the hope and tragedy it held for the explorers, soldiers and colonists who came from Mexico, and to the deserts over which came, at last, the American trappers and traders.

To the north, it reaches out to the founding of all the 21 California missions and of Monterey, San Jose, Los Angeles and San Francisco. Presidio Hill also looks to the south, to the peninsula of Baja California, whose settlement and subsequent decline foreshadowed events in California.

From the West, over the open Pacific Ocean, which the Spaniards called the South Sea, first came the ships of the discoverers and colonists, and then, as Spain weakened and collapsed, the ships of the British, the French and the Russians, and most importantly, the ships of adventurous American merchants.

The era from 1769 to 1835 was rich in faith and purpose. That it also at times was heavy with sorrow and neglect only proves that men and not events shape history. One of those men was Fr. Junípero Serra, with whom our story begins.

CHAPTER ONE

THE RING OF FAITH

A graying Fr. Junípero Serra, who had brought Christianity to California, sat humbly on the floor of a cabin of the ship *San Antonio* and slowly and with a tired hand composed a letter to his old friend and companion, Fr. Francisco Palóu, at Loreto, the president of the Franciscan missions of Baja California. It was dated: "At the South Sea, in front of the Port of San Diego, April 16, 1770."

"It is now a full year since I received news from the College, or from his Most Illustrious Lordship," he wrote, "and soon it will be a year also, since I had my last letter from your reverence. Blessed be God! When you can I would appreciate your sending us some Mass candles and incense. . ."

It was about 7 o'clock in the morning, and the *San Antonio* had been towed by launch with the tide out to the entrance of the port, and was awaiting a change in the wind to sail north, to once more seek the bay of Monterey. Serra wrote he would hand his letter over to the sailors in the launch, when they were ready to pull away, in the hope it eventually would reach Loreto.

In the many months that had passed since he and the Spanish expedition had left by land from Loreto and by sea from La Paz, to raise the first cross in California and found Mission San Diego de Alcalá, more than a third of its members had died of scurvy,

THE BELL WAS A SYMBOL of a way of life that has vanished from California. Worship, work and play were regulated by the ringing of bells in a world made up of small units where faith was the only source of strength and security.

3

The Franciscans' old "Mother" San Fernando Church in Mexico City.

supplies had failed to arrive when the *San José* was mysteriously lost at sea, and they had experienced an attack from Indians who mocked their attempts to convert them. Don Gaspar de Portolá, the commander, had blazed El Camino Real, or the King's Highway, up through California in an effort to locate the bay of Monterey, so extravagantly described 166 years before by the explorer, Sebastián Vizcaíno, but failing to recognize it, had returned, disappointed, to San Diego, ready to give up the entire expedition and abandon California.

But the return of the *San Antonio* on her second trip up the coast had changed the course of history. She had been bound with supplies for Monterey, in the confidence that a mission and fort already had been founded there, but had turned around and unexpectedly put into San Diego Bay. The first precarious settlement at San Diego was saved; Monterey would be found, and another mission started there as ordered by His Majesty, the King of Spain, and his Illustrious Lordship, Don José de Gálvez, the visitor-general of New Spain. This time Monterey would be sought by sea as well as by land. Serra chose to go on the *San Antonio* while Fr. Juan Crespí would go a second time by land, with Capt. Portolá. Frs. Fernando Parrón and Francisco Gómez would remain as ministers at San Diego, with the protection of some soldiers.

The *San Antonio* picked up a wind off Point Loma but the voyage proved to be a long and trying one. The wind as usual blew mostly out of the north and west and the *San Antonio* beat against it, helplessly at times, and as Serra wrote:

"For days far from getting near to Monterey, we were getting farther and farther away from the goal of our desires. The result of it all was that the voyage lasted a full month and a half; and on May 31st, we entered and dropped anchor in the port — the object of so many controversies. We recognized it without any question, as being, both as to its underlying reality and its superficial landmarks, the same and unchanged spot where our ancestors the Spaniards landed in the year 1603. It is plain justice that we should definitely put out of our minds all thought, or any lingering fancy, of the port's having disappeared, or being no longer in existence. These false notions have been circulated by reports emanating from the recent land expedition."

The arrival, on a Friday, the first of June, was an occasion for further rejoicing; they found Portolá and Crespí, and the rest of the land party, already there, having arrived eight days before after a relatively easy march overland from the semi-arid southland up through a country vividly green and fresh with spring. Serra invited all hands to Mass and the erection of a cross on the following Sunday.

"The day came," he wrote.

4

"A Little chapel and altar were erected in that little valley, and under the same live-oak, close to the beach, where, it is said, Mass was celebrated at the beginning of the last century. Two processions from different directions converged at the same time on the spot, one from the sea, and one from the land expedition; we singing the divine praises in the launch, and the men on land, in their hearts.

"Our arrival was greeted by the joyful sound of the bells suspended from the branches of the oak tree. Everything being in readiness, and having put on alb and stole, and kneeling down with all the men before the altar, I intoned the hymn Veni, Creator Spiritus at the conclusion of which, and after invoking the help of the Holy Spirit on everything we were about to perform, I blessed the salt and the water. Then we all made our way to a gigantic cross which was all in readiness and lying on the ground. With everyone lending a hand we set it in an upright position. I sang the prayers for its blessing. We set it in the ground and then, with all the tenderness of our hearts, we venerated it. I sprinkled with holy water all the fields around. And thus, after raising aloft the standard of the King of Heaven, we unfurled the flag of our Catholic Monarch likewise. As we raised each one of them, we shouted at the top of our voices: 'Long live the Faith! Long live the King!' All the time the bells were ringing, and our rifles were being fired, and from the boat came the thunder of the big guns.

"Then we buried at the foot of the cross a dead sailor, a caulker, the only one to die during this second expedition."

One more official step remained to be taken, to reconfirm the discovery of California by Juan Rodríguez Cabrillo in 1542. As described by Serra, the officers proceeded to the act of taking formal possession of that country in the name of the King, unfurling and waving once more the royal flag, pulling grass, moving stones, and other formalities according to law — all accompanied with cheers, ringing of bells, and cannonades. The next day the expedition moved a rifle shot from the beach and there established a fort and mission which they named San Carlos de Monterey, in honor of the first name of both the King and the Viceroy. From then on, for as long as he lived, Serra would make his headquarters in the north but he always was to look back with nostalgia on San Diego as "the mother mission" of California.

The great news of the saving of San Diego and the founding of Monterey must get back to Mexico. Josef Velásquez, a soldier, and a sailor whom history has not identified, volunteered to make the 1200-mile journey back through San Diego and down the Pacific trail in Baja California that led to Velicatá and then along the chain of old Jesuit missions, now administered by the Franciscans, to Loreto, the mission settlement and port on the Gulf of California, known to the Spaniards as the Sea of Cortés. They finally found Gov. Matías Armona and Fr. Palóu at Todos Santos, far south on the Pacific side of the peninsula, on Aug. 2. The governor immediately wrote a message to be rushed to the Viceroy, the Marqués de Croix, at Mexico City.

Sketch of Loreto Mission when at its height in Baja California.

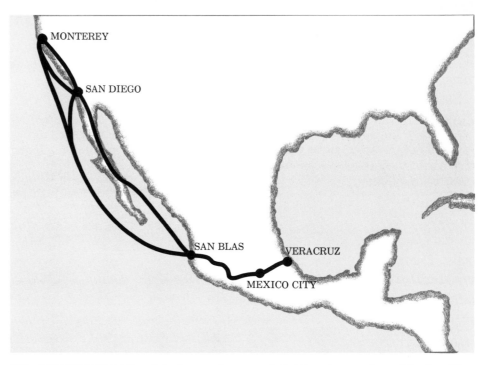

EL CAMINO REAL, with the settlement of California, ran from Mexico City to San Diego and then Monterey, by land and by sea. The news of the saving of San Diego was raced by ship directly from Monterey to San Blas, Mexico.

At Monterey, the *San Antonio*, her supplies unloaded, prepared to return to Mexico on July 9. With her went Capt. Portolá, his work in California at an end, and Miguel Costansó, the engineer, who wrote such detailed reports of the Indians and the topography of the new land. With the wind at her back, the *San Antonio* made a quick passage down the coast, and rounding Cabo San Lucas, drove across the open sea on the long slant to San Blas on the mainland of Mexico, arriving on Aug. 1. She had sailed 1700 miles in 24 days. San Blas, situated about 180 miles south of Mazatlán, was to play a vital role in the development of San Diego and the Spanish domination of California. The town where conquerors once walked sat on one of the rocky hills forming the open bay and overlooking tropical lagoons and the dark estuaries that run through groves of mangrove and coconut and banana trees. Orchids abound and roses grow wild.

At San Blas, Portolá hurried his own messenger to the Viceroy. A horseman left the feverish, summery heat of San Blas and following a branch of El Camino Real, climbed inland through jungle lushness to Tepic, 45 miles away, and then up one of the world's greatest mountain gulches to Guadalajara, from there riding the high plateau of Mexico to the capital of New Spain. He arrived on Aug. 10, 1770, after a ride of more than 600 miles. The messenger from Gov. Armona was still unreported.

It was a great day for Spain. Her dominions had been extended many hundreds of miles up the Pacific Coast, to meet the threat of the advancing Russian fur hunters and to thwart any territorial ambitions of the English and the French.

San Diego and Monterey were crude camps in a pagan land. There were 40 people, including converted Indians from Baja California, at Monterey, and 23 at San Diego. But Mexico City of the 18th Century was a city of magnificent cathedrals, great universities and many monasteries and hospitals, most of them standing to this day. The dean of the massive Cathedral, which stands on El Zócalo, or the major plaza, and is visited by all American tourists, was requested to order a solemn ringing of the Cathedral bells. Then, one by one, all the churches of Mexico City followed suit, until the city echoed and re-echoed with the sound of a thousand bells. People poured into the streets, wondering what all the excitement was about. As Palóu wrote in his biography of Serra,

"when they were informed, they joined His Excellency in the rejoicing. The principal inhabitants went to the palace to offer their congratulations, which the Viceroy and the visitor-general received together . . . both gave thanks to God for the successful outcome of the conquest and the expeditions sent to effect it, by which the dominions of our Catholic Monarch had been extended for more than 300 leagues in the northern part of this America."

But that wasn't all. The Viceroy wanted everybody in New Spain to know about it, so he ordered the printing and distribution of an account, which still survives, and which was sent to every part of the viceroyalty and to Old Spain as well.

El Camino Real, on the Atlantic Coast, now ran from the sandy, humid port of Veracruz, up the old route of the great conqueror, Hernán Cortés, to the snow-rimmed valley of Mexico, and then, on its northern branch, to San Blas, and then jumping across a

WHEN CALIFORNIA WAS FIRST SETTLED, and crude camps erected in a wilderness thick with Indians, Mexico City was a cosmopolitan metropolis with universities and fine churches. The cathedral still stands on the Zócalo.

Mounted Spanish soldier as drawn by the artist Walter Francis.

vast expanse of open and hazardous sea, picked up again at San Diego and stretched on to Monterey. It was a thin line of 2300 miles often staggered with death and disease.

For Gálvez, especially, this was a triumphant moment. As a member of the Council of the Indies, he had been sent to New Spain to reform its administration, and he conceived and carried out the planning of the expeditions to settle California and assure the Spanish claim. And Gálvez was not one to shun greatness. Efficient and zealous, even to the point of aiding in the scraping of the bottom of the ships for the expedition and in the packing of supplies, he could, at the same time, be mean and petty. He forbade card playing and punished some of the soldiers by ordering them on the expedition to San Diego and Monterey, and referred to the Indians as "poor Israelites" whom he had to lead to some promised land. It was he who carried out for Spain the expulsion of the Jesuits from Baja California and afterward persisted in hunting through their missions for gold, silver and pearls which he was firmly convinced had been hidden from him. This story of hidden Jesuit treasure has lived through the years. He became so rabid on the subject a companion accused him of insanity, and Gálvez had him cast into prison. At one time he threatened to bring 600 apes from Guatemala and dress them in uniforms and use them to maintain order. Later, in Sonora, he again was accused of insanity by secretaries, one of whom became a viceroy himself, and again threw his accusers into prison. But, despite it all, California owes much to this vain, erratic but capable man. He eventually returned to Spain and became minister of state for the Indies, dying in 1787.

Portolá, with his return to San Blas, stepped out of the history of California. Born in Catalonia of noble rank, he had seen military service in Italy and Portugal, as well as in the New World. In 1776, he was appointed governor of the city of Puebla, apparently serving until 1783, when he received salary advances in order to return to Spain. He died in 1786.

Of the other members of the little band of brave men who broke the way for settlement of California, some remained to write stirring chapters of adventure and faith, and some, suffering personal tragedy and death, followed Portolá out of the story. Don Pedro Prat, the surgeon who had disregarded his own health at San Diego in the effort to defeat the scurvy that so ravaged the ranks of those who came by sea, lost his mind and had to be sent back to Guadalajara. Vicente Vila, a lieutenant in the Royal Navy and commander of the unhappy *San Carlos*, which lost nearly all its crew on its way to San Diego, returned to San Blas, with his ship, and died soon afterward. The map he made of San Diego Bay lies in the Archives of the Indies, in Seville, Spain. Fr. Juan Vizcaíno, wounded in the first Indian attack on Presidio Hill, never recovered and was forced to leave his companions and return to Mexico.

The work must go on. Within six days of the arrival of the news about San Diego and Monterey, the Viceroy had provided for support of the new establishments and the five more missions that were to be founded as quickly as possible above San Diego. San Fernando College was asked to supply 10 more Franciscan fathers for these missions besides 20 more for the old and new missions of the peninsula. Serra, in his letters, also requested that two bells be supplied for each mission to be founded, and thereafter for more than 65 years, the lives of all those in California, Indians as well as Spaniards, were to be regulated by the ringing of bells that called them to work and to worship.

THIS IS WHERE CHRISTIAN CIVILIZATION BEGAN on the West Coast in 1769. The Junípero Serra Museum looks down on the green slope of Presidio Hill. Rows of humps mark crumbled adobe of old presidio walls, buildings. Hill was cut away later for dirt to divert the river.

CHAPTER TWO

THE FIGHT TO LIVE

The rejoicing that rang over Mexico City had little echo at San Diego. Presidio Hill, the birthplace of Christian civilization on the Pacific Coast, remained a place of sickness and disappointment. Fr. Palóu was to comment that, from the beginning, the fathers stationed at San Diego had to "sustain themselves with the bread of affliction and the waters of distress." Those who had been left behind, when Serra and Portolá went to Monterey, kept close to the tight stockade of poles they had erected on the sloping hillside. The bright promise of the first days of their arrival, when the land had seemed so fertile and productive, with the river running and grapes growing in profusion, had quickly dimmed. Remaining with Frs. Párron and Gómez were Sgt. José Francisco Ortega, a man who later was to be reckoned with in the history of California, eight soldiers, a few muleteers and a number of Baja California Indians. Still in the harbor at that time was the expedition's other ship, the *San Carlos*, which, with the *San Antonio*, had been the first vessels to enter San Diego harbor in more than a century and a half, but her crew wasn't much help to the little band on Presidio Hill. Besides Capt. Vila, only five sailors had survived the scurvy. Impatient with the failure of replacements for the crew to arrive, Vila borrowed two soldiers and two muleteers and sailed for San Blas.

THE DOUGHTY SAN CARLOS *is shown in this painting by Walter Francis as it was leaving La Paz on the expedition to California. The* San Carlos *for many years shuttled supplies between San Blas and San Diego and Monterey.*

The situation at San Diego was relieved temporarily in June when Capt. Fernando Javier de Rivera y Moncada, who had commanded the Leatherjackets from Loreto on the original march to San Diego, returned from Baja California with 20 additional soldiers, and cattle and supplies. Of Rivera, much yet was to be heard. Of the next year little is known about happenings at San Diego. The records of this period were burned sometime later in an Indian uprising. But by March 12, 1771, apparently the padres had at last been able to convert a few of the antagonistic, stubborn Diegueño Indians who lived in the village of Cosoy, or Kosoi, among the trees at the foot of Presidio Hill. The first new converts, or neophytes, were pitifully few compared to the almost overwhelming number of heathens, or gentiles. The threat of abandoning San Diego arose once more.

It was on this date that the *San Antonio* arrived again from Mexico, with 10 additional fathers for the new missions of Alta California, and Fr. Gómez, now in poor health from the rigors of the past year, decided to give up and go home. He was followed soon after by Fr. Parrón. The *San Antonio* proceeded to Monterey, and on the way south brought to San Diego, Don Pedro Fages, the commander of the Catalán Volunteers from Spain, who had been appointed military commander of Alta California.

Writing to the Viceroy, Fages gives us our first real glimpse of life in San Diego:

"I find this mission has made a good beginning as regards temporary buildings and cultivation. Also, the cattle, which Capt. Fernando Rivera left here when he departed, are in good condition. There are 82 cows, 7 bulls, 8 heifers to two years, and 13 calves. I find also 13 mules. There are only 13 soldiers with the corporal, who it seems to me, are necessary for the protection of the mission. The drove of cattle from Lower California, besides 60 mules, guarded by 20 soldiers and 6 muleteers, have arrived. This will enable me to facilitate the founding of the Missions of San Gabriel and San Buenaventura. This I shall do at once, and distribute to each mission the requisite cattle and mules. Thus I shall leave them in good state of defense."

The good beginning was a modest one, certainly. Some but not much progress had been made on a presidio and mission. A chapel of poles with a tule roof, and a dwelling for the fathers, were built inside the walls, and adobe bricks were made by Indian workmen for a new and larger church. For some reason or other, this particular church evidently was never built.

Fages was a man with a purpose, and he was to clash continually with the zealous Serra and the other padres over the handling of the Indians, the assignment of soldiers, the distribution of mules and administration of the missions themselves. Industrious and loyal, he nevertheless was short-tempered and quarrelsome. His haughty manner led only to trouble which was to bring a crisis in the raw affairs of California.

As commander of the Catalán soldiers, Fages had little regard for the local Leatherjackets from Loreto, who, nevertheless, generally were more accustomed to frontier living. His treatment of the soldiers evidently was responsible, at least in part, for the desertion of nine soldiers and a muleteer from San Diego. Fages sent Fr. Antonio Paterna, there waiting assignment, out after the deserters, with a humiliating pardon signed in blank, to induce them to return. It worked. But Fages in a later letter to the Viceroy complained about continuing desertions. The excitement and adventure of discovery and exploration had ended, and ahead was dull guard duty at lonely outposts of civilization. Even Loreto must have seen like a cosmopolitan center to soldiers camped on the side of Presidio Hill and looking down on dirt-covered huts of sullen Indians.

The soldiers of California, he wrote, were "perverse and obstinate," and the corporals and sergeants "complied little with their obligation of punishing soldiers in proportion to their misdeeds." Three soldiers raped two young pagan Indian girls near San Diego and Fages sent one of them as a prisoner to Velicatá and sent the others to Monterey in chains. In answer to demands to return home , he would read the royal ordinances, remind them of their duties, and tell them "you are on a campaign and you cannot make such a request."

Rivera had gone to Velicatá once more, to obtain additional cattle and supplies, and he led 19 or 20 soldiers and a train of 80 mules and 10 horses, and carried with him reports of what had transpired at San Diego and Monterey. On the way they fought a skirmish with Indians, killing two of them. Evidently he was to deliver cattle and supplies to Monterey, but perhaps in resentment over the selection of Fages as military commander, took them only as far as San Diego. Serra was shifting fathers around, to bring together as working companions those from the same regions of Spain, and thus it was that Fr. Luis Jayme, of the island of Majorca, where Serra was born, was assigned to San Diego with Fr. Tomás de la Peña y Saravia. Jayme was fated to become the first martyr of the mission period of California history.

The mission at Monterey had been moved to Carmel and new missions started, San Gabriel Arcángel, east of Los Angeles, and San Antonio de Padua in the valley of Los Robles in Central California, in 1771, and San Luis Obispo de Tolosa, in 1772, but troubles between Serra and Fages continued. They got into a dispute at San Diego over the founding of another mission, San Buenaventura,

Principal bays and points noted in history of Baja California.

15

long planned at what is now Ventura, and the padres lamented that Fages "considers himself as absolute and that the missionaries count for less than the least of his soldiers, so that the missionaries cannot speak to him on the slightest matter concerning missions. He stated that he is in charge of all; that the missionaries have nothing more to do than obey, say Mass, administer the sacraments; that all the rest devolves him upon him as commander." At last, in late 1772, Serra determined to go to Mexico City, aboard the *San Carlos* to see the new Viceroy, Antonio María Bucareli y Ursúa, and bring about a solution to their troubles. He left on Oct. 20 on the long journey by sea and by land.

Starvation again threatened San Diego and Fr. Dumetz was sent south for more supplies and Fages sent a pack train down from the north with emergency flour. Writing under date of May 21, 1772, Fr. Crespi, says:

"I passed by way of San Gabriel Mission and found that the Fathers had tightened the cord around their waist . . . At San Diego, I found very few victuals. There were only seven *fanegas* of corn and about 200 pounds of flour. The guards for a long time maintained themselves with half a pint of corn and only 20 ounces of flour a day; the Fathers likewise, with a little milk. They say that thus they have passed most of the year, without lard, without tallow, without even a candle of this kind, and even without wine for the Holy Masses, so that Holy Mass is celebrated only on Sundays and on days of obligation. God grant that Fr. Dumetz arrive promptly with help for these missions and that the ships bring up supplies, otherwise, we are lost."

The end of this period of starvation came with the re-arrival of the two most welcome ships in the South Sea: The *San Carlos* and *San Antonio*, in August, 1772. Dumetz also returned, accompanied by Fr. Peña, and the first flock of sheep for California.

A change in the administration of the missions in Lower California also brought Fr. Francisco Palóu, Serra's old companion, to San Diego. The missions in Lower California had been founded by the Jesuits, but when the Jesuits were expelled under secret orders, they had been handed over to the Franciscans under the leadership of Serra. Now they were turned over to the Dominican Order and Palóu rode the Pacific Trail to join the leader he so admired and so loved. He was to remain near Serra's side to write about his life and his death. Among those with him was Fr. Vicente Fuster, of the Province of Aragon, Spain, who was to remain at San Diego. Little by little, the mission and settlement were growing, and in Palóu's official report is found a situation that has plagued San Diego all the years since — water.

"This mission . . . is situated on a high elevation about two gunshots from the beach, looking toward Point Guijarros and the mouth of the port named San Diego, which is in 32 degrees and 42 minutes north latitude. The beach,

Frs. Palóu, Lasuén, Fuster listed as leaving Loreto for California.

as also the vicinity of the mission, is well peopled by savages, since within a district of 10 leagues there are more than 20 large rancherias, and one other adjoining the mission . . . by degrees they came to join the mission, so that already 85 adults and children are baptized, seven of whom died recently, while 12 couples were married and are now living in the village composed of dwellings that are made of poles and tules . . . The pagans of other rancherias also frequent the mission and are present at the *doctrina* or catechism, attracted by their fondness for hearing the neophytes sing.

Wood, leather shoe worn by early fathers at San Juan Capistrano.

"Within the stockade is the church or chapel, constructed of poles and roofed with tules, as also the habitation of the two missionaries, having the requisite rooms partly of adobe and partly of wood and roofed with tules.

"Likewise, within the stockade, is a similar structure that serves as the barracks for the soldier guards and as a storehouse for the supplies. For defensive purposes, within the stockade, are two cannons of bronze. One looks toward the port, and the other toward the Indian rancheria. On one side of the stockade, in the wall, is an opening for the foundations of a church 30 yards (varas) long. For this some stones and 4,000 adobes have already been prepared. The foremen of the work are the Fathers, and the workmen are the neophytes, who labor with pleasure. The work has now stopped for want of provisions; the neophytes saw themselves obliged to retire in search of wild fruits, until the ship arrives.

"As this mission lacks water for irrigating the extensive and fertile land which it possesses, the inmates must suffer want, unless the crops turn out well. The first two years have proved this. In the first year, the river rose so high (though it has running water near the mission only in the rainy season), that it carried away all that had been sown. In the second year, planting was done farther back of the stream. During the greater part of that season, however, the water was scarce so that the plants perished. Only five *fanegas* of wheat were secured, and these were used for sowing in the locality about two leagues from the mission, because from experience it was learned that in said place rain was more frequent. The country has been surveyed for a distance of 10 leagues in every direction; but no running water for irrigation has been discovered. Only for the livestock is there in various places sufficient water and abundant pasture.

"The savages subsist on the seeds of the *zacate* (wild grass) which they harvest in the season. From these they make sheaves as is the custom to do with wheat. They also live by fishing and by hunting hares and rabbits which are plentiful. The Missionary Fathers have sent to San Blas for a canoe and a net so that the new Christians might subsist on fish. If this succeeds, it will, no doubt, be a great relief.

"Of the cattle which came for these new missions from Lower California by order of Inspector-General José de Gálvez, this mission was allowed 18 head, large and small. In the beginning of last October it had 40 head. It then owned also 74 head of sheep, 55 goats, 19 pigs, 15 mares, 4 fillies, 1 colt, 8 tame horses, 1 jackass, 6 donkeys, 4 riding mules, and 18 pack mules with the necessary outfit.

Padre hat at San Luis Rey, one of two left from mission days.

"The mission possesses 12 plowshares and other iron implements. There is also a sufficient supply of tools for carpenter and for masons, and a forge for the blacksmith, although there are no mechanics to teach these crafts."

Serra sailed for San Blas and riding on the way to Mexico City, fell so ill at Guadalajara that the "fathers ordered me to receive the sacraments and I was in danger of death for many days." He recovered, but was stricken again, at Querétaro, but rose once more

Map of Port of San Blas, used by French navigator, La Perouse.

to push his way to the capital and to fight for the authority of the missionaries. He arrived Feb. 6, 1773, but it was many days before he could see the Viceroy. Serra won nearly every point he sought in his 32-point *Representación*, and also out of the meeting came the *Reglamento* which formed the basis for governing Alta California for many years.

Serra asked for the removal of Fages as military commander, and suggested he be replaced with Sgt. Ortega, whom he described as honorable and honest, and a good penman, and because he had a "God-fearing conscience, his accounts would be correctly kept." Fages was removed but the Viceroy did not believe Ortega had sufficient rank for such a post. Instead, Rivera, a captain, was appointed military commander and Ortega was promoted to lieutenant and put in command at San Diego. Soon after, on Jan. 1, 1774, San Diego was raised to the status of a Royal Presidio.

Among other points won by Serra was the removal of soldiers at request of the missionaries, in moral cases involving Indians; the recruitment of married soldiers; that Capt. Juan Bautista de Anza, at the presidio of Tubac, in Arizona, be permitted to open a land route from Sonora to California; and most important to the fathers, reaffirmation of the "immemorial custom" that the management, command, and punishment of the Indians except in crimes of blood, and the education of baptized Indians, be left entirely in the hands of the missionaries. It was declared that the missionaries had the right to control the mission Indians as a father controls his family. This point was the key to the whole Indian problem, and its application was to bring both praise and criticism to the padres down through the years.

LAGOONS, JUNGLE AND RUINS combine at San Blas, the port town on the Mexican coast which once supplied San Diego. San Blas died away but is coming back once more as a resort area. The ruins are the old customs house.

18

The new regulations contained the steps by which San Diego was to grow into a pueblo and then a city. Historian Hubert Howe Bancroft said that while the first object was to be the conversion of the natives, the next most important was their gathering in mission towns for purposes of civilization; as the little towns may someday become great cities, great care should be taken in the selection of sites; the commander was authorized to assign lands to communities, and also to such individuals as were disposed to work, but all must dwell in the pueblo or mission; missions may be converted into pueblos when sufficiently advanced, retaining the name of the patron saint; no vessels were to be admitted to California ports except the San Blas transports and the Manila galleons on their lonely circle route from the Philippines to Acapulco; no trade with either foreign or Spanish vessels was to be permitted; the mission of San Diego could be moved if deemed best, and importantly, all records and archives must be carefully cared for, and finally these instructions were to be kept profoundly secret.

Kissing the feet of every friar at the College of San Fernando, begging their pardon for any bad example he may have set, and bidding them farewell forever, Serra started back on the return journey to California and the overwhelming task to which he had pledged the rest of his life.

Fages and his Catalán Volunteers were withdrawn. But he was far from out of the history of San Diego. Rivera was back in his native Compostela, on the mainland, when he received the news of his appointment. There is no indication he was very happy about it. He had longed to retire, because of illness, and had gone into debt buying an *hacienda*. Borrowing money, he went to Mexico City, saw Bucareli, then returned to bid his family goodbye once again. After still more years of hard service he was to die violently but gallantly along the Colorado River.

New life came to San Diego. The age of settlement opened. Rivera went to Sinaloa to begin recruiting married soldiers, who were to take their families with them to the frontier. He gathered together a party of 55 persons and they crossed over from San Blas to Loreto aboard a new ship, the *Concepción*. There, he ordered Ortega to come south to Velicatá and escort the families to San Diego and to Monterey, while he went ahead to assume his new command. These were the first real colonists of California, arriving 18 months before those to be taken north to San Francisco over the desert route by Anza, and they trod the now established Pacific trail that Serra and Portolá had first broken on their way to San Diego five years before. More settlers — carpenters, blacksmiths, mechanics — were to follow soon by sea as well as by land.

List of early Leather-jackets on duty at San Diego and Monterey.

The first colonists arrived at San Diego on Sept. 26, 1774.

Ortega's march up Baja California with hopeful but distressed families was anything but easy or pleasant. In his report to Rivera he said some of the guard, in particular one Francisco Lugo, had shown themselves "predisposed toward sedition," and "I warned the leaders that I would turn them over to the commandant in irons. With this, they calmed down and lowered their heads and I was able to maintain peace." He said that upon arriving at the Presidio of San Diego, the soldiers had found "it repulsive to take care of the '*caballada*' (the animals), and the families are in great need." Some of the women had already been left in Santa Maria. "Having rehabilitated the unmarried personnel, I gave assistance to those families with what I could, and they were somewhat relieved." This letter to Rivera was dated Oct. 3, San Diego. Four months later the wife of Ortega gave birth to a son, and as far as it is known this was the first white child born in San Diego. Though pregnant, she had made this long trek with him. The exact date is uncertain, as mission records of that period were destroyed, but the event was recalled later and recorded from memory in the mission registry. The child was given the name of José Francisco María. Most of the colonists moved on to Monterey.

Thoughts of moving the mission from Presidio Hill became more insistent. All cultivation now was further up the valley, according to Palóu, "on the banks of the river, though out of danger from the floods, about two leagues from the mission, for it had been noted that in said locality the rains begin earlier and last longer than at the mission. Furthermore, in case of lack of rains, water could be drawn with little labor from the river. The place was named *Nuestra Señora del Pilar*." This location, of course, is at the site of the present mission. The missionaries also had another reason for wanting to move the mission: to separate the lightly-clad Indian women from the restless and at times rebellious soldiers. Fages himself had been considerably disturbed by this situation and wanted the Indians moved away from the Presidio, but Serra was opposed to separating them from the influence of the mission. Palóu had gone to San Gabriel, accompanied by Fr. Peña, who had been unhappy in San Diego, and Fuster was made assistant to Fr. Jayme. Nothing was done for a time about moving the mission, but Jayme was not to let the matter drop, thus setting the stage for the tragedy that the missionaries were to remember all their stay in California.

CHAPTER THREE

THE TEST BY FIRE

Fr. Luis Jayme walked through fire to become the first Franciscan martyr in the pagan land of New California. He couldn't believe that the Indians, whom he loved, would burn and attack a mission, or that they would kill him without thought or mercy. But they did, with uninhibited cruelty.

Fr. Jayme joined in the appeal to move the mission. "As long as the mission is here, it will never have a firm basis due to the lack of water from which it suffers," he wrote to Serra. But, he added confidently, "The Indians here, as more come, become humbler, and the gentiles show greater desire to be baptized." The removal was ordered by the Viceroy in 1774, and effected in August of that year, and Serra commented that "we gladly take notice of the many new Christians who have followed the Fathers to the new place, doubtless recognizing its advantages." But the little military force now had to be divided.

The new mission structures, six miles up the valley, on a slight promontory, at the site of a rancheria known to the Indians as Nipaguay, or Nipawai, were not much improvement over the ones on Presidio Hill. The site was at a bend of the river, where it swings northward, and from it, the fathers could command a broad view of the valley in both directions. In the distance they could see the sharp outline of Presidio Hill.

THE FIRST PADRE to achieve martyrdom in California was Fr. Luis Jayme. He was struck down and killed by his "children" when 600 Diegueño Indians attacked and burned the first mission buildings constructed in Mission Valley.

*Painted, hand-lettered
sheepskin prayer book
is 3 feet in size.*

Serra's report said that by December the mission comprised a church of poles, with a tule roof, 53 by 17 feet; an adobe house with rooms for the fathers, 56 by 12 feet; an adobe granary, a house of poles and tile for shepherds and muleteers; an adobe smithy, a servants' house of poles, and 13 native dwellings. A corral for mares and horses was located a league away, at a place they called *Rancho de San Luis*. This was further up the river. The end of the year indicated that at last progress was being made in converting the Indians to Christianity and bringing to them the benefits of civilization. There had been 106 baptisms and there were 19 Indian families living around the mission.

But underneath, an undercurrent of trouble rippled through the sierra. Resentment had burned deep over the soldiers' frequent molestations of Indian women. Events began to pile up. The more immediate reasons for the attack that was to come were the flogging of some Christian Indians for attending a pagan dance; an Indian claim that Fr. Fuster had threatened to burn their rancheria if it were not moved away from the immediate vicinity of the mission, and, lastly, the seizing of two Indian leaders on a charge of robbing one of their own women of some fish. Those accused were called Carlos, chief of a group of Christian Indians at the rancheria, and Francisco, his brother. But they escaped and took five others with them. Pursuing soldiers captured two of the five and returned them to the mission. Those captured warned that they had learned the Indians in the interior were being aroused and planned to kill the missionaries as well as the soldiers.

Fr. Pedro Font, who visited the tragic scene later, wrote in his diary that the Indians had given Jayme . . .

"Warning several times . . . but he always refused to believe them, thinking that it would be impossible that his Indians would do such a thing to him because he loved them greatly and favored them in every way he could. Indeed, he even became angry with the Indian who last told him of it, threatening that if he ever came again with such a tale he would order him punished."

But Indian runners were spreading out to villages all over the southland and as far as the Colorado River, even among the warlike Yumas, urging a concentrated uprising to get rid of the Spaniards once and for all before all Indians were converted by force and while Spanish forces were divided. Neophytes at the mission were enlisted as a virtual "fifth column." An attack was planned simultaneously on both the mission and the presidio. There were 11 Spaniards at each place; four at the presidio were ill and two were in the stocks for punishment. Lt. Ortega and some of the soldiers had gone to San Juan Capistrano to locate a site for another mission. The guard at the mission consisted of four soldiers.

The time of the attack was set for soon after midnight, in the early hours of Nov. 5, 1775. It was a bright moonlit night.

The Indians gathered in small bands at selected villages, then slipped down the river bed close to its banks, unseen and unheard, and, climbing the hillsides and circling the mission, they infiltrated silently into the grounds. Font tells us that:

"Since it was night and the soldiers of the guard of the mission were in the quarters sleeping (for thus they performed their duty there, those evil vagabonds!), the Indians first stole what they wished from the church, breaking in pieces with a stone the chest of the vestments, which they carried off, and likewise two images of the *Purísima Concepción* and *Señor San Josef*, dispatching their women to the mountains with the plunder. Then taking some firebrands from the guardhouse, they began to set fire to the same guardhouse, to the church, and to the houses of the fathers, which, being built of tule and logs, easily caught fire."

Fr. Fuster has left us a moving and detailed story of what happened that night, which he wrote as a report for Serra on Nov. 28:

"On the 5th day of this present month of November, about one o'clock at night, there was such a throng of Indians, both gentiles and Christians, who came to the Mission, that as far as the soldiers could judge they must have numbered more than 600. The first they did was to circle the rancheria, then the mission, from the four sides; then they pillaged the church of its precious articles, and after that they set fire to it. Next came the guardhouse and building where Fray Luis had his quarters. I slept in the storehouse or granary, which was the last place they set fire. Amid the yelling and discharges of the guns, half-asleep, I made my way out of the building, hardly knowing what it was all about. Since I had to cross over to the other side God kindly kept watch over me. I made a dash for it and got there safely. Then I asked the soldiers: 'What is this all about?' Hardly were the words out of my mouth then I saw on all sides around me so many arrows that you could not possibly count them. The only thing I did was to drop my cloak and stand flat against the wall of the guardhouse, and use the mantle as a cover so that no arrows might hit me. And this, thanks be to God, is what I succeeded in doing. There we were surrounded on all sides by flames."

Fuster retreated to his own quarters and the soldiers to an adjoining room, where they began to fight back. Shutting himself in, along with Lt. Ortega's older son and a nephew, Fuster wrote that he started to implore the Divine Mercy through the intercession of Mary Most Holy, St. Diego, and many other saints "to free us from the hosts of the enemies besetting us on all sides — namely, the Indians and flames." Gradually regaining his composure, he remembered Fr. Jayme and ran through the flames to enter his burning quarters, feeling all over the bed in the dark but failing to find him. With the fire leaping up on all sides, the little band retreated to the middle of the courtyard.

In this letter Fr. Jayme pleads to move the mission up the valley.

"Scarcely had I got there when I heard a gunshot in the smithy, and saw the blacksmith Felipe Romero running towards us. He told us that we should

25

commend the soul of the other blacksmith, José Arroyo, in our prayers to God, because they had already shot and killed him. They said Felipe managed to escape because he shot his gun at a gentile and killed him; whereat the others scattered, and he had a chance to join the rest of us ... Seeing that we were all lost and could not escape in any direction, I said to the soldiers: 'Let us go to the cookhouse and barricade ourselves with these bales of clothes that I have here.' ... They got together their bags of bullets and other implements of war, and in a body we ran for it. When we reached the cookhouse two soldiers set about dragging the bales so as to close off the front part. While busy with that work they were badly wounded by the Indians, but God granted that the entrance way could be blocked to mid-height. ... As soon as we reached the cookhouse our enemies saw us, and with united forces they hurled such a storm of arrows, rocks, adobe and firebrands that it seemed they were determined to bury us under them. The two soldiers who alone were fit to fight kept up a constant fire, and just eight paces away we could see a gentile stretched out dead from their bullets. The walls of the fathers' buildings already afire served the Indians as a protection. The buildings were quite close at hand; hence the enemy could fire on us with more precision. I could not possibly give Your Reverence any adequate account of the arrows which came singing straight for my head and stuck in the adobes. Thank God not one of them hit me. But this much I can say: one arrow hit square into the pillow I was holding up as a protection for my face. I immediately removed the arrow from the pillow — the one I was using to protect myself. As some relief to their jangled nerves the soldiers handed over to me the sack of gunpowder. Your Reverence can well understand the strain under which we all were when we could see fire all over and around us from the firebrands they were hurling at us and the danger of an explosion from the gunpowder...."

Fuster promised that if they ever got out they would fast nine Saturdays and offer up Mass to the Heavenly Queen nine times.

"We were all longing for daylight — there was plenty of the other kind — and that night seemed to us as long as the pains of purgatory. The arrows stopped coming for awhile, but not the rocks and firebrands. Yet this very cessation caused me anguish, because I reckoned they were merely resting up to make a more furious attack at dawn. And sure enough my suspicions were well grounded. Scarcely had dawn appeared then they let loose such a storm of arrows as to overwhelm us. I could hear numbers of the enemy, who had until recently been my trusted children, giving orders that now they should once and for all make an end of us, and encouraging their own ranks for the final charge. But God so decreed that a discharge of our guns just in the nick of time disheartened them and caused them to scatter...."

At the sign of flight, loyal Christian Indians, who had been gathered near the mission for Mass that same day, set off after the attackers with their own weapons, without evidently being so reckless as to use them, explaining later they had watched the long battle but had been reluctant to come to the fathers' assistance because of a fear of the dark.

In all this time, Fuster had not seen or heard anything of his friend and companion, Jayme, and he asked the Indians:

"My sons, where is Father Luis? They each replied: 'Father, I do not know.' And their response was like a sharp sword going right through my heart. Then came all the Christian women, sad-faced and dejected. At the sight of them I was both sad and glad. I can assure Your Reverence that my mind was tottering and weak, with all sorts of pictures disturbing it. Then one after the other the Indians who live regularly at the mission came along, and those from the two rancherias. . . And I noticed those from the mission came without their arms while the others had them. I began to suspect a trap, but this was quickly dispelled when they began to speak and tell me they had chased away the enemy and that I should have no fear or misgivings. I came out from that ill-fated cookhouse, and stood in front of them. They all came up and embraced me and acknowledged me as their father. Just what my feelings were I cannot properly describe, hardly knowing whether anguish or joy was uppermost in my mind. As soon as my thoughts cleared somewhat my first anxiety was for Father Luis. And so I told the Indians to go and see where the father was; others I told to look for the horses, and others to go to warn the presidio, others again to fetch water for the wheat granary which was still on fire. All this they did with the utmost dispatch, dividing themselves off into groups to do my bidding."

One of the Indians sent to search for water found Jayme's body in the bed of the river.

"I questioned: 'Alive or dead?' 'Dead,' he replied. Just think, Your Reverence, what must have been my grief and sorrow at hearing that he was already dead. But since God so wished it I told them to go bring him up. Very soon they had done so. If the news that he was already dead was a blow to me, how much harder was it to bear when I saw he was quite unrecognizable. He was disfigured from head to foot, and I could see that his death had been cruel beyond description and to the fullest satisfaction of the barbarians. He was stripped completely of all his clothing, even to his undergarments around his middle. His chest and body were riddled through with countless jabs they had given him, and his face one great bruise from the clubbing and stoning it had suffered. The only way my eyes could recognize him as Father Luis was from the whiteness of his skin and the tonsure on his head. It was indeed a stroke of fortune that they did not take his scalp off with them as is customary with these barbarians when they have killed their enemies."

The shock was too much for Fuster and he fainted, falling across the body of his friend. The Christian Indians bathed his temples with water and brought him back to consciousness. "What anguish and sorrow were mine my pen cannot describe. Before my eyes was the comrade I had lost, and whom I loved and revered so much, and I could see to my shame, how shining were his virtues and what a weak imitation were my own poor efforts."

Though Fuster makes no mention of it, Palóu believes that Jayme virtually invited death by rushing out with arms extended to meet the onrushing Indians with his customary greeting: "Love God, my children!" Only those outside the stockade, or who went outside, were killed. Two Indians were sent to the presidio and soldiers finally arrived. They had slept or dozed through the entire affair. They put together five stretchers, two for the bodies of the men who had been killed and three for the two soldiers and master carpenter

Old cannon which protected California from Indians, Englishmen.

27

who had been wounded. The two soldiers, however, were able to ride to the presidio along old Friars Road that follows the north side of the valley, but the carpenter had to be carried; he was so badly hurt he died within five days. The Indians took charge of the little procession of dead and wounded and, Fuster said, "by slow stages we arrived at the presidio. I made my way on foot walking by the side of the dead. We reached the presidio, and the many sighs and tears of the people brought a fresh tide of sorrow to my own heart . . . " Fuster buried his old friend as well as the carpenter under the floor of the church at the presidio. Jayme was only 35 years old at the time of his death.

Thus a man educated as a lector of philosophy on a distant Mediterranean island came to his end on the sandy bed of an unfriendly river in San Diego. His body was moved twice and now lies under the sanctuary of the present mission. The efforts of more than a year had been wiped out in one night. Across the road from the present restored mission structures, and just above a large tranquil pool of water in a sand pit crowded in with heavy growth, a concrete cross, scarred and broken, stands neglected in a patch of weeds. This spot is where some believe Fr. Jayme met his death. Lost in the fire were the leather-bound registers of baptisms, marriages and deaths and also the book containing the list of converts. Some of these records were restored from the memory of the fathers. Nothing was left but ruins, and the fathers were forced to ask residence in the presidio. The veneer of Christianity had proved to be a thin one. And so it was to remain for many years. The Indians weren't much in the way of fighters either. The two soldiers who escaped the initial attacks were able to beat off the whole 600.

In a sense, the attack was a vindication of the fears expressed years earlier by Fages. In their failure to follow up the initial attack, the Indians lost an opportunity to perhaps permanently destroy all of the Spanish settlements in California. In the whole coastal strip of more than 400 miles there were only 75 soldiers guarding five missions and two presidios. The force gathered for the attack in San Diego had divided as it approached the mission, half going ahead to the presidio, which was to have been attacked first from above, the flames there to signal the moment for the charge on the mission, but the impatient and emotionally aroused Indians set the torch to the mission too soon. Those approaching the presidio feared the guards already had been aroused and turned and fled back to join those at the mission. Otherwise, probably all, at both the presidio and mission, would have been slain.

Ortega hurried back to San Diego and all through the rest of the month they lived in the fear and expectation of another attack. So

Cross marks spot where it is believed Fr. Jayme met martyrdom.

28

it wasn't until late in November that soldiers could be spared to take word of the disaster to Rivera at Monterey and Serra at Carmel. Relations between Rivera and the missionaries already had become strained and Font says that Rivera went to Serra and in his brusque manner told him of the death of his friend:

"Fr. President, I have just received a fatal notice from San Diego which obliges me to put myself on the road thither immediately, and it is that the Indians have revolted, burned the mission, and killed Father Luis. Only one thing pleases me very much, and it is that no soldier was killed, thanks be to God!"

Serra's reaction, apart from his personal sorrow, was one of exhultation in his belief that "the blood of the martyrs is the seed of the church," and he fell to his knees and exclaimed "Thanks be to God, that land is already irrigated; now the conversion of the Diegueños will succeed." Subsequently, Serra was to plead for mercy for all of the Indian attackers.

LESS THAN SIX MILES separated the San Diego Mission and the fort on Presidio Hill. But the mission was attacked and burned and not a single person at the presidio was aware of it. All were asleep at their posts.

Old front of the church at San Gabriel Mission as it looks today.

Spanish forces began to converge on San Diego, but things moved slowly in those days. Rivera went to San Gabriel Mission first and enlisted the help of Capt. Anza, who reached there after crossing the Borrego Desert on his way to San Francisco with a band of settlers to found a new colony. Rivera and Anza led 35 soldiers to San Diego, accompanied by Fr. Font. Two ships worked up the coast from San Blas, and Viceroy Bucareli shortly was to order troops sent up from Baja California.

The question was why the fire and shouting at the mission did not alert those at the presidio. Fuster commented that "the mission is in full sight from there, as everyone admits. Yet they not only did not send assistance, but they did not even see the fire. Now this will seem an extraordinary happening; to anyone who takes a look at the location of the two places it will cause much surprise." Font, in his diary, gave this view: "The sentinel on duty at that hour in his declaration excused himself by saying that it was true he saw the light, but thought it was the light of the moon." But, as Font pointed out, by the time of night when the attack took place the moon would have been in the west, not in the east in the direction of the mission. "But it is nothing new for the soldiers to fulfill their obligations thus."

The sentinel's excuse was that he did not recognize the difference, "seeing that the light came up from the east, because when he was put on sentinel duty he was charged only with looking after the prisoners, and since he was facing them and watching them, and therefore the light was at his back, although he saw it on one side, he did not turn to see where it came from."

Font was outraged.

"So, this defense appeared to *Señor* Rivera to be sufficient, and he exonerated the sentinel and did not even arrest him, but charged the uprising to the lieutenant of the presidio, Don Antonio Francisco Ortega, and his bad conduct, although in the matter he was not at all to blame, for at that time he was occupied in the founding of Mission San Juan Capistrano. But since he was on very good terms with the fathers, he was very much disliked by *Señor* Rivera, who pays more attention to the soldiers than to the fathers. And so on this occasion there was opportunity for passions to arise."

Altogether it was found that Indians from 40 rancherias, both Christian and pagan, took part in the attack. Some of the mission structures were ransacked before the general attack, indicating treachery on the part of the Christianized Indians. Font, a Franciscan, had no use for any of them and was critical of Serra, "In fine, the mission of San Diego is the worst of all those which the fathers of San Fernando have in these new establishments, and likewise its Indians are the worst." He said they were like the ones who had attacked Anza in Coyote Canyon "both in perverse intentions and bad hearts, as well as because they are of degenerate bodies, ugly, dirty, disheveled, filthy, ill-smelling and flat-faced." The Colorado River Indians did not join the conspiracy, still being under the influence of the friendship which had been established with them by Anza. Their turn was to come later.

Though Rivera remained at San Diego to capture the offenders, Font says all the captures were effected by a sergeant "while Señor Rivera was at the presidio eating the little food which the fathers had and wearying them by the disrespect with which he treated them."

Title page of Fr. Pedro Font's diary on experiences in San Diego.

From time to time scouting parties brought in Indian culprits and they were punished by 50 lashings, one of them dying. Another committed suicide. Among those captured was Francisco, but Carlos eluded his pursuers until months later, when he finally walked into the presidio and sought asylum in its church. Rivera, by note, demanded that the fathers hand him over. They refused. Rivera, angered, drew a sword, and forcing his way in, seized the prisoner. His excuse was that the structure was a shack, or converted warehouse, and therefore not a sacred church. Fr. Fuster promptly declared Rivera excommunicated. This caused a turmoil. Eventually Serra upheld Fuster in the excommunication, and Rivera handed the prisoner back to the missionaries. They in turn formally released him to the authorities. All was forgiven. What finally happened to Carlos is not clear.

Anza had been impatient to get back to his own responsibilities, and left, but he and Rivera were to clash repeatedly in the months ahead. Anza finally prepared a record against Rivera, and leaving instructions with the lieutenant on how to proceed "if Rivera be pronounced crazy, according to the signs of dementia which he has given by his conduct," went to Mexico to make his report to the Viceroy on conditions in California.

CHAPTER FOUR

DEATH ON A RIVER

The year was 1776. On the other side of the vast continent, beyond the barriers of desert, mountain and plain, a people threw off their ties with Europe — the bonds of more than 200 years. Concord and Lexington and Boston were followed by a Declaration of Independence. The 13 colonies on the eastern seaboard, no longer dependent on an exhausted Britain for protection, formed their own union, the United States of America. A new nation and a new spirit of progress and adventure were rising. Mountain men were pushing ever west, and new enterprising ships of commerce began to appear in New World sea lanes so long dominated by Spain. All this was far removed from the little struggling settlements on the Pacific Coast. But peace was to be shattered by an Indian uprising along the Colorado River that threatened the Spanish hold on California and fatefully shut off a land connection with New Spain. Thus the hold of Spain, and later of Mexico, on California, remained a weak and tenuous one. In time, ambitious Americans were to break through by sea and by land.

Rebuilding of the San Diego Mission was begun with the help of sailors under Capt. Diego Choquet of the *San Antonio*, with Rivera's reluctant assurance of protection. All went well until Rivera, becoming alarmed by rumors that a new Indian uprising was imminent, withdrew the guard from the mission and beat a

THESE YUMA INDIANS look anything but warlike. It was the Yumas who destroyed two presidios on the Colorado River, slaughtering perhaps 50 persons. This sketch was by an artist with an American Boundary Expedition.

Fr. Lasuén, who served at San Diego, became missions' president.

hasty retreat to the presidio. This so angered Choquet that he also withdrew his crew and sailed for San Blas. All work on the mission stopped and its fate hung in the balance, until it again was saved, this time by the arrival of a new force of soldiers, who had been recruited by Capt. Pedro Fages and sent up from Guadalajara. They bore letters from the Viceroy expressing his sorrow over the tragedy at San Diego and making the first order of business restoration of the mission and the refounding of Mission San Juan Capistrano. Fr. Serra rang the bells upon hearing the joyous news; Rivera assigned a new guard, and himself hurried north to direct the founding of two other new missions, at San Francisco and Santa Clara, as previously had been ordered.

This was good news, too, for Fr. Fermín Francisco de Lasuén, who had come to California with Palóu and had been destined for assignment at San Juan Capistrano. Impatient with the long delay in its establishment, he had petitioned to return to Mexico, but his plea was rejected, and he was kept at San Diego, fortunately for the future missions of California.

Bucareli agreed with Serra that it was "more fitting to win over the rebellious neophytes than to punish them," and he said he was notifying Rivera that the Indians were to "receive kindness and good treatment rather than punishment and destruction of their villages which they had to expect because of their revolt. I have likewise made it known to the commandants that the chief aim of the present moment is the re-establishment of Mission San Diego and the founding of the new Mission San Juan Capistrano" . . . . and "it is my mind that the 25 men I ordered recruited in Old California for the better protection of those missions in New California, should serve as reinforcements of the presidio. I ordered that a sufficient guard be placed at the Missions San Diego and San Juan Capistrano, until Lt. Col. Don Juan Bautista de Anza returns and I receive fresh information. Then new and appropriate action will be taken . . ."

When the captain of the *San Antonio* reported to the Viceroy that Rivera had retreated merely upon hearing rumors of Indian dangers, which did not materialize, it was too much, at last for Bucareli. He put into effect the wishes of the King of Spain for a new hand in control of California. In a letter to Serra, Bucareli expressed his displeasure over Rivera's action in suspending reconstruction of the ruined San Diego Mission, "especially because of the light excuse given, as I learned from a letter written to me by Naval Lt. Don Diego Choquet, commandant of the packet boat *El Príncipe*, (the *San Antonio*)." Bucareli said that he supposed

Rivera had carried out his latest orders, but if not, the new governor would. The new governor was Felipe de Neve.

Neve had been nominal governor of both Baja California and Alta California, but as his capital was at Loreto, it had little meaning, and he was ordered to Monterey as governor, and Rivera was sent to Loreto as lieutenant governor. The ascendency of New California over the Old was established. He arrived at Monterey on Feb. 3, 1777, with a letter of instructions. He also carried an order from the King informing him that a Capt. Cook had been dispatched from England on two vessels on a voyage of discovery to the South Sea and he was not to let him enter any port.

By Oct. 17, 1776, the new buildings were ready for occupancy. During the next year Fr. Fuster was shifted to San Gabriel and Fr. Juan Figuer joined Lasuén at San Diego. A report of 1777 lists a church 80 by 14 feet, built of adobe with a thatched roof, two dwellings for the fathers, a refectory or dining hall, a granary, kitchen, harness room and a dormitory for boys and young men, and a corridor along the front of the padres' quarters and the storeroom. Adobe had replaced poles but the roofs yet were not of tile. The mission was kept alive by help from the other missions. The first baptism took place on Dec. 8, 1776, and in all there were now 440 baptized Indians living at the mission.

It was not a peaceful land, for all of that. The Pamo Indians of Santa María Valley, it was learned, were making arrows and enlisting the help of four other bands for another surprise attack. Lt. Ortega sent a warning to Chief Aaaran, and back came his challenge: Come on and fight. Sgt. Guillermo Carrillo took him up, and with eight men raided the Pamo rancheria, killing two Indians, burning two others who refused to come out of their hut, and seizing 80 bows, 1500 arrows and many clubs. The Indian bravery melted away. Other warriors surrendered and were flogged on the spot. The four chieftains — Aachil, Aalcuirin, Aaaran, Taguagui — were bound and taken to San Diego, tried on April 6, and convicted of plotting to kill Christians. Ortega pronounced the sentence,

"Deeming it useful to the service of God, the King and the public weal, I sentence them to a violent death by two musket shots on the 11th at 9 a.m., the troops to be present at the execution under arms, also all the Christian rancherias subject to the San Diego Mission, that they may be warned to act righteously."

Ortega instructed Frs. Lasuén and Figuer to "prepare the condemned, for the good of their souls, in the understanding that if they do not accept the salutary waters of holy baptism, they die on Saturday morning; and if they do — they die all the same!"

A CALIFORNIA DRAGOON, clad in buckskin, with leather shield and lance, is depicted fighting Indians. It is believed that this sketch was made by a Spanish sailor, José Cardero. It is in the Naval Museum at Madrid.

This would have been the first public execution in California. Evidently it was never carried out. Bucareli's policy was one of mercy and anyway, Ortega had no authority to impose such a sentence. From all that can be gathered, the ringleaders later became proper Christians.

In the mountains, inter-tribal warfare flared up. Supposedly Christianized Indians joined with a band of pagans in an attack on a rancheria called Jalo, in which 12 were killed, and it developed that the leader was the same Carlos who had instigated the attack on the San Diego Mission in which Fr. Jayme was killed. Carlos also was suspected of being one of the Indians who attacked the presidio soon after it was founded, when Serra almost met the same fate as Jayme. Three of the leaders in the Jalo attack were put to hard work, but after a long series of arguments as to what to do with them, Ortega took them out at night and banished them to Baja California. This saddened Serra because to him it meant the Indians would die away from their homes and be unable to go to confession because there would be no one to understand their language.

In 1778, Serra received permission to confirm, as California had no Bishop, and he went to San Diego and confirmed 610 persons. But there was a drought that year and the next, and prospects for the mission again looked gloomy indeed. The fathers were beginning to feel frustrated and wanted to retire to San Fernando College. Fr. Lasuén remained, however, and he was to succeed Serra as president.

The missionary pioneering spirit was far from dead and it received new strength along the Colorado River in the lonely explorations of Fr. Francisco Garcés, who had been the first white man to wander up through the northern wastes of Baja California into the Imperial Valley from where he sighted a gap in the coastal range. This was Coyote Canyon which leads out of Borrego Valley to San Carlos Pass in the San Jacinto Mountains, and he took Anza over this route in opening the Sonora-California land route to San Gabriel Mission and Monterey. He made a friend of Chief Palma of the Yuma Indians, a relationship developed by Anza. Now, Garcés was back on the trail, entering the vast interior mountain regions through Cajon Pass and penetrating as far north as

THIS SHOWS THE LOCATION of the Yuma massacres. Four padres were among the half hundred persons slaughtered by Yuma Indians when Spaniards made the mistake of combining pueblos and presidios in single settlements.

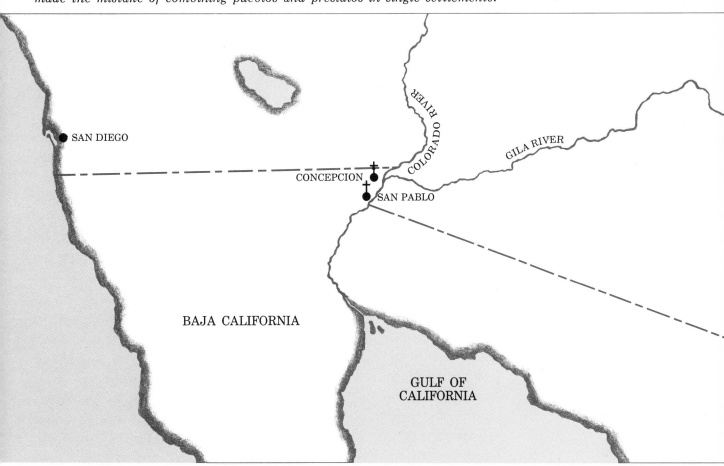

San Joaquin Valley, and then returning to the Colorado-Gila junction by way of the Mojave Desert.

Forces were shaping up for new tragedy, this time involving the Yuma Indians. The Diegueños of San Diego were members of the same Yuman linguistic family, but did not equal the Yumas in physical appearance and fierceness.

Yuma monument to Fr. Francisco Garcés, friend of desert Indians.

Establishment of settlements on the Colorado near the Yuma crossing on the Sonora-California route, below the confluence of the Gila and Colorado Rivers, was decided on; though through unwise influences, a decision was made to establish a new system uniting missions, presidios and pueblos, and putting Spaniards and Indians in the same compound, in direct opposition to the laws of Spain. The authority of the missionaries was restricted to religious matters, and the control and direction of the natives given to the military and civilians. Garcés protested and Anza, who knew the Yumas best, sent warning that such a settlement could not be established without the strongest kind of protection. But all this was ignored by the new commandant of the interior provinces, Gen. Teodoro de Croix, and the pueblo of La Purísima Concepción, at the site of the old Fort Yuma, was founded in 1780, and soon after, the pueblo of San Pedro y San Pablo Bicuñer was begun eight miles to the southwest. Both were on the west bank of the river. Colonists arrived and lands were distributed in disregard of Indian rights or claims.

The Yuma Indians, who had kept out of the uprising that burned the mission at San Diego, took a new look at their situation. Even though their chief, Palma, had been to Mexico City with the respected white captain, Anza, and seen its majesty and been welcomed by the Viceroy, all they got out of it were some trinkets. The bedraggled colonists were just people and poor ones, not lords. Santiago de Islas, in command, tried to pacify the increasingly resentful natives by installing Palma's brother as governor of the lower Yumas, but soon turned around and put him in the stocks. Bands of arrogant Indians roamed through the pueblos, carrying clubs and showing contempt for the settlers. And up from Sonora came Capt. Rivera, now in charge of recruitment, leading a new company of 40 recruits, their families and 1000 cattle, who were to be settled in the new pueblo of Los Angeles and at the new mission and presidio of Santa Barbara. At the Colorado, refusing to take too seriously the fears expressed by the missionaries and in contempt of the hostility of the Yumas, he sent the main company and military force on to San Gabriel, and with about a dozen men, crossed to the east side of the Colorado and camped opposite Concepción, to rest the cattle. He had made a fatal mistake. He had placed the river, impassable without help, between himself and the small forces at the presidio. Their strength had been divided. The time for war was at hand.

On Tuesday, July 17, the Indians struck. The first attack was launched against the lower village of San Pedro y San Pablo. The slaughter was quick and terrible. The Frs. Juan Díaz and Matías Moreno, a sergeant and most of the soldiers and male settlers met instant death. All the women and five men, including two Indians were taken prisoners. The buildings were burned and everything destroyed.

At the village of Concepción, all was quiet, the people unsuspecting. Father Garcés was saying Mass. The Indians fell upon them, slaying the commandant Islas, a corporal, and most of the men found in the adjoining field. But the two padres at the mission, Frs. Garcés and Juan Barraneche, were spared. Across the river, the camp of Rivera was attacked on the following morning. Rivera and his men had thrown up some barricades and they fought to the end, with no hope of rescue and no quarter expected. The frontier at last claimed Capt. Fernando Javier de Rivera y Moncada. He had only wanted to retire to the quiet of his *hacienda*.

A Fr. Juan Domingo de Arricivita, who wrote a summary of the tragedy for the Franciscans, said regarding Rivera's last hours:

"He made a kind of a trench and got ready his soldiers and arms, and on the morning of the 18th a multitude of Yumas assaulted him in a mob. They were received by the mounted soldiers with a volley from the guns which had full effect, killing many but as the crowd was very great, at the firing, they rushed upon the horses and disabled them with blows, and the riders falling they threw themselves upon him, and in this way killed some. For this reason the rest united in the trench, but it gave little shelter, and it did not protect them, and although they defended themselves vigorously, causing much loss to the Yumas, overwhelmed by the multitudes, they were all killed. Thus ended the captain who manifestly underrated the Indians, and whose reckless confidence delivered him into their hands; for if he had had an adequate guard, his boldness would have punished them; and his sad fate is clear proof that the destruction of the towns would not have occurred if the measures had been taken which experienced people proposed."

The Indians weren't through. They made a second attack on Concepción. Chief Palma had ordered them to bring the two priests, Garcés and Barreneche, to him unharmed, but the raid was led by a Christian Indian deserter from Altar, who, according to the Franciscan report, shouted that "If these remain alive, all is lost, for these are the worse." They were slain on the spot. The Yumas preferred to kill rather than capture. If they had time they decapitated their victims. If not, they took scalps, though they seemed to hold them in some dread. They liked to capture young women but generally did not abuse them. In the

Flintlock pistol made in London in 1790 found in county desert.

The Coco-pas were encountered in the Lower Colorado River area.

Pima women of the Colorado Desert shown in early American sketch.

two days of slaughter they killed between 46 and 50 persons and took 91 prisoners, mostly women and children. Fr. Moreno's body was decapitated.

The dead lay where they had fallen, under the hot summer sun. More than a month later, the soldiers who had escorted the settlers as far as San Gabriel drew near the Colorado on their march back to Sonora and picked up reports of the disaster. At Concepción they found the burned buildings and saw the bodies still lying in the plaza. The Indians, one of them wearing the uniform of the dead Rivera, made a quick attack on them, wounding the leader, *Alférez* Limón, and his son, and killing two men who had been left a distance back with some cattle. They retreated to San Gabriel by way of Santa Olaya in Baja California, and back up through Borrego Desert and Coyote Canyon.

The Spanish reaction was strong but two months elapsed before any rescue expedition could be organized and arrive at the scene. The task was handed to Don Pedro Fages, now a lieutenant colonel, and after a council of war at Arizpe in north central Sonora, he and his soldiers left from the site of Hermosillo on Sept. 16. Although they packed cannon, and at one time were to face 1500 armed Indians, the first objective was to obtain release of all captives that might still be alive. Within five days they had picked up the trail of warring bands, and after one brief engagement, two women and one infant, who had been held slaves, were rescued. On Sept. 22, they rescued 16. On Oct. 18, they halted along the banks of the Colorado. The Yumas sent a captive soldier to the Spaniards, and Fages reported in his diary:

"Miguel Antonio Romero came to meet us. He brought a letter from Captain Palma, in which the letter said that if we came in peace, he was also thus inclined. When we had come to the exact edge of the river — on the bank, at the top of the cliff, there were about 500 Indians armed with bows, arrows, spears, and some with guns, while many other Indians were coming and going from neighboring villages — we negotiated with Palma for the exchange of the captives for maize, blankets, beads, and cigarettes, etc. We secured the return of 48 captives, including men and women, adults and children. To two Indians who came to our side of the river we gave some boxes of cigarettes. By these men we sent to Captain Palma one of my peaked hats (galloned with silver and having a cockade), a shirt, and some boxes of cigarettes, to keep them contented. He reciprocated with some muskmelons, watermelons, squashes, about three *almudes* of maize, and three of *yurimury*. The scene of the murder of Captain Rivera and some of his companions was identified. Their bodies had been consumed, but that of Rivera was unmistakably identified by the break in one of the shin-bones. Several papers were found which I ordered gathered up, although they were torn to bits."

Then the expedition received some rather unwelcome assistance. More than 600 Indians of neighboring tribes of Jalchedunes,

Pimas Gileños and Coco-maricopas united for an opportune attack on the Yumas, which they carried out with considerable killing and burning. The Spaniards joined in, and among the Yumas, Chief Palma and his brother were both wounded. But in view of the spreading warfare, and the burden of the women and children, the Spaniards adopted "a course agreeable to the service of God and King, and to the welfare of all," and retired temporarily from the Colorado. At Sonoitac the women and children were sent to Altar, Sonora, and the expedition returned to seek the remainder.

Indian tribes were numerous along the Colorado. Here are Papagos.

It was Dec. 3 before any more were rescued, this time seven women, in exchange for other prisoners held by Fages. The Yumas still had one white woman prisoner, named María Juliana Sambrano, of Altar, as hostage, and the Spaniards two, while a new peace parley was undertaken. Fages' diary continues:

"The two Indian women were held by us, so that the next day the Yumas should bring the remaining Christian women who were yet in their power. This they promised to do. The band of Indians which gathered on the other side of the river numbered about 600. Among other things, they said that they felt resentment on account of the Indians whom we had killed on the preceding days; to which we replied that they had first raised arms against us. With this they were convinced, saying that we had done quite properly. They also assured us that if we wanted to fight, they were ready, for they would die at the very spot where they had killed Captain Rivera and his companions. They declared to us that they realized the mistake that they had made, and that they were mortal, and not wood or stone; but that if we desired peace, they wanted the same thing."

The exchange was made the next day. All had been rescued. Now came the task of giving a Christian burial to those who had died in the massacre. On Dec. 7, Fages notes:

"Very early this day I set out for the ruined town of San Pedro y San Pablo de Bicuñer with Capt. Tueros, Ensign Don Manuel Antonio de Arbizú, 10 volunteers, and 34 presidial soldiers, leaving the rest of the garrison for guards of the camp and the horses. On our way we came to the villages of the petty chief and his Yuma band, which were all deserted. Arriving at dawn at the foot of the town mentioned, we found the body of Rev. Fr. Juan Díaz, which was still recognizable by the tonsure, which had not yet disappeared; and, as two people were with us who had been present at the time of the outrage, and declared that it was indeed he, I had his bones gathered up in my presence and put into a sack made of leather along with the body of the Rev. Fr. Moreno, which we found behind the church, and which, although the bones only remained, I ordered gathered up and placed with those previously mentioned. A holy crucifix was found, and some little pieces of the holy girdle, as I doubt not, all of which I gathered up with particular care. In examining the outskirts of the town, we found many bones of settlers and soldiers who died in the uprising of the people of the Yuma nation. I immediately had these bones burned and the ashes collected, except those of the reverend fathers, which I kept separate, as I have stated. The ashes I speak of were put into two other sacks. I had the great bell of the town taken up, and loaded into a hamper."

The bodies of Garcés and Barreneche were found three days later near Concepción:

"Captain Don Pedro Tueros had the satisfaction of finding them; they were buried very close together, as if they had been interred side by side exactly in line, and laid out with their under-garments on, and they were not much decayed, especially the body of Fr. Garcés. On the bank where they were buried, a quantity of very fragrant camomile had grown. We were informed that an Indian woman who esteemed them highly had performed the kindly deed of burying them. We carefully gathered up these bodies, the sack of bones, and the bell which we had left behind on the seventh instant

THE ORIGINAL EDITION OF FR. PALOU'S life story of Fr. Junípero Serra contained this map of the old missions of Baja California and the ones founded by Serra in New California. It was first published in 1787.

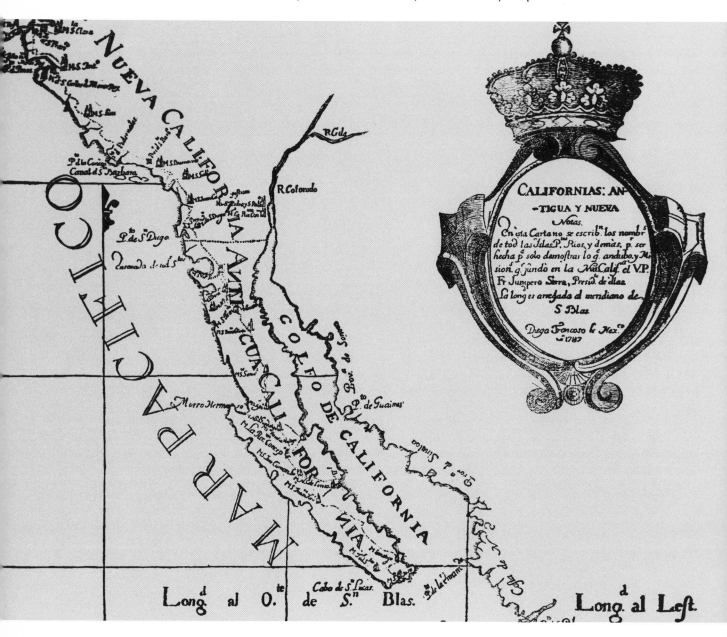

to go to the fight at the camp . . . and another bell which we found today. We halted at the town of San Pedro y San Pablo Bicuñer, and deposited the bodies and the bones of the four reverend fathers on the altar of the church, which, although burned, still had its walls almost intact, especially those of the high altar. Upon this altar candles were lighted, and, the troop and the rest of the people being gathered together, except the guard, we recited the holy rosary in concert with the Rev. Fr. Cenizo."

The remains of the four priests were placed in large metal cigarette cases and carried back to Sonora. Serra described his reaction to the Yuma disaster in a letter to Lasuén:

"As to what happened on the Colorado River — both in regard to the new experiment in mission management and in regard to the frightful disaster that followed — what can I say? All that we can do is to offer our sympathy for the sufferings of so many poor fellows who met their death there and bow before the inscrutable will of God. If they now kill the Indians, nothing more can be expected from the Colorado River which was so much advertised and the center of so many hopes. . . . Our poor Don Fernando (Rivera), he who was so cautious in the matter of Indians; he who was as sturdy as an oak tree and with so large a force of armed men was killed in one fell blow! Alas! What are we to say on the matter? God alone knows. There is little more to be said. Blessed be the name of the Lord."

Why the Indians gave up their captives so easily can only be guessed. The captives told a story corroborated in part by some of the natives, that the Yumas had been frightened away from the scene of their crimes by reports of nightly processions of white-robed figures with crosses and lighted candles marching through the desolation of Concepción. Night on the desert does strange things with the imagination and even now, looking out over the wastelands, pink and yellow in the moonlight, one can easily believe they can see the tall and warlike Yumas of old as they ran through the sharp desert nights with fire-brands held close to their bodies to keep them warm.

Nothing happened that winter, and because of spring floods along the river, it was decided to wait until September before attempting to capture and execute the Yuma chieftains and bring about permanent peace. But just as the campaign was about to begin, with 168 men in the field, Neve got orders by messenger appointing him commandant-general of the interior provinces and Fages was to succeed him as governor of California. There were a few desultory skirmishes but nothing was solved. The Yumas remained independent and unsubdued. No pueblos or missions were ever re-established on the Colorado. It remained a hostile land.

CHAPTER FIVE

Norte.

Plan

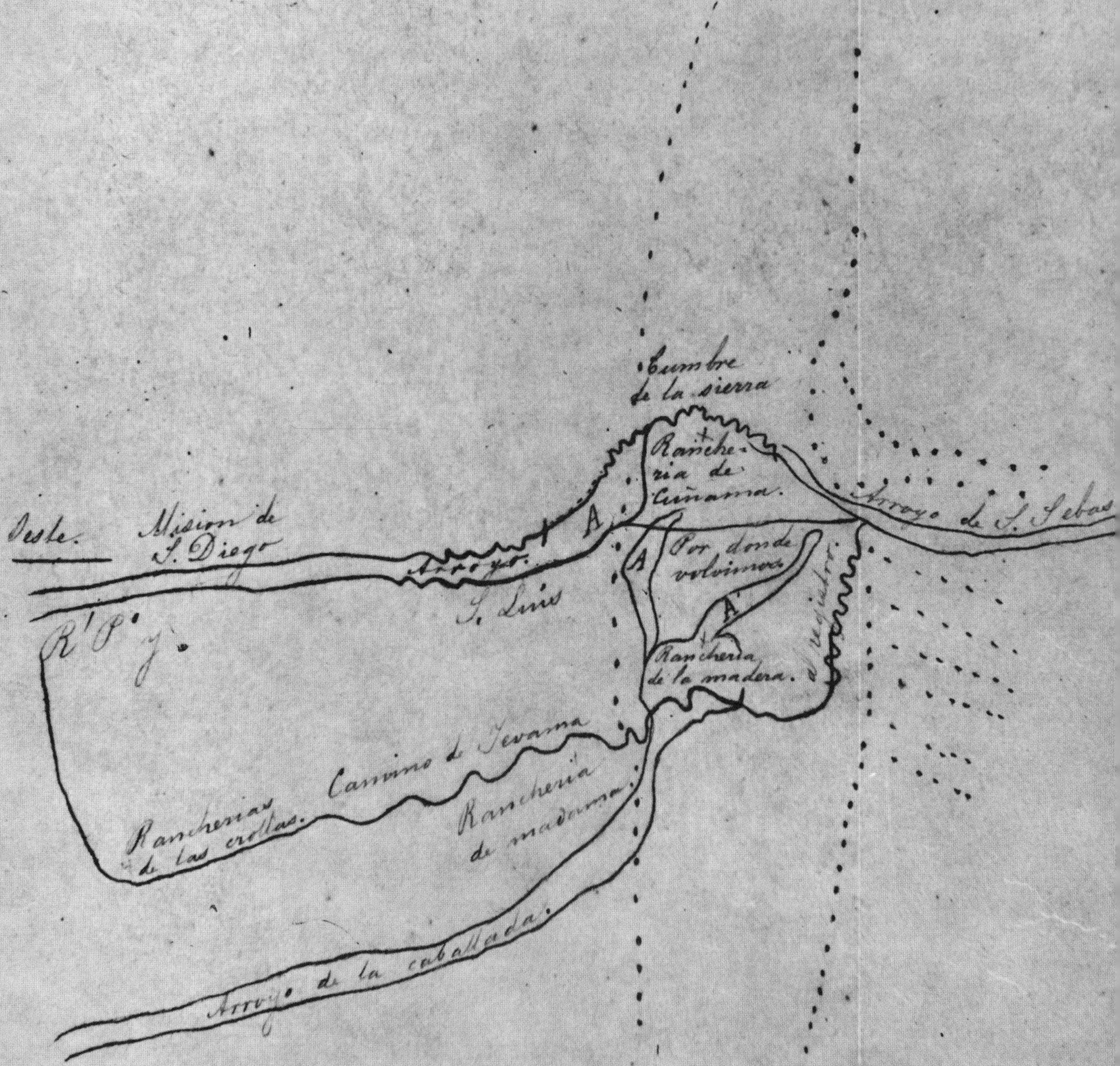

Oeste.   Misión de
          S. Diego

Cumbre
de la sierra

Ranche-
ria de
Cuñama.

A

Arroyo de S. Sebas

Arroyo.
S. Luis

A   Por donde
     volvimos

A

R'P'J.

Rancheria
de la madera.

Ranchería
de madera

Rancherias   Camino de Jevama
de las crollas.

Arroyo de la caballada.

Donde señalan los puntos es la cumbre de la sierra y c—
—an á S. Sebastian. Donde señalo A, son aguages corrientes, —
—tos. Pasto en abundancia toda la cumbre.

Velasquez (firmado).

Sur.

Es copia exacta tom—
del original.

OPENING THE LAND

The news of the tragedy along the Colorado River struck fear to the hearts of the settlers along the coast, and the missionaries felt their holy work again was in jeopardy. As for San Diego, still considered a frontier, unable to support a large colony and its Christian Indians largely scattered and forced to live among the pagans, a strong feeling of danger persisted, but the will to survive and to progress would not die.

Gov. Felipe de Neve had begun the task of bringing some order to the affairs of California. When he arrived he found the presidios to be mere collections of huts surrounded by fences of sticks and inadequate as a defense against even the arrows and clubs of the Indians. He pushed construction work and by July of 1778, a wall of stone, 537 yards in circumference, 12 feet high and 4 feet thick, was completed at Monterey, while at San Diego stones were collected for foundations but little real progress made. The Mission of San Diego did complete a new adobe church, 90 feet long by 17 feet wide and high, and strengthened and roofed with pine timbers.

"At the end of this first decade of its history," Bancroft writes, "the Spanish settlements in California consisted of three presidios, one pueblo, and eight missions. There were at these establishments besides the governor, two lieutenants, three sergeants, 14 corporals,

THIS IS A COPY OF FIRST MAP of interior sections of San Diego County. It shows the Fages trail over the mountains and was drawn by a soldier named Josef Velásquez, on the instructions of his leader, Gov. Pedro Fages.

49

about 140 soldiers, 30 *sirvientes*, 20 settlers, five master-mechanics, one surgeon, and three store-keepers, 16 Franciscan missionaries and about 3000 neophytes. The total population of Spanish and mixed blood was not far from 500. The annual expense to the royal treasury of keeping up these establishments was nearly $50,000, or some $10,000 more than was provided for by the regulation of 1773."

San José had been laid out as the first pueblo, and Neve was anxious to get on with colonizing California instead of leaving all its development to the missionaries. He and Serra were not to see eye-to-eye on many things, particularly in the ever-present conflict between civil and religious authority. Neve thought that one missionary at each mission was enough and he directed his soldiers not to get friendly with the padres or to pay any attention to them. Serra commented bitterly that "my going around and confirming is interfering with his sleep." Neve attempted to establish a policy of initiating self-government among the Indians and they were ordered to annually elect their own *alcaldes* and *regidores* to maintain order within their own ranks and villages. The fathers felt this was premature, the Indian tribes were still barbaric and hardly to be considered as "emerging people." Serra cited cases where the system had failed to work. He recalled that "At the San Luis Mission, (San Luis Obispo) the *alcalde* kidnapped another man's wife and took off with her, and it was quite some while before they arrested him. The Missionary Father followed the same course of action . . . and handed him over to the corporal. He was punished, but in so light a fashion that the corporal himself acknowledged that it was not in accordance with his crime. . . . At San Diego, I do not speak. They have had to put up with a great deal from their *alcaldes*, but fortunately the presidio is near. May God help them."

In 1781, a new regulation, or *reglamento*, for the governing of California, and providing for its occupation and settlement, went into effect. It had been drawn by Neve and approved by the viceroy as well as the king. While the regulations seemed clear enough at the time, those pertaining to pueblo land titles were to contribute to legal disputes down to the present day. The colonists, or *pobladores*, were to be *"gente de razón"* or, as it were, civilized people. The Indians would have to come in another way and some provision for this eventuality was made. The pueblos must form a square and streets agreeable to the laws of Spain. Settlers were to be recruited from the older provinces and each was to be granted a house-lot and a tract of land for cultivation, with necessary livestock, implements and seed, all to be repaid within five years; they were to receive some annual cash from the government, to be repaid in clothing and other articles; to have use of community or government lands for pasturage and obtaining wood and water, and to be free from taxes or tithes for five years. Those already living in California, as well as discharged soldiers, were entitled to the same benefits except for cash and cattle. In return, the settlers were required to sell the surplus products of their lands to the presidios; each settler must keep himself, horse and musket in readiness for emergencies; they must take their land within the pueblo limits of four square leagues, according to Spanish law and custom, and should not try to monopolize the pueblo wealth by owning more than 50 animals of any one kind; must not encumber or mortgage their property, and must join the pueblo in tilling common land, from which community expenses were to be met, and in constructing dams, canals, roads and streets, and necessary town buildings.

The families who were to begin the community life of San Diego, under Neve's regulations, were to be granted two mares, two cows, two sheep, two goats, all to be breeding animals; a yoke of oxen or steers, a plough share or point, hoe, wooden spade with steel point, axe, sickle, wood knife, musket, leather shield, a cargo mule and two horses — all given under condition of repayment in horses and mules "fit to be given and received." For the community at large there were to be mules corresponding to the total number of cattle owned by all inhabitants, a seed jackass, a common one, and three she asses and three sows, a forge, six crowbars, six iron spades or shovels and the necessary tools for carpenter and cast work.

In 1781, while Cornwallis was surrendering at Yorktown on the far-distant Atlantic seaboard, Neve was issuing his instructions on which was founded *El Pueblo de Nuestra Señora, la Reina de los Angeles del Río de Porciúncula*. The early colonists, collected from among the idle and displaced of the frontier of Sinaloa and Sonora, were not a promising lot. As time went on, California became somewhat of a penal colony. It was prison or California, and many preferred prison. One governor commented that the future of the new pueblos might better be assured if the settlers were sent at least two million leagues away from California and kept there for 200 years. Serra was opposed to the founding of the early pueblos, or towns, on principle. The Franciscans felt colonization would result only in pressure against the unprepared Indians and their lands. All through Mexico the land grabbers had followed close on the heels of the missionaries. But thus was a civilization built. And this was the California to which Fages was returning as governor.

He left the Colorado and instead of taking the Anza route northward across the Borrego Desert and up through Coyote Canyon to San Gabriel and then down to San Diego, he challenged the great sierra. The coastal range shutting off San Diego from the overland route had long been a barrier to development. The mountains seem to rise with stark grandeur right out of the desert floor. Only the Indians had penetrated this vastness — except for Fages himself. Ten years before he had wound up through the mountains from San Diego, in pursuit of deserters, and descended the sharp eastern slopes to the desert. He returned

THOUGH OFTEN BESTED BY HIS WIFE, mountains and deserts held few terrors for Pedro Fages, a governor and military commander of early days in California, who broke this trail over the sierra to San Diego Presidio.

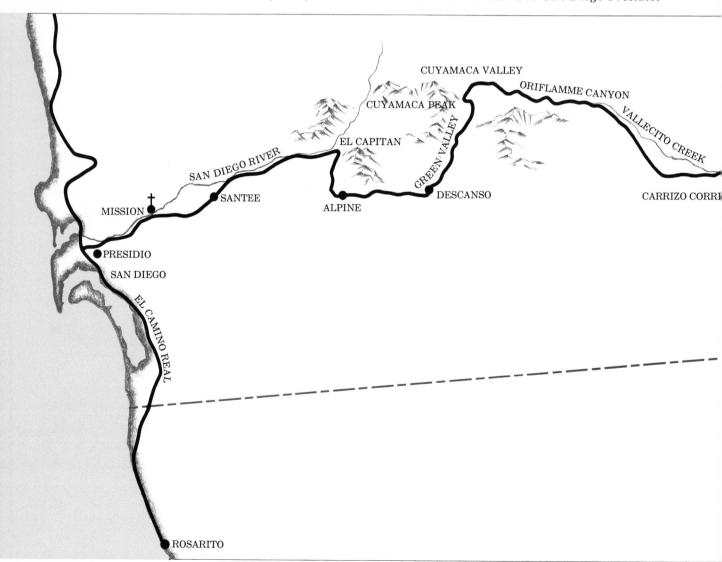

by the regular Anza route through Coyote Canyon. Now he turned to climb the sierra from the east with the assurance of a man who knew what he was about. He left the Anza trail at San Sebastián, now known as Harper's Well, at the junction of the San Felipe and Carrizo Creeks, almost in the center of the vast, dry and forbidding desert that spreads out from the Colorado River to the coastal range. From this point across the desert and over the mountains to San Diego was a distance of nearly 150 miles, a route starting from below sea level, in the bed of a lost sea, and passing up through a 5000-foot pass in wooded, green and wet mountain areas, and then down gently sloping valleys to the freshness and fogs of the ocean shore. From San Sebastián he went south along the Carrizo wash, one of the dry beds that carry flash floods through the desert, and rounding the arid, rocky Fish Creek Mountains, followed it west as it entered the desert valleys that rise in a series of low but giant steps, through what is called the Carrizo Corridor, toward the base of the high Oriflamme Mountains that form part of the coastal range. They were following, as the explorers usually did, a well-worn Indian road. Capt. A. R. Johnson of the American Kearny Expedition passed over the same route in 1846, and reported "the constant seeing of pieces of pottery shows that Indians have traversed it time out of mind."

Well of the Eight Echoes with wide Carrizo Corridor in distance.

In time this corridor was to become an historic route for American migrations westward, on the Sonora road from Mexico to Los Angeles, and then for the San Antonio-San Diego mail route and the Butterfield Stage route. From the dry-alkaline Carrizo they followed Vallecito Creek, passing Agua Caliente, "another spring on the slope of a little ridge," and pushing on into Vallecito Valley, which Fages identified as San Felipe Viejo. The harshness of the desert below was softening a little here, with evidence of springs and considerable greenness, and the farsighted Fages could see its possible future importance. It had conditions requisite for establishing a mission, and he later was to propose that a garrison be located here. In American times it became a stopping place on the mail and stage routes to San Diego and Los Angeles.

Vallecito, the second step on the ladder out of the harsh desert.

From there Fages led his men up through a small, rocky pass, La Puerte Grade, on to another step, Mason Valley. They were drawing up along the base of the high Oriflamme Mountains and a point of decision. Here the Carrizo Corridor ends. And here two trails split away. Breaking off to the right, or east, from Mason Valley is Box Canyon, a small, narrow rock-erupted gulch. The Americans under Gen. Kearny broke a wagon trail through this

Mason Valley is last step of Carrizo Corridor before mountains.

Box Canyon through which pioneers broke trail to Warner's Pass.

canyon and into another series of flat, wide valleys slowly turning to the north and northwest. Blair Valley, Earthquake Valley and San Felipe Valley form a low-level route leading to Warner's Hot Springs, in north central San Diego County. Here, again, one road led to San Diego and another to Los Angeles.

But Fages had other ideas. He turned directly west up the steep-walled Oriflamme Canyon, and then "winding from hilltop to hilltop," reached the summit of the Cuyamaca Mountains. This route later became the road of the Jackass Mail from San Antonio. Hero Eugene Rensch, tracing the route in an article in the California Historical Society Journal, says that:

"The trail Fages and his men followed on their ascent from the mouth of the canyon, 2500 feet in elevation, into Cuyamaca Valley, 2100 feet above, may still be traced along the ridge just south of a fork which enters Oriflamme Canyon from the northwest. It is deeply worn and is marked by stones piled one atop the other in Indian fashion; on one of the lower *mesitas*, or hilltops, old campsites are visible, with their grinding holes, broken pottery and scored earth."

The Spaniards accepted the rigors of the desert with little complaint. Many of them, as well as their fathers and grandfathers, had been born on the northern frontiers of New Spain. Most of this is a vast dry country known as the Sonora Desert which surrounds the Gulf of California, extending from northwest Mexico into southern Arizona, southeastern California, and down along the eastern side of the peninsula. The Colorado basin was known to the Spaniards as "*La Palma de la Mano de Dios,*" or the "Hollow of God's Hand." Only the silt delta built up by the flow of the Colorado River keeps the waters of the gulf from flooding the Imperial and Coachella Valleys. The lowest point in the Colorado is the Salton Sea, 273 feet below sea level.

Oriflamme Canyon, on the Fages' trail over coast mountain range.

Going through the heavy sands or over the baked ground of the Carrizo Corridor, as the explorers did so many years ago, the overwhelming silence seems to accentuate the desert's harshness. Distances become uncertain, as the dry, rocky hills fade into the haze of the horizon. Here and there are patches of green, indicating the presence of water seeping up from underground lakes fed by the streams which in rainy periods course down from the coastal mountains and sink through the sands. Harper's Well is more than 100 feet below sea level. The route into the Corridor, along Carrizo Creek Wash, is between 300 and 400 feet above sea level; the first step, the Carrizo Valley, is about 800 feet above sea level; the second step, Vallecito Valley, about 1500 feet, and the third step, Mason Valley, about 2000, lifting at its end to 2500 feet. The east entrance of the Corridor is wide; the west end is closed by the Oriflamme Mountains. There are only narrow paths of escape. The Oriflamme Mountains themselves form a gigantic mass, cut here and there by sharp canyons, and covered with small granite rocks seemingly crushed and powdered by time. In the early morning the mountains light up in the flame of the sun's direct rays; as the day wears on, they grow cold and desolate, and in the evening, as the marcher approaches, they seem to grow in size and loom up with a forbidding darkness. Always luring the explorers on in their long marches across the deserts toward the mountains, would be the cuts or clefts indicating possible passage ways. The deserts and their mountains with their changing moods appear beautiful to the visitor in a car or jeep. But Fr. Pedro Font, speaking for those who had to find a way across them, described the great hills of rocks as "the sweepings of the world."

Rensch believes the summit of the trail was reached southeast of Cuyamaca Lake, high in wooded country, and from there they started south through the carpeted valleys that flow easily down the wide mountain slopes toward the coast, going through Green Valley, Descanso Valley, across Little Descanso, and then into Viejas Valley, turning north just east of Alpine to reach the San Diego River. The rough map of the Fages route, drawn a year earlier by Josef Velásquez, a soldier, and the wording in the Fages' diary, indicate, however, that they may have followed a more westerly route and approached the San Diego River from the north. The mountain areas were criss-crossed with Indian roads or trails. At the river, at the mouth of Conejos Creek, they saw the village of the Great *Capitán*, or *El Capitán Grande*, now covered by the waters of El Capitan Reservoir. They went down the San Diego River to El Monte Park and then southward into El Cajon Valley, which the Spaniards knew as Rancho Santa Monica, a grazing ground for cattle of the San Diego Mission. They arrived at the mission on April 20, 1782, after making the journey of 150 miles in seven days.

Indian grinding holes at Green Valley along high, age-old trail.

The mountains had been conquered. Fages records that the next morning at the mission —

"We heard Mass in the mission, and setting out from there after midday, arrived at the presidio of San Diego two leagues away, at about four in the afternoon, and halted there. The lieutenant in command, Don José de Zúñiga, and his Ensign Velásquez, came about a half league to meet us. This royal presidio is in good condition as is the troop. They are building a little church in the center, and round the presidio a mud wall."

Official interest in this overland route to San Diego was kept alive for many years and San Diego was now tied directly to the Anza trail by the Fages trail. But the massacre on the Colorado

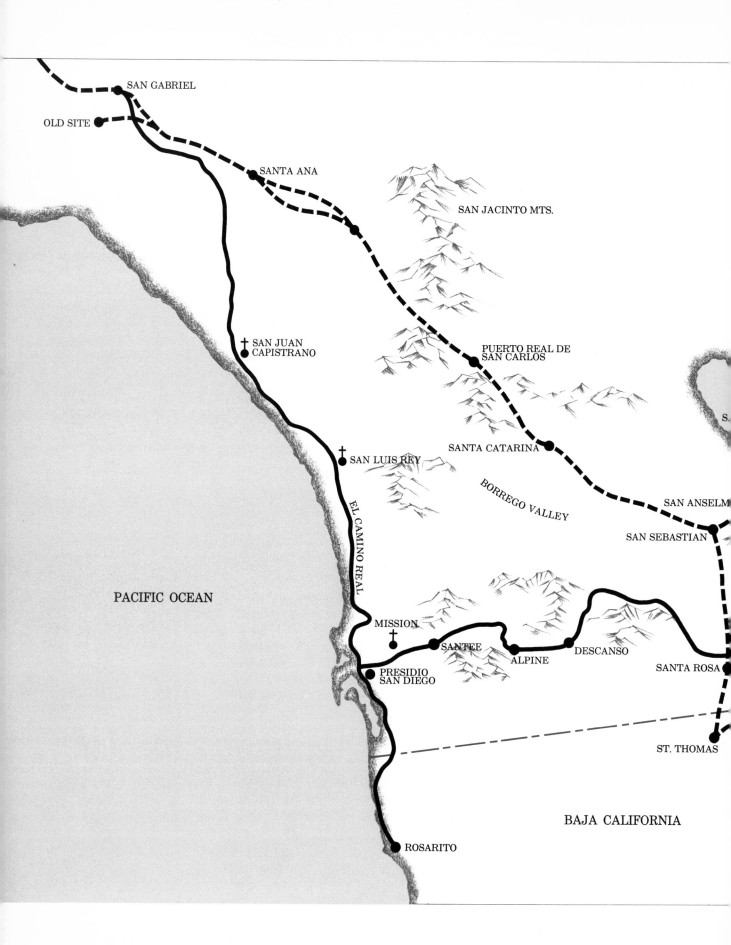

OLD SITE

SAN GABRIEL

SANTA ANA

SAN JACINTO MTS.

† SAN JUAN
CAPISTRANO

PUERTO REAL DE
SAN CARLOS

† SAN LUIS REY

SANTA CATARINA

EL CAMINO REAL

BORREGO VALLEY

SAN ANSELM

SAN SEBASTIAN

PACIFIC OCEAN

MISSION
†

SANTEE

ALPINE

DESCANSO

SANTA ROSA

PRESIDIO
SAN DIEGO

ST. THOMAS

BAJA CALIFORNIA

ROSARITO

S.

all but closed the land approach to California for as long as Spanish rule continued. The reopening of these routes was to come with the advance of the Americans.

What was San Diego like, when Fages returned as governor of California, after so long an absence? Lt. Ortega had been made commander of the new presidio at Santa Barbara and Lt. Zúñiga had been named as his successor at San Diego. The garrison by regulation was to consist of five corporals, 46 soldiers, a sergeant and a lieutenant. The presidio of San Diego was the command post of a military district embracing the missions of San Diego, San Juan Capistrano and San Gabriel, and each was to have a guard of six, with four to be on guard at the new pueblo of Los Angeles. This left 24 soldiers at the San Diego presidio. There were also a carpenter, a blacksmith, and a few servants.

The presidio district, over which San Diego was given command in 1780 and which was made effective the next year, embraced most of the present area of Southern California and part of Mexico, extending north to Santa Monica and San Gabriel, northeast through the San Bernardino Mountains to the Mojave Desert, east to the Colorado River, and south to Palóu's Marker. This was a marker placed by Fr. Palóu in the mountains 50 miles southeast of San Diego to mark the dividing line between Franciscan jurisdiction in New California and Dominican authority in Old California. Almost eight million persons now live in this area. The military force reported it had 44 swords, 48 lances, 49 muskets, 11 pistols, 47 leather jackets, 49 leather shields, 52 saddles, 50 horses, and 107 mules. It wasn't much, as Bancroft says:

"Respecting the presidio buildings . . . the records are silent . . . but I suppose that the palisades were at least replaced by an adobe wall enclosing the necessary buildings, public and private. Here on the hill lived about 125 persons, men, women and children. Each year in summer or early autumn one of the transport vessels entered the harbor and landed a year's supplies at the embarcadero several miles down the bay, to be brought up by the presidio mules. Every week or two, small parties of soldier couriers arrived from Loreto in the south, or Monterey in the north . . . with items of news for all. Each day of festival a friar came over from the mission to say Mass and otherwise care for the spiritual interests of the soldiers and their families; and thus the time dragged on from day to day from year to year with hardly a ripple on the sea of monotony."

There is some evidence the presidio was enclosed only on two or three sides until at least 1792.

Diary of Pedro Fages' expedition which broke trail to San Diego.

THE SPANISH TRAILS OF SAN DIEGO COUNTY. The Anza trail led through Borrego Valley to San Carlos Pass and San Gabriel. The Fages trail left the Anza trail and crossed the sierra. El Camino Real linked missions.

Soldier of Monterey sketched by member of Malaspina Expedition.

Wife of a Monterey soldier as she appeared in early settlement.

In the early years of the 1780's considerable progress was made at the mission. Frs. Lasuén and Figuer sent a lengthy report to the Fr. President saying that 671 Indians now belonged to the mission, the new church was 84 feet long and 15 feet wide, and had adobe walls three feet thick; the library had been enriched, and church goods included four linen surplices for the altar boys and a black stole for burials. By 1783 Fr. Lasuén reported that new structures included a granary, a refectory, guest rooms, a harness room, a kitchen and a pantry, and these buildings and the soldiers' quarters occupied three wings of a quadrangle. Each wing measured about 155 feet in length. The fourth side was closed by an adobe wall 11 feet high. Outside the quadrangle there was a tank for tanning hides. Mission records listed 966 baptisms, 232 marriages and 216 deaths.

A year after Fages' arrival at San Diego, Serra came down by ship from Carmel and remained for a month. His work was nearing an end. He had won most of his battles, but had paid the penalty. He was tired and troubled by pains in his chest. It was to be his last visit to the "mother mission."

With the Indians quiet, for a time, the only excitement was provided by Fages' domestic troubles. The governor brought his wife, Doña Eulalia de Callis, and his son, Pedro, up from Mexico, and she, being born of high position in Spain, was welcomed with respect and the joyous ringing of bells wherever she went on her long journey northward. She was the first lady of position to settle in California. There has been some historical suspicion that Fages' numerous promotions were due, in part at least, to the influence of her family. She was shocked at the almost naked condition of the Indians, gave her clothes to them until warned she wouldn't be able to replace any, and after giving birth to a daughter, started a campaign to induce her husband to return to Mexico. Their quarrels became a topic of widespread interest, particularly when the governor was banished from her bedroom for three months, and then later accused by her of showing more than platonic interest in an Indian maid servant. The friars intervened in the battle, and siding with Fages, after due investigation into her charges, ordered her into silence. When called away on gubernatorial duties, Fages insisted that his wife retire to San Carlos Mission, and wait his return, and when she at first refused, he broke down the door to their home and said he would tie her up and carry her there. She gave in, but her conduct at the mission, where she interrupted church services and flouted the authority of the friars, led to a threat to have her flogged and chained. Though she had said she would see him in *el infierno*, or hell, before she would go back to him, she finally subsided and eventually they were re-united in their home. The last we know of the matter is an official plea which she sent to the Royal *Audiencia*, asking her husband's removal as governor on the grounds the climate was injurious to his health, and of his efforts to prevent the document from being forwarded to Spain. The noble commander, known as "The Bear," evidently had been overmatched.

While New California was still in the throes of growth, time was beginning to take its toll in Old California. Governor Arrillaga made an inspection of the peninsula and reported he found hunger and desolation everywhere. Pablo Martínez, in his "History of Baja California," writes that a "terrible drought had ruined the crops and there was no food except meat, and this at very high prices due to the taxes that were charged. The mining industry had been completely paralyzed and for the greater part the colonists had left the region." Antigua California was sinking back into pre-conquest conditions, from which it has not yet fully emerged. Since taking over the Baja missions from the Fran-ciscans, who had got them from the Jesuits, the Dominicans had added three more, El Rosario, in 1774; Santo Domingo, in 1775; and San Vicente, in 1780, all on the Pacific trail to San Diego. There were now 21 missions in the peninsula. In a report on the situation, after an inspection trip, the haughty, crusty Fages made the following observations:

"All the Indians of California are lazy, incompetent and stupid. Their sole aspiration is to steal. The women do some spinning and weaving under the guidance of the missionaries. The cereals that they raise scarcely serve for the maintenance of the inhabitants. Pearl diving is the principal source of wealth, but does not prosper for lack of manpower. If the Indians should be given the earth he would not be capable of cultivating it, lazy as he is."

Now, as to the general conditions of the older mission establish-ments, particularly those in the south of the peninsula, Fages had this to say:

"The frequent change of missions is prejudicial to the progress of their interests; but the principal cause of ruin is the lack of water. The moving of natives from the missions of the north to the south has proved to be useless, because even though the Indians may have identical customs, they contract venereal diseases and die.... The missions of San José, Santiago, Todos Santos, San Javier, Loreto, Comondú, Cadegomo, Guadalupe and Mulege are on the way to total extinction.... There are missions among those named that go for months or years with no more than a few baptisms ... in all there are three times as many adults who die as there are babies born."

It had been a long time since the Jesuits broke the arid ground of Baja California and step by step built the little thin chain of

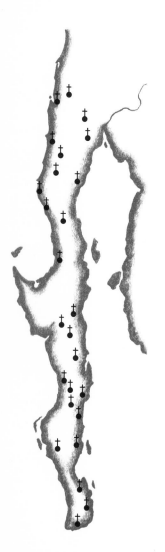

Jesuits, Franciscans and Dominicans built Baja California missions.

missions which provided the Franciscan ladder to New California. The Jesuits were expelled and the Franciscans soon willingly gave up the Baja missions to the Dominicans. The Dominicans lacked the pioneering drive of the Jesuits and the practical, work-a-day philosophy of the Franciscans. Their work was of the mind more than of the hand.

What was happening in Old California was to foreshadow the fate of the missions in New California.

This period saw several other explorations of San Diego County. The Spaniards began to chart the harbors they had claimed and to push explorations of the forbidding mountain ranges. Don Juan Pantoja y Arriaza, pilot on *La Princesa*, ferrying supplies between San Blas and the California ports, charted San Francisco Bay and the Santa Barbara channel, as well as San Diego Bay. His map and report, dated 1782, contains some place names appearing in history for the first time: *Punta de La Loma de San Diego* and *Bajos de Zúñiga*, or Zuniga Shoal, named after the new commandant at San Diego. *Punta de los Muertos*, or Dead Man's Point, is shown at the foot of San Diego's Market Street. It is not known for certain whether he referred to the burial place of the victims of scurvy from his own ship and the accompanying *La Favorita*, or perhaps the burial place of the scores who died on the original Serra-Portolá expedition. The first is the more accepted and more likely. Ships of the Serra-Portolá expedition anchored nearer where the San Diego River discharged into the bay and camp was made on a hillock. The dead were buried nearby.

The charts made by Pantoja were to show up in strange hands, French, English and American, in a new era of trade and exploration. The early efforts of Spain to keep all things secret didn't seem to be very binding on later seafaring men.

The mountains behind San Diego were challenged again, this time from the west by Velásquez, who it will be remembered drew the first rough crude map showing the Carrizo Corridor through which Fages had come, though he identified it as *Arroyo de San Sebastián*. The map shows two rivers, the San Diego and the Sweetwater, the latter identified as *Arroyo de la caballada*, or the watering place for livestock. Between the two rivers, but nearer the Sweetwater, he shows what evidently was another well-travelled Indian road, *Camino de Tevama*. This led up into the high mountain timber and pasturage. Two years later he broke trail for Fages in a new crossing of the sierra, this time in search of a more southerly crossing that might open a trail to the Colorado below the territory of the feared Yumas.

Velásquez kept a journal of the exploratory trip dated April 27, 1785, San Diego, and it starts as follows:

"Journal which I composed by order of the governor, Don Pedro Fages, from the notes which His Lordship has made personally from the frontier, across the sierra, ranging from the mouth of the Colorado River to the Gulf of California, passing through the lands of the Indian nations, Camillares, Cucupaes, Guipecamaes, Cajuenes and Yumas, noting this and the return, crossing the aforesaid sierra up to arrival at this presidio."

They went south down the lower bay along the Mission Highway, or El Camino Real, connecting the missions of New and Old California, for two leagues, which could be anything from six to 10 miles, and after coming to a brook, went upstream heading east. In three days of marching east, following stream beds, they came to a "very beautiful plain with grass and water and a warm spring besides." The Velásquez journal is difficult to follow, as he seemed more interested in incidents than geography, though the plain, which to them meant a valley, could have been no place other than Jacumba Valley. Jacumba has the only hot springs in that section of the county and was the site of an Indian rancheria. Meeting some Indians there, they inquired as to the best route over the mountains:

"I asked them where there was a good road to cross the sierra and go down to the river. They answered that there were three routes: one to the north, one to the east and another to the southeast. The first went over many hills and the horses couldn't make the descents. The second was better although it was rocky. The third was somewhat good but waterless. Having noted this it seemed to me more appropriate to try the second and keep nearer our course."

At the summit of the mountains they climbed a ridge from where they could see "the flats or plains through which the Colorado runs." They went down a long gulch through which they thought they could pass in a few hours but "there were so many boxed-in curves that night closed in upon us. . . In it we went down to the plain without finding water." There the road divided and they took the one to the northeast to avoid getting bogged down in the estuaries of the Colorado River. They went a considerable distance into Baja California, encountering heavily-wooded areas along the estuaries of the Colorado, sighting the sand dunes which stretch away to the little hills along the river which were the sites of the pueblos destroyed by the Yumas, and meeting bands of as many as 500 Indians. They were unable to find Santa Olaya, where Anza had watered, but Velásquez scouting ahead, did find a lagoon of good water. The journal reads:

"On the banks of this water, stood a rancheria which the Yumas were assaulting. Although I didn't see any dead there, I did indeed see the trace where they went out fighting, and at the distance of a shotgun shot, I began to see dead men. I saw these only along the road and on the sides of the hummocks. I saw seven bodies besides these seen by men herding the train. There were many buzzards about.

"These Yumas were mounted, and, according to their tracks, there were over twenty charging and killing up to the foot of the sierra which the horses couldn't climb. Those who escaped, according to the trace I saw when I climbed the hill, ran, spilling their grain and throwing away their weapons."

Velásquez hastened to tell Fages what he had learned, and Fages decided it was time to take leave of that region, and building frequent bonfires, so that other sections of his force and pack train could follow as quickly and directly as possible, they picked up the old Anza trail that led from Santa Rosa of the Flat Rocks, or Yuha Wells, near the U.S.-Mexican border in Imperial Valley, and headed for Harper's Well, or San Sebastián. From there they followed the Fages trail to *Valle de San Felipe* and then up Oriflamme Canyon to Cuyamaca Valley, and the Indian rancheria of Cuna-mac. On the way they had a brush with Indians, losing three of their horses, having one of their men wounded, and in turn, shooting to death the chief of the attackers, and learning that these same Indians had slain the deserting soldier whom Velásquez had sought on his first trip into the mountains two years before.

Fages had found that conditions hadn't changed very much at San Diego. Conversion was slow and uncertain, and even the majority of those accepting Christianity had to continue living in pagan rancherias, and more frequently than not, they became backsliders. Fages noted that, "The missionaries, having to deny their neophytes the provisions whilst the Indians were increasing the acreage, stormed Heaven with ceaseless petitions for rains, whenever their field needed them, until they succeeded. Thus it is since 1779, that some good harvests have been gathered."

But as for the Indians themselves, as good Christian prospects, Fages sadly lamented:

"Indeed, this tribe, which among those discovered is the most numerous, is also the most restless, stubborn, haughty, warlike, and hostile toward us, absolutely opposed to all rational subjection and full of the spirit of independence. The truth is that by the indefatigable tolerance and prudence of the missionaries together with their constant gentleness and other apostolic traits and supported by corresponding and opportune solicitude of the government, the Indians have been kept quiet, peaceful, and subdued for seven or eight years. Nevertheless, it must not be overlooked that a considerable armed force must needs be at hand in sufficient numbers to repress their natural and crusty pride."

CHAPTER SIX

MISSION of SAN CARLOS and BAY of CARMEL
UPPER CALIFORNIA.

Smith Elder & Co Cornhill.

FR. SERRA'S DEATH

At Carmel, Serra looked out from his beloved mission of San Carlos and knew that his work was coming to an end. In a sense, his death was to mark the closing of a period of exploration and isolation. In the 15 years since he had led the Franciscan fathers up into New California, no foreigners had broken into the rich and quiet land. A few Spanish settlements had been established but, in reality, California belonged to the nine missions which stretched along the coast from San Diego to San Francisco. The threat of Russian advances from Alaskan waters, which had brought about the belated Spanish decision to possess and settle California, persisted. And knowledge of Spain's growing weakness, as a result of military defeats in Europe, was attracting a rising interest in California and the American West Coast on the part of the French and the English. And then there were the brash Americans, whose ships were beginning to appear in shipping lanes around the world.

These events seemed far removed from the peaceful mission on the rim of Carmel Valley which Serra had made his headquarters. Most important to him in the 15 years had been the conversion of more than 4600 heathens who were now living at the missions as Christians. This was a harvest worthy of a giant of the church. He was tired now, ill, and 70 years old. His legs, which had troubled him over the years since his arrival in Mexico in 1749 at the age

HISTORY IS INDEBTED to a British naval officer, William Smyth, for this sketch of Mission San Carlos at Carmel. He was with the HMS Blossom *when it visited Monterey in 1827-28. He later became an admiral, geographer.*

of 36, were getting worse and he had difficulty in standing. "The nights I pass without much sleep, but the reason for this may not be so much my legs as the chief at the presidio." By this he meant his old antagonist, Gov. Neve.

The church at Carmel, now restored, rose-tinted in the shadows and with a yellow-green moss clinging to the damp walls and red tiles of the roof, sits on a site cut out of the sloping hillside of a green-carpeted valley opening on a little round bay that receives the full force of a plunging surf. The high hills are heavily wooded and near the shore of the bay are salt water marshes and cypress trees twisted by the constant winds. The freshness and greeness carried memories of that far-off island in the Mediterranean Sea on which Serra was born. In the old church yard at that time was a tall wooden cross that marked the grave of Fr. Juan Crespí, the companion who had come with him from Majorca and had shared his zeal and his disappointments. Crespí had died a year before at the age of 60.

It was a reflective period for Serra, and upon hearing the good news from Lasuén at San Diego, that at last the mother mission seemed to be getting on firm basis, he wrote that he was "especially pleased . . . with what you have to say about the happy delivery of Anna, sterile for so many years: I mean your fine mission with its many encouraging and copious fruits and blessings." But with dry humor, he added that he foresaw greater things ahead, and "the best thing for us to do is to give the saints something to be busy about. They have had plenty of rest, you know."

The pains in his chest were increasing in intensity, but on Aug. 19, as he had done each year for 14 years, he celebrated a High Mass in honor of St. Joseph. It was on this feast day that a ship had arrived with supplies and saved the first Christian settlement at San Diego in 1770. Fr. Palóu was with Serra at his death and he has told the story in these words, in part:

"On August 26, he arose, weaker still. He told me he had passed a bad night. As a result, he desired to prepare himself for whatever God might decree with regards to him. He remained secluded the entire day, admitting not a single distraction. That night he made his general confession to me amid many tears, and with a clear mind just as if he were well. When this was over, after a brief period of reflection he took a cup of broth and then went to rest, his wish being that no one remain with him in his little room.

"As soon as morning dawned on the 27th, I went to visit him and found him saying his breviary, since it was his custom always to commence Matins before daybreak. On the road he always began it as soon as morning dawned. He said he would like to receive the Most Holy Viaticum, and that for this he would go to the church. When I told him that was not necessary, that his cell could be fixed up in the best way possible and that the Divine Majesty would come to visit him, he said, 'No,' that he wanted to receive

Interior of Carmel Mission where Fr. Junípero Serra lies buried.

Him in church, since if he could walk there, there was no need for the Lord to come to him."

He walked to the church, a distance of more than 100 yards, accompanied by the commandant of the presidio, the soldiers of the mission and all the Indians of the town and mission. Fr. Palóu goes on to say:

"When he was finished, he returned to his little cell accompanied by all the people. Some shed tears from devotion and tenderness, others out of sadness and sorrow because they feared they would be left without their beloved father. He remained alone in his cell in meditation, seated on the chair at the table. When I beheld him thus absorbed, I saw no reason to enter to talk to him.

"I saw that the carpenter from the presidio was about to go in, but I stopped him. He said the father had called for him to make a coffin for his burial, and he wanted to ask him how he wished it made. This affected me. Not permitting him to enter and talk with the father, I gave him orders to make it like the one he had made for Father Crespí.

"During the night he felt worse, and he asked to be anointed. He spent the entire night without sleep, the greater part of it on his knees, while he pressed his chest against the boards of his bed. When I suggested that he lie down awhile, he answered that in that position he felt more relieved. Other short periods of the night he spent seated on the floor, leaning against the lap of some of the neophytes. All night long his little cell was filled with these neophytes, drawn there by the great love they had for him ... When I saw him in this state of exhaustion and leaning against the arms of the Indians, I asked the surgeon how he thought he was. He answered, since the father appeared to be in a very critical state, 'It seems to me that this blessed father wants to die on the floor.'

"I went in soon after and asked him if he wished absolution and the application of the plenary indulgence. He answered 'Yes,' and prepared himself. On his knees he received the plenary absolution, and I gave him also the plenary indulgence of the Order, with which he was most happy. He passed the entire night in the manner described. The feast of the Doctor of the Church St. Augustine dawned, Aug. 28, and he appeared relieved. He did not experience so much congestion in his chest. During the whole night he had not slept or taken anything. He spent the morning seated on the rush stool, leaning against the bed. This bed consisted of some roughhewn boards, covered by a blanket serving more as a covering, such as was customary at our college. Along the road he used to do the same thing. He would stretch the blankets and a pillow on the ground, and he would lie down on these to get his necessary rest. He always slept with a crucifix upon his breast, in the embrace of his hands. It was about a foot in length. He had carried it with him from the time he was in the novitiate at the college, nor did he ever fail to have it with him. On all his journeys he carried it with him, together with the blanket and the pillow. At his mission and whenever he stopped, as soon as he got up from bed he placed the crucifix upon the pillow. Thus he had it on this occasion.

An enlargement from Guerrero painting of Fr. Junípero Serra, of 1784.

About 10 o'clock in the morning on that feast of St. Augustine, the officers of the frigate came to visit him. They were the Captain and Commandant, José Cañizares, who was very well known to Serra since the first expedition in 1769, and the Royal Chaplain,

Don Cristóbal Díaz, who also had met him at Monterey in 1779. He received them with extraordinary greetings, and ordered that a solemn ringing of the bells be given in their honor.

"To them, he said, 'Do me this favor and work of mercy; throw a little bit of earth upon my body, and I shall be greatly indebted to you.' And casting his eyes upon me, he said: 'I desire you to bury me in the church, quite close to Father Fray Juan Crespí for the present; and when the stone church is built, they may put me wherever they want.'

"Within a short time he asked me to sprinkle his little room with holy water, and I did. All of a sudden very frightened, he said to me: 'Great fear has come upon me; I have a great fear. Read me the Commendation for a Departing Soul, and say it aloud so I can hear it.' I did as he asked, while all the gentlemen from the ship assisted. Also present were his priest companion, Fray Matías Noriega, and the surgeon, and many others both from the ship and from the mission. I read for him the Commendation for a Departing Soul, to which the Venerable Father, though dying, responded as if he were well, just sitting there on his little rush stool. As soon as I finished, he broke out in words full of joy, saying: 'Thanks be to God, thanks be to God, all fear has now left me. Thanks be to God, I have no more fear.'

"He walked to his little room where he had his bed. He took off only his mantle and lay down over the boards covered with a blanket, with his holy crucifix mentioned above, in order to rest. We all thought he was going to sleep, as during the whole night he had not slept any. The gentlemen went out to eat. Since I was a little uneasy, after a short time I returned and approached his bed to see if he was sleeping. I found him just as we had left him a little before, but now asleep in the Lord, without having given any sign or trace of agony, his body showing no other sign of death than the cessation of breathing; on the contrary, he seemed to be sleeping. We piously believe that he went to sleep in the Lord a little before two in the afternoon, on the feast of St. Augustine in the year 1784, and that he went to receive in heaven the reward of his apostolic labors."

Two funeral services were held, one on Sunday, Aug. 29, and a second on Sept. 4. The mission bells tolled throughout each day and at half hour intervals the *San Carlos* fired a salvo which was

Restored cell in which Junípero Serra spent his last hours.

THE PRESIDIO OF MONTEREY was sketched while under construction by a sailor-artist of a Spanish scientific expedition which visited California in 1791. The sailor, José Cardero, left many other sketches of life of the times.

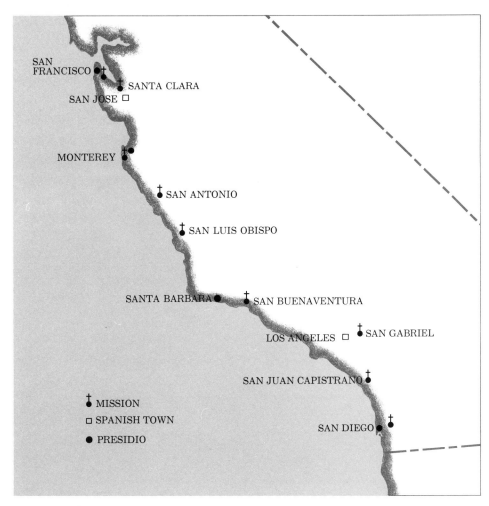

THIS WAS CALIFORNIA at the death of Fr. Junípero Serra. There were nine missions, four presidios and two pueblos. All this had been done in only 15 years. To him, San Diego was always the "Mother Mission" of California.

answered by the guns of the presidio. The room at the San Carlos Mission in which Serra died has been restored. It is a cell about 12 feet square, with thick adobe walls, a tile floor, and one narrow window. There is the bed of rough planks, with wooden pegs for legs, and one blanket, "to mortify the flesh." Serra's body lies between those of his two companions, Crespí and Lasuén, in front of the church sanctuary.

Palóu temporarily assumed the presidency of the California missions, though he was reluctant to do so, and a year later the College of San Fernando selected Fr. Lasuén of San Diego as president. Serra had left California with nine missions – San Diego, San Juan Capistrano, San Gabriel, San Buenaventura, San Luis Obispo, San Antonio, San Carlos, Santa Clara, and San Francisco. There were now four presidios – San Diego, Santa Barbara, Monterey and San Francisco, and two towns, or pueblos – Los Angeles and San Jose.

California was a closed province — bounded by Baja California and Mexico on the south, and locked off by high mountains and deserts on the east. To the north were the Russians. But the sea was an open door. On the morning of Sept. 15, 1786, two French vessels, the *Boussole* and the *Astrolabe*, under command of Jean Francois de Galaup, Comte de La Pérouse, put into Monterey. These were the first foreign ships to visit a California port. On a scientific and exploring journey around the world, they were received by Gov. Fages with grace and assistance in the way of supplies. The Frenchmen had been given careful instructions on what they were to do and report, and particularly, as regards the possibilities of the fur trade which the Russians had been exploiting far to the north.

Capt. Cook in his round-the-world voyage had reported on the extent of the sea otter fur trade along the northwest American coast, of which the Spaniards were aware but failed to do much about it. The instructions to La Pérouse, couched in careful language, expressed France's deep friendship and regard for Spain but, in the true spirit of foreign relations, suggested he look around and see just how many forts and guns were protecting California — just in case:

"If in the survey which he is to make of the north-west coast of America he finds at any points of that coast forts or trading-posts belonging to His Catholic Majesty he will scrupulously avoid everything which might give offence to the commandants or chiefs of those establishments; but he will use with them the ties of blood and friendship which so closely unite the two sovereigns in order to obtain by means thereof all the aid and refreshment which he may need and which the country may be able to furnish. . . . So far as it is possible to judge from the relations of those countries which have reached France, the actual possession of Spain does not extend above the ports of San Diego and Monterey, where she has built small forts garrisoned by detachments from California or from New Mexico. The *Sieur* de La Pérouse will try to learn the condition, force, and aim of these establishments; and to inform himself if they are the only ones which Spain has founded on those coasts. He will likewise ascertain at what latitude a beginning may be made of procuring peltries; what quantity the Americans (Indians) can furnish; what articles would be best adapted to the fur-trade; what facilities there might be for a French establishment, all this relating of course chiefly to the northern coast."

After an investigation, La Pérouse came to the conclusion that the fur trade could prove more profitable to the Spaniards than the richest gold mines of Mexico and reported that Fages said he easily could furnish 20,000 skins a year and even more with new establishments to the north.

On a visit to San Carlos Mission, La Pérouse wrote that:

". . . after having crossed a little plain covered with herds of cattle, . . . we ascended the hills and heard the sound of bells announcing our coming. We were received like lords of a parish visiting their estates for the first time. The president of the mission, clad in cope, his holy-water sprinkler in hand, received us at the door of the church illuminated as on the grandest festivals."

It was all very colorful, but La Pérouse, though he had praise for the character, zeal, and motives of the missionaries as individuals, and acknowledged the shortcomings of the aboriginal Indians, thought the Franciscan establishments bore an unhappy resemblance to the slave plantations of Santo Domingo.

"With pain we say it, the resemblance is so perfect that we have seen men and women in irons or in the stocks; and even the sound of the lash might have struck our ears, that punishment being also admitted, though practiced with little severity."

The French were soon on their way, crossing the Pacific, visiting the Philippine Islands, coasting past Japan and China, losing 11 men to savages at the Navigator Islands, and then, after touching at Botany Bay on the coast of New Zealand, where the rest of La Pérouse's journal was left behind, vanishing from sight. Nothing further ever was heard of the ships or crew.

La Pérouse's report of the extent of Russian operations along the northern American coast caused Spain once again to stir into some kind of action. Two ships were sent as far as the Alaskan coast, and José Martínez reported seeing Russian and English activity. He was sent back the next year, found one American and three English ships at Nootka Sound, and an armed trading post on shore. He seized the English ships, confiscated their cargoes, took some of the officers prisoners — and brought about a diplomatic crisis which almost caused another war between Spain and England. But Spain, already in decline and unable to call on her ally, France, torn by revolution, eventually gave up and withdrew all her claims to territory north of the present California line.

Spain did send a scientific expedition of its own to California, which compiled extensive data which, however, in so typical a manner, found its way into the files of no concern. This was the expedition led by Capts. Alejandro Malaspina and José Bustamante y Guerra, and which is known historically as the Malaspina Expedition. Most of the scientific work was done at Monterey in 1791, and the expedition never stopped at San Diego, but, evidently, working with available information gathered in California and from previous expeditions, it reported that San Diego "offers to view a pleasant variety of trees, shrubs and fragrant plants, and

Location of Nootka Sound on Vancouver Island in North Pacific.

Next page, THE THIRTEEN COLONIES had formed into the United States, but still little was known of the vast interior of America. The Spaniards held the West Coast and Southwest. The interior was referred to as Louisiana.

71

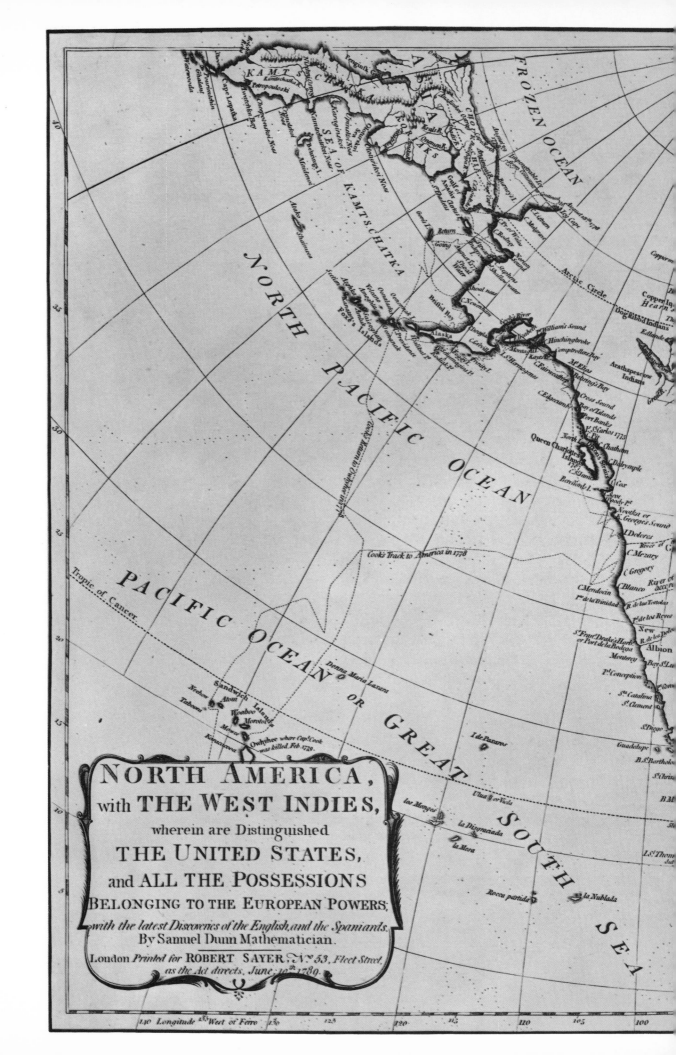

FROZEN OCEAN

KAMTSCHR

SEA OF KAMTSCHATKA

NORTH PACIFIC OCEAN

Arctic Circle

Copper In.
Hearn's

Dog Ribbed Indians

Arathapescow
Indians

Cooks Track to America in 1778

Tropic of Cancer

PACIFIC OCEAN OR GREAT

SOUTH SEA

Denna Maria Lazara

Sandwich Islands
Atoui
Neehow
Tahoora
Woahoo
Morotoi
Mowee
Karakakooa Owhyhee where Cap.t Cook
was killed Feb.t 1779

I de Pazaros

las Mongos

Ulua ij or Viela

la Disgraciada

la Mesa

Rocca partida   la Nublada

NORTH AMERICA,
with THE WEST INDIES,
wherein are Distinguished
THE UNITED STATES,
and ALL THE POSSESSIONS
BELONGING TO THE EUROPEAN POWERS;
with the latest Discoveries of the English, and the Spaniards.
By Samuel Dunn Mathematician.

London *Printed for* ROBERT SAYER, N.º 53, Fleet Street,
as the Act directs, June 10.th 1789.

140 Longitude 135 West of Ferro 130   125   120   115   110   105   100

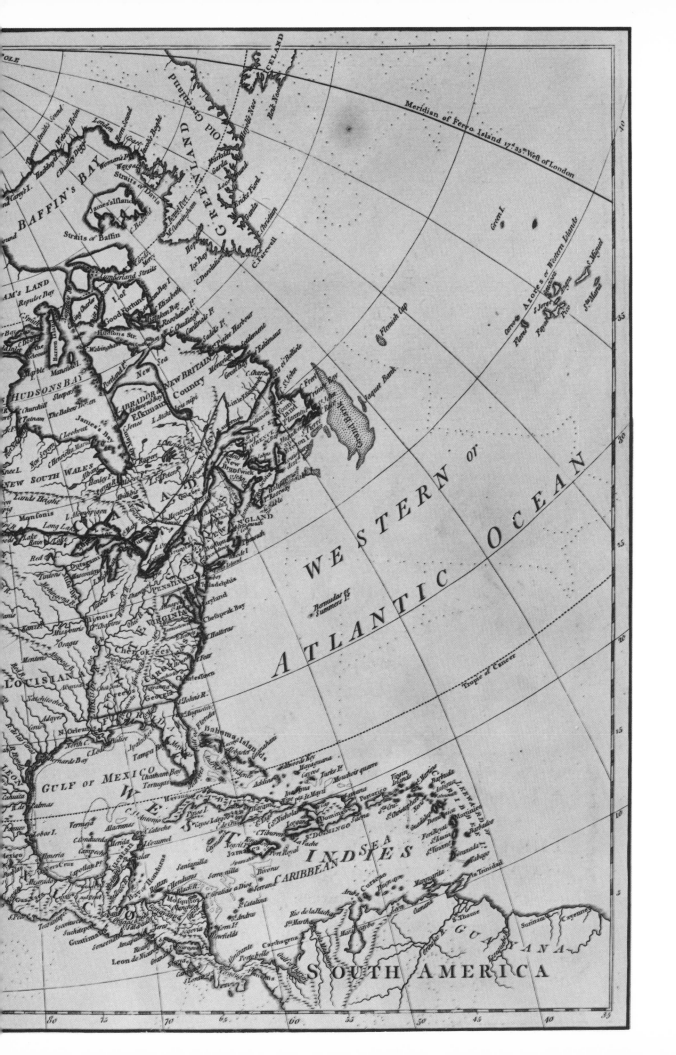

near the beach some beautiful meadows," . . . and with cooling winds to soften the summer heat, "nature always different, always wonderful, had lavished here her gifts for the well-being of man." Artists with the expedition produced some excellent drawings of California bird and animal life, Indian costumes, and the way of life and dress in the early Spanish days. In the following year a man, identified as a naturalist named José Longinos Martínez, with an escort of soldiers, reached San Diego, and reported that "the summit of the little mountain on the point of the Port of San Diego is strewn with opaque garnets." This didn't seem to excite anyone.

The situation at San Diego was quiet. Little happened to disturb the routine of frontier life. Work at the mission progressed and affairs at the presidio were under the capable direction of Lt. Zúñiga. In a letter to his mother, the thoughtful and devoted Zúñiga wrote that:

"He had the pleasure of informing her that in the course of the past year a beautiful church had been commenced at the presidio under his charge and an image in honor of the pure and Immaculate Conception provided for; that he had been instrumental in accomplishing the work and had himself personally labored as a mason and as a carpenter and had painted the whole with his own hands; and that he thanked God that she would thus see that her son, who had done things that were evil, was now zealous in doing things that were good."

Twenty-one years after the founding of the first mission, there were about 1000 white persons in California. In the San Diego district, which included the Missions of San Diego, San Juan Capistrano and San Gabriel, as well as the Royal Presidio, there were 220 persons. The presidio population was about 125. The pueblo of Los Angeles had 73 men and 51 women.

In the north, Fages, tired and ill, resigned his post as governor, and this brave but quarrelsome officer, a reckless horseman and eager hunter, passed out of the history of California. He hoped to go back to his home in Spain but it is believed he died in Mexico.

It is to an Englishman that we now turn, for the next chapter in the story of San Diego.

CHAPTER SEVEN

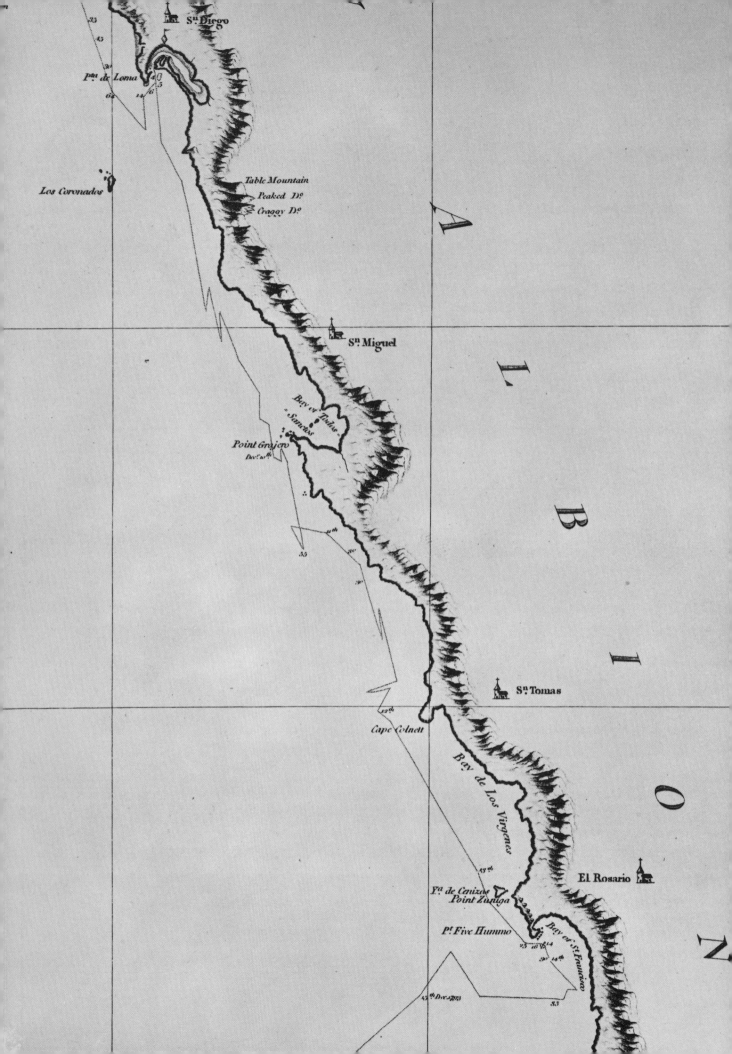

Sᵗ Diego

Pᵗ de Loma

Los Coronados

Table Mountain
Peaked Dᵒ
Craggy Dᵒ

Sⁿ Miguel

Bay of Todos
= Santos
Point Grajero

Cape Colnett

Sᵗ Tomas

Bay de Los Virgenes

El Rosario

Yª de Cenizas
Point Zuñiga

Pᵗ Five Hummo

Bay of St Francisco

A L B I O N

GEORGE VANCOUVER

The Spaniards withdrew behind a wall of secretiveness and suspicion — the world was not to know about California, if they
could help it. The first foreigner to break through this wall for a
thorough look at San Diego was a British sea captain, George
Vancouver. He found San Diego a dreary and lonesome place,
poorly protected, its people indolent and incapable of resisting
any real invasion. What an irresistible temptation to foreigners!

Though the Spaniards claimed California through the discoveries
of Juan Rodríguez Cabrillo in 1542, the English couldn't forget
that Sir Francis Drake had been along the coast, as a gentleman
pirate, in 1579, had gone ashore, tacked up a claim on a brass
plate, and named the country New Albion. It was time for another
look at the northwest American Continent. George Vancouver,
who had been with the famous Capt. James Cook on his round-
the-world explorations, was named to command a small fleet,
armed, but carrying surveyors, map makers, astronomers, botanists
and geologists, and this expedition has left us detailed descriptions
of San Diego and the mode of life in Spanish California times.
He had instructions similar to those of the Frenchman, La Pérouse,
to investigate the fur trade, as well as to chart the coast and all its
waterways, and investigate and report on all Spanish settlements.
His reports on both Upper and Lower California were to uncover

THE ENGLISH kept a close watch on California in the early days. George
Vancouver scouted the coast and drew this map. He was the first of many
foreigners who visited San Diego in the years it was a Spanish possession.

77

the weakness of the Spanish hold and the little progress which had been made on colonization and development.

Vancouver's three vessels — the *Discovery*, the *Chatham* and the *Daedalus* — were on the American coast in April of 1792 and conducted what probably was the last search for the fabled Strait of Anian, a navigable passage which must connect the Atlantic and Pacific Oceans and which had intrigued mariners since the days of Cortés and Cabrillo. They didn't find it, but near the mouth of the Columbia River they did find an American brig, the *Columbia*, of Boston. Capt. Robert Gray, upon sighting the British ships, hoisted an American flag and fired a salute of welcome.

The *Columbia* had been the first American ship to encircle the globe. Capt. Gray left Boston in 1787 and after trading for otter furs along the Northwest Coast, went on to China and then around the world. Now he was on another voyage, in which he discovered the Columbia River, picked up a cargo of furs which he sold for $90,000 worth of Chinese goods in Canton, and returned to Boston after an absence of three years, and with a rich profit. The success of his trading was not to be overlooked.

In all, Vancouver made three different visits along the coast, and entered San Diego Bay on Nov. 27, 1793. His ships were the

POINT LOMA has been the subject of much historical dispute as to whether it was ever wooded. This sketch by George Vancouver in 1793 indicates there was a heavy growth of brush but evidently no sign of a forest or trees.

first foreign vessels ever to visit here. As far as he was concerned, St. Diego or San Diego, was part of New Albion, as he persisted in calling California.

The ships dropped anchor without the slightest indication of having been seen, let alone being welcomed. Certainly everybody couldn't have been asleep. Finally, Vancouver dispatched a Lt. Swaine up the harbor to the presidio to inform the commanding officer of the arrival of the ships and to inquire if any dispatches had arrived for them by land.

The presidio guard was acting very cautiously. Vancouver's arrival had been anticipated and careful instructions had been received. While Swaine was on his way to the presidio, a messenger brought to the *Discovery* a polite letter from *Señor* Don Antonio

Grajera, a lieutenant in the Spanish cavalry and commandant at San Diego, requesting to be informed of the business that had brought the little squadron within the limits of his command.

When Swaine returned with the news that he had been received with politeness and hospitality, Vancouver answered Grajera's letter and announced he would pay his official respects the following day. All very formal. Vancouver tells of his visit:

"This visit, accordingly took place, accompanied by Lts. Puget and Hanson. On landing we found horses in waiting for us, on which we rode up to the presidio, where we were received with that politeness and hospitality we had reason to expect from the liberal behaviour of the commandant on the preceding evening. His friendly offers were immediately renewed, and were accompanied by similar assurances of assistance from *Señor* Don José Zúñiga, the former commandant, who had recently been promoted to the rank of captain of infantry, and appointed to the charge of an important post on the opposite side of the Gulf of California, for which he was then preparing to depart."

Yes, the Spanish were polite, but, Vancouver continued:

"These gentlemen informed us that having been given to understand it was my intention to visit this port they had long expected us, and that about four days before, on being informed of the probability of our arrival, they had, to their great mortification, received at the same time from *Señor* Arrillaga (the acting governor, Capt. José Joaquín de Arrillaga) such a list of restrictions as would inevitably deprive both parties of that satisfaction that could not otherwise have failed to render our stay here very pleasant."

The orders which presumably embarrassed the reception committee prohibited the transaction of any business on shore, excepting the procuring of wood and water; that when the above supplies were furnished, which was to be done with all possible expedition, it was expected that they were to depart immediately. Vancouver remained for 12 days. He wrote in his journal that:

"The profound secrecy which the Spanish nation has so strictly observed with regard to their territories and settlements in this hemisphere, naturally excites, in the strongest manner, a curiosity and a desire of being informed of the state, condition and progress of the several establishments provided in these distant regions, for the purposes of converting its native inhabitants to Christianity and civilization."

George Vancouver, the English explorer who visited old presidio.

However, he did have in his possession a copy of the chart of San Diego Bay made in 1782 by Pantoja and which evidently had been reproduced by Alexander Dalrymple, official hydrographer of the British East India Company. This map had also turned up in the hands of La Pérouse. Vancouver noted some corrections in distances and soundings. San Diego, he found, didn't present much of a military threat.

"The Presidio of San Diego seemed to be the least of the Spanish establishments with which we were acquainted. It is irregularly built, on very uneven ground, which makes it liable to some inconveniences, without the obvious appearance of any object for selecting such a spot. The situation of it is dreary and lonesome, in the midst of a barren uncultivated country, producing so little herbage that, excepting in the spring months, their cattle are sent to the distance of 20 or 30 miles for pasturage. During that season, and as long as the rainy weather may continue, a sufficient number are then brought nearer for the use of the presidio and mission; and such as have not been wanted are again sent back to the interior country when the dry weather commences; which, although more productive in point of grass, is not very prolific in grain, pulse, fruits, roots, or other culinary vegetables. I understood that they are frequently obliged to resort for a supply of these articles to the mission of San Juan Capistrano, which abounded in vegetables and animal productions, consisting of great herds of cattle, flocks of sheep, and goats; and I was assured it was one of the most fertile establishments in the country."

A botanist with the expedition, Archibald Menzies, also kept a detailed journal, which is now in the British Museum, and he tells of the visit to the presidio.

"When we arrived at the presidio we were met on the outside of the gate by the Commandant and Capt. Zúñiga and the Guard was under arms to receive Lt. Puget as commander of the *Chatham*. We were conducted to the Commandant's house which is on the opposite side of the area facing the gate and we must do him credit to say that it is on the whole a much neater dwelling than any we saw at the Northern Settlements, but the

A SPANISH MAP OF SAN DIEGO BAY made by Juan Pantoja in 1782 fell into foreign hands. In the center is a French version in possession of La Perouse Expedition, next the English version of the Vancouver Expedition.

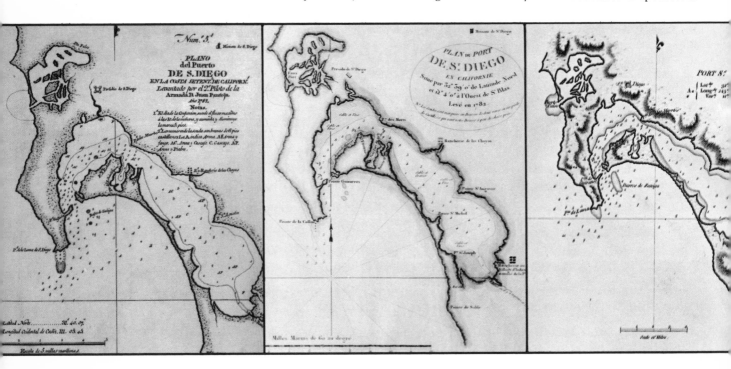

soldiers' barracks which are arranged contiguous to the wall round the square are wretched hovels. The church is in the middle of one side of the square and though but small is neatly finished and kept exceedingly clear and in good order, but the presidio in general we conceived much inferior in point of situation, regularity and cleanliness to that of St. Barbara though the latter is more infant a settlement. This is situated on the western declivity of a rugged imminence and guarded only by three guns mounted in carriages before the entrance."

Despite the official barriers against cooperation, the Spaniards and the Englishmen seemed to enjoy each other's company. Menzies said that Capt. Zúñiga and the commandant came down to visit the *Daedalus* and afterward had lunch on the *Discovery*. "They were both remarkably pleasant and intelligent men and seemed very partial to our little convivial parties." The mission fathers also sent a quantity of fruit and kernels, one being noted as *simmondsia californica nut*, commonly known as goat nut, with an almond-like taste, which Menzies said was a natural produce of the country and praised for its medicinal properties, and which was taken to England and planted in His Majesty's Royal Garden at Kew.

Ancient French organ which was brought to San Gabriel Mission.

Fr. Lasuén, the president of the missions, happened to arrive at San Diego during the visit of the ships and hastened aboard to pay his respects to Vancouver.

"This venerable father, though upwards of 60 years of age," Menzies wrote, "in executing the duties of his calling is exposed in his journeys from mission to mission to great fatigue and frequent hardships — he is sometimes obliged to sleep out in the open air in the valleys or mountains whenever night overtakes him and that too in the most inclement season, and he runs no little risque (sic) of being attacked and cut off in his route by savage tribes, yet this duty he cheerfully performs with a degree of zeal and perseverance that excites admiration and that at a time of life when his age and constitution more justly claim the comfort and care of retirement."

Vancouver gave Lasuén a small organ and it was taken to Monterey. Menzies told of the shortage of water and was informed that crews of early Spanish ships found water by digging in the sand southward and near the entrance of the harbor. Even in 1792, crews of Spanish ships bound south for San Blas were warned to take aboard plenty of water at points northward before touching at San Diego. Menzies also made a curious observation about an island lying south of San Clemente, which the Spaniards said was a new one and had not been laid down on their charts. No such island has ever been known to exist.

The way of life in California, according to Vancouver, was not calculated to produce any great increase in white inhabitants:

"The Spaniards in their missions and presidios, being the two principal distinctions of Spanish inhabitants, lead a confined, and in most respects

81

a very indolent life; the religious part of the society within a cloister, the military in barracks. The last mentioned order do nothing, in the strictest sense of the expression; for they neither till, sow, nor reap, but wholly depend upon the labour of the inhabitants of the missions and pueblos for their subsistence, and the common necessaries of life. To reconcile this inactivity whilst they remain on duty in the presidio, with the meritorious exertions that the same description of people are seen to make in the pueblos, is certainly a very difficult task; and the contradiction would have remained very prejudicial to their character, had I not been informed, that to support the consequence of the soldier in the eyes of the natives, and to insure him their respect, it had been deemed highly improper that he should be subjected to any laborious employment. This circumstance alone is sufficient to account for the habitual indolence and want of industry in the military part of these societies.

"From this brief sketch, some idea may probably be formed of the present state of the European settlements in this country, and the degree of importance they are of to the Spanish monarchy, which retains this extent of country under its authority by a force that, had we not been eye-witnesses of its insignificance in many instances, we should hardly have given credit to the possibility of so small a body of men keeping in awe, and under subjection, the natives of this country, without resorting to harsh or unjustifiable measures. The number of their forces, between port San Francisco and San Diego, including both establishments, and occupying an extent in one line of upwards of 420 nautical miles, does not amount to 300, officers included; and from San Diego southward, to Loreto, not above 100 more, exclusive of the garrison and settlers residing at that port. These are all that are employed for the protection of the missions. Those of the Dominican order, to the southward of San Diego, are 16 in number, each of which is guarded by five soldiers only. Of the Franciscan order, to the northward of San Diego, there are 13; some guarded by five, whilst others have eight, 10 or 12 soldiers for their protection in those situations where the Indians are more numerous and likely to prove troublesome. . . . The presidio of San Diego and Santa Barbara are each garrisoned by a company of 60 men; out of which number guards are afforded to the missions of the same names. The garrison of Monterey, generally, I believe, consists of a company of 60 or 80 men, and that of San Francisco 36 men only. These soldiers are all very expert horsemen, and, so far as their numbers extend, are well qualified to support themselves against any domestic insurrection; but are totally incapable of making any resistance against a foreign invasion.

"With little difficulty San Diego might also be rendered a place of considerable strength, by establishing a small force at the entrance of the port; where, at this time, there were neither works, guns, houses, or other habitations nearer than the presidio, which is at the distance of at least five miles from the port, and where they have only three small pieces of brass cannon.

"Such is the condition of this country as it respects its internal security, and external defence; but why such an extent of territory should have been thus subjugated, and after all the expence and labour that has been bestowed upon its colonization turned to no account whatever, is a mystery in the science of state policy not easily to be explained."

The Spaniards, Vancouver concluded, had merely cleared the way for the "ambitious enterprises of those maritime powers." By placing establishments so far from each other, and failing to

George Vancouver thanks Viceroy for his welcome in California.

strengthen the barrier to their valuable possessions in New Spain, "they have thrown irresistible temptations in the way of strangers to trespass over their boundary." He foresaw that a well-conducted trade, especially in furs, "between this coast and China, India, Japan and other places, may on some future date, under a judicious and well-regulated establishment, become an object of serious and important consideration to any nation that shall be inclined to reap the advantage of such commerce."

It was time to leave. Vancouver's ships sailed back across the Pacific and upon returning to London, instead of being able to live out his days in honor, Vancouver fell into disgrace, due partly to an incident that took place on his ship. He was accused of flogging a midshipman who was a young nobleman by the name of Thomas Pitt, a member of the great Pitt family. Flogging was common on ships of war, and during a four-year period the records showed there were 95 cases of flogging on the *Discovery*. The law of the sea was harsh, and as his was an independent command far off in the Pacific, there was no time or means of applying to the admiralty for court martial. Whether he actually had young Pitt flogged is not known. Such an act against a man of high birth was considered unthinkable. The ship's records merely note that Pitt was sent back to England from Hawaii, on another ship. When Vancouver himself returned, he found young Pitt had become Baron Camelford. He challenged Vancouver to a duel, which was refused, but later Pitt had the satisfaction, if it could be called that, of caning him. A wild and irrational person, young Pitt eventually was accused of taking part in a mutiny, was expelled from the naval service, and later met death in a duel. But Vancouver never recovered from the humiliation. In his late years he completed five of six books on his journeys, dying on May 12, 1798.

The Spanish government was now genuinely alarmed. Something would have to be done to defend California. The presidios were to be strengthened and no warships large enough to seize San Diego were to be permitted to enter the bay. The building of a fort on Punta Guijarros, or Ballast Point, a necessity even Vancouver had seen, was ordered. There was considerable talk, as usual, but not much action. But when Spain and England went to war in 1797, though the news was late in reaching as far away as San Diego and Monterey, precautions were taken to thwart any British invasion, which all felt sure was coming. All British ships were to be seized at once; at the first sight of the enemy, military forces were to be concentrated at specific points, and all livestock driven inland. Men drilled in the presidio squares and messengers

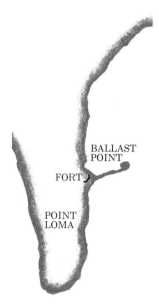

Location of Fort Guijarros on Ballast Point as it was in 1800.

Voucher for nails, labor on esplanade of Fort Guijarros in 1808.

scurried importantly up and down the state. The Indians were placed on the alert by assuring them the English were far worse than the Spaniards.

Keeping up the defenses of San Diego always had been a problem. Four years before the threat of a British invasion Gov. Diego de Borica had advised the viceroy that three sides of the presidio were in a weakened condition, owing to the bad quality of timber used in roofing for the abutting structures, while the warehouses, church and officers' quarters on the fourth side were in good condition. Lumber was shipped down from Monterey on

THE SPANIARDS were meticulous record keepers and this old report shows the number of inhabitants at the Presidio of San Diego. It is signed by Lt. Manuel Rodríguez who added many exciting chapters to presidio history.

Provincia de Californias. Jurisdicion de S.ⁿ Diego.

Estado que manifiesta el numero de Yndios y Gente de razon existente en cha Jurisdicion segun el Padron de fin de este año de 1798, con distincion de Hombres, mugeres, Muchachos y Muchachas.

	Indios.					Españoles, y otras ca...				
	Hombres	Mugeres	Muchachos	Muchachas	Totales	Hombres	Mugeres	Muchachos	Muchachas	Totales
Presidio de San Diego	2		2		4	70	32	44	27	173
San Diego	561	644	158	163	1.526	5				5
San Gabriel	445	455	357	211	1.468	9	6	9	4	28
San Juan Capistrano	389	402	115	201	1.107	9	5	9	7	30
San Miguel	54	87	26	38	205	13	10	7	7	37
San Luis Rey	58	59	46	47	210	6	5	5	6	22
	1.509	1.647	704	660	4.520	112	58	74	51	295

San Diego 31. de Diciembre de 1798.

Manuel Rodriguez

the *Princesa*, and on Nov. 8, 1796, an esplanade, powder magazine, a flag, and a barracks and quarters for married personnel of Catalán Volunteers were blessed by the friars amid artillery salute.

Workmen and timber also were sent from Monterey for the new fort on Ballast Point, while Santa Barbara furnished axle trees and wheels for 10 carts to haul lumber and rocks. Engineer Alberto Córdoba inspected the defenses in 1796 and found that the safety of San Diego would have to depend on the enemy being ignorant of its weaknesses.

The arrival of 25 additional Catalán Volunteers raised the strength of the San Diego company to 90 men, and the population on Presidio Hill now totaled more than 180 persons. No foreign invasion ever materialized though the captors of a Spanish vessel claimed that some of their men were on the coast in 1797, as crewmen of two English vessels, and entered San Diego Bay and took soundings by moonlight.

Antonio Grajera, who had succeeded Lt. Zúñiga, had his troubles with women and liquor which affected his mind and health, and he was ordered home, dying two days out of the port while aboard the *Concepción*. Death also took Fr. Fuster, who had survived the attack on the San Diego Mission. He died Oct. 21, 1800, at San Juan Capistrano Mission. A band of 200 Indians attacked *Alférez* Grijalva while he was returning from San Miguel Mission with three natives accused of murder, and Grijalva's horse and one Indian were killed. Eight foundling children came up from Mexico to live at San Diego and an earthquake, on Nov. 22, 1800, cracked the warehouse and a number of the military houses in the presidio. The presidio commandant tried to induce Spanish youths to learn trades. They were insulted at the suggestion of going to work.

Despite all the work that had been done on the presidio, in the effort to strengthen it, its abandonment was urged in 1802 by Lt. Manuel Rodríguez, the acting commandant who soon was to take over officially as captain. In a letter dated Jan. 13, he reported to Gov. Arrillaga that the presidio was in great danger, as the water was coming over the summit of the lomas and gradually eating away the walls, and unless something was done right away they would fall in ruin. In order to build a new presidio, he said it would be necessary to have one or two professors in the art of building as the person occupying this position at the time apparently was not equipped to know just what should be done, which could be judged by the small quantities of adobes and lumber that he had asked.

"Every year, daily repairs are made to this presidio due to the circumstances of its poor location and being the oldest of all such establishments. . ."

This letter also mentioned that a room added to the barracks and the five houses built for the married Volunteers a few short years before were already falling into ruin due to their hurried and poor construction.

Besides water, there was another factor which was causing great damage. The wind kept knocking down the front walls, which Rodríguez had repaired twice before, and it was considered fortunate that no serious injuries had been sustained. The tiles on the roofs of the principal buildings as well as of all the surrounding houses were falling off, leaving the rooftops broken and useless.

Rodríguez concluded by saying that it was absolutely necessary that a new presidio be erected, but this time to be situated where the wind and water would not affect it. Nothing much happened. And by 1806 even the cannons had been eroded and the wood on the esplanade had so rotted that it was impossible to roll the cannons. Besides, the ammunition didn't fit the cannons.

Now, significant to the history of California, and of San Diego, was the appearance in northern California waters of the American ship *Otter*, from Boston. She showed up at Monterey on Oct. 29, 1796. She carried six guns and 26 men. But she wasn't interested in fighting but in trade: The fur trade. Two years later four American sailors who had been left in Baja California by the American ship *Gallant*, were brought to the presidio at San Diego and put to work, while waiting for a vessel to take them to San Blas for eventual passage home. In 1799, a British sloop-of-war, the *Mercedes*, stopped briefly at San Diego, but as the war was over, the visit passed without incidence. A year later, on Aug. 25, 1800, the first American ship entered San Diego Bay. She was the brig *Betsy*, out of Boston and under the command of Capt. Charles Winship. She took on wood and water and sailed away, carrying $100,000 worth of furs obtained on the northwest coast. Her destination was Canton, China.

CHAPTER EIGHT

Ship Alexander of Boston,
Robert S. Pulsifer, Master
Going out the port of Havre de grace.

THE BOSTON SHIPS

It was the Boston men who ended the isolation of San Diego and introduced American goods and influences into California. The New England maritime merchants and sailors of Boston and Salem and Marblehead took the American flag to every major port in the world, opened many new routes of trade, and in the long view, gave to America the command of the seas. Most of them went to sea while barely in their teens, and expecting no favors but hard work, asking nothing of others or their government but the right to sail the oceans without hindrance, they built their fortunes on danger and chance, and produced the wealth that enriched New England and all of the struggling United States. Their mansions still stand on Boston's Beacon Hill and around Salem's Washington Square, with the dignity of a Century and a half.

The men of Salem, most of them Puritans with several centuries of hard living behind them, pushed their ships on the long runs to the mysterious lands beyond the eastern horizon, across the Atlantic Ocean and around the Cape of Good Hope, to Arabia, India, and Sumatra and the Spice Islands, and then China. The reports of the *Columbia* on the possibilities in the fur trade, and the subsequent successful voyage of the *Otter*, diverted many of the ships of Boston from the Atlantic to the Pacific. They drove their way down the coast of the Americas and around Cape Horn,

THE GALLANT SHIPS OF BOSTON led the way to California. This is an old painting of the Alexander. *Records indicate she probably was the same* Alexander *that enlivened the fur smuggling days in and out of San Diego port.*

the most difficult and most terrifying passage in the world, and then sailed up the Pacific Coast, defying the Spaniards at Valparaiso and Lima, and then sweeping as far north as Nootka Sound. Turning back south they hunted for furs at San Francisco, Monterey, Santa Barbara, San Diego and the offshore islands, and along the Baja California bays. After a final call at San Blas, on the mainland of Mexico, and with hulls stuffed with rich pelts, they squared away for the run across the Pacific to the Hawaiian Islands, or the Sandwich Islands, as they were known. In all, 18 months to two years had been spent on the Pacific Coast. Hawaii, or O whye, as it was often phonetically spelled in those days, became the heart of the Pacific, and on its shore you could buy anything from Lowell shirting to New England rum, and even the first constitution of the Kingdom of Hawaii as drawn by Kamehameha III, reflected New England religious influence with its declaration that "no law shall be enacted which is at variance with the words of the Lord Jehovah." At Hawaii, after resting on its warm sands and among its friendly people, they would pick up a cargo of sandalwood and proceed to China. China was the rich market for sandalwood and seal skins, and in particular, for the most beautiful of all furs — that of the sea otter. Seal skins were taken in tremendous numbers in warm southern waters, by both Salem and Boston ships, and traded in at Canton. Seal

CHINA HAD A CLOSE RELATIONSHIP with San Diego in Spanish times. Canton of the 1800's was lined with hongs, or warehouses, in which foreign goods, including otter furs from the American coast, were traded for silk.

90

skins sold anywhere from 80 cents to $2, while an otter fur brought from $30 to as much as $120.

The Chinese never heated their homes; they merely piled on clothing. The wealthiest clad themselves in the most valuable fur, that of the otter; the middle class, in seal skin, and the poor, in wadded cotton. Foreigners generally were not welcome in China and cargo-laden ships stopped at Portuguese Macao for "chop" or permission from Chinese officials to proceed to Whampoa, where they were forced to drop anchor and ferry their goods by small boats 12 miles upstream to the hongs of Canton. Though restricted, American traders and seamen got along well with the Chinese and established a relationship that lasted well into the 20th Century. Canton was a place to stir any young Puritan from the cold shores of New England. The river was filled with flower boats with their painted windows and carved in the shape of flowers and birds; mandarin boats with colored silk pennants, and tea-deckers with topsides lacquered in bright colors and with square sails of brown matting. Thousands of persons lived on the little sampans that choked the river shores. At night, the light from paper lanterns cast a soft glow over a strange world. From Canton back to New England was a long way. The ships would catch the northeast monsoon down the China Sea, passing the Borneo coast, sliding through the tight Banka Straits close to the Sumatra coast, and after squeezing through the Sunda Straits and passing Java Head, entering the open water for the crossing of the Indian Ocean to Madagascar. From there it was around the Cape of Good Hope, a stop at St. Helena's Island in the mid-central Atlantic, and the long open haul to Cape Cod.

The ships in the Canton trade were not large, which reduced losses by storm and accident, and the fewer the sails to handle the less the trouble. But they were fast and safe. They were armed and willing to fight, as the Spaniards at San Diego were to learn. The Spaniards tried to close the door to California but it didn't work. In the early days, when the possibilities of the fur trade were first realized, more than 10,000 skins valued at three million dollars had found their way from California to China on the Manila Galleons, to be traded for quicksilver, the first being collected and shipped through San Diego in 1786. But various restrictions, rivalries, unreliability of Indian hunters, and official ineptitude, virtually brought the legitimate trade to a halt. The way was open for a contraband trade that appealed to American adventurers.

The sea otters which they hunted were found all along the coast in the cold Japanese current from the Aleutian Islands to Sebastian Vizcaíno Bay half way down the peninsula of Baja

California. Its jet black or deep velvety brown fur cost the lives of hundreds of men, the loss of many ships, and brought nations to the brink of war. The Russians, first in the trade and all the time pushing further and further south, were the most greedy and the most merciless. They enslaved the Aleut Indians as huntsmen, chained their women as hostages, and with spear and rifle slaughtered all the herds they could find. To the Russians, "the Czar is far away, and God does not care."

Camphor wood chest brought from China in early fur trading days.

In return for the fur, the Chinese traded many kinds of fragrant teas, soft crepes, silks, sugar, carved chests, nankeens, rare china-ware and fans — all in demand in the expanding civilization along our eastern seaboard. For the Americans, the Indians caught otter and traded the pelts in exchange for mirrors, bright pieces of cloth, sheets of copper, scarlet coats, shoes, buttons, blankets, nails, second-hand keys for necklaces, and old government muskets and blunderbusses. For the practical mission fathers, as the trade developed, there were goods and supplies from New England factories that Spain and Mexico had never been able to supply, all of which was to have a profound effect on the future of California.

The situation in the Northwest was fraught with danger at all times, as the Indians were barbarous and deceitful. At least two American vessels met disaster in those waters. At Nootka Sound the ship *Boston* anchored near a native village, where its tall chief, splashed with red paint and wearing a robe of otter fur, invited the crew to go salmon fishing. When most of them had gone the chief signalled his warriors and they boarded the ship. The captain was beaten and thrown overboard and finished off by other Indians in canoes. All on board were slain and their severed heads arranged in a neat row on the quarterdeck. The ship was beached and ransacked. Most of those who had gone fishing were ambushed and killed. Two men held as hostages later were rescued.

Strange dress of the fierce Nootka Indians of Northwest Coast.

John Jacob Astor, a German immigrant who was building a fortune on furs, sent another vessel, the *Tonquin*, under Capt. Jonathan Thorn, on leave from the U.S. Navy, with a crew of 21 and 33 passengers to build and establish a fort, named Astoria, at the mouth of the Columbia River. The ship then proceeded to Nootka Sound, where Capt. Thorn invited natives to come aboard for trading. A row ensued, blows were exchanged, and the Indians left. The next day they were back, all smiles. But hidden in furs were knives and each native had marked his man. The officers and crew were knifed and thrown overboard, and 500 natives crowded onto the ship to loot her. Suddenly she blew up. Evidently some sailors had hidden in the hold, and chose to ignite the powder magazines and blow themselves up with the ship to avenge the death of their companions.

The Yankee trader was a sharp one, and they had to watch each other as closely as they did the foreigners. San Diego began to see the sails of many foreign ships, despite everything the Spaniards could do to control illicit trade. American ships traded off the lonely sections of the coast out of reach of officialdom, and at other times put into harbors with sad stories of being short of water and provisions, or being desperately in need of repairs, all generally being merely excuses to remain in port to contact the settlements and buy furs from soldiers, citizens or Indians, generally under cover of darkness. As a matter of fact the padres of Spain and the Puritans of New England got along famously, and when not under the annoying eye of military authority, often traded and bargained, enjoyed convivial hours and many toasts to each other's health and happiness.

The 104-ton brigantine *Betsy*, the first of the fur hunting ships to enter San Diego Bay, told port authorities that she had just come from the Hawaiian Islands, and was enroute to China but desperately short of water and wood. Capt. Charles Winship was granted time in port to provision the ship, but in a letter to his brother in Boston he indicated he had not been to the Islands but had been cruising the California coast for otter. Two months later the *Betsy* showed up at San Blas, not China. Here, the captain had another story. The main mast had been broken in a terrible storm and he had only put into San Blas because he hadn't been able to find San Diego. The *Betsy* left San Blas in a hurry, with the appearance of Spanish ships, so much so that Capt. Winship and the supercargo, or business agent, Joseph O'Cain, were left behind. Winship died there at the age of 23, while O'Cain managed to get back to Boston and, in command of another vessel, changed the course of the entire otter trade.

The *Betsy* reached Canton under the command of the first mate, a Capt. Brown, and he disposed of its cargo of furs, later coming under some suspicion himself. Sullivan Dorr, a representative at Canton for the famous Dorr shipping family of Boston, reported that "as to Capt. Brown's pillaging the owners of the *Betsy*, I can't say; there is sufficient room in this country to cheat owners and it is not improbable that Brown allowed a high price for tea and received a private compensation for so doing . . . you cannot be too scrupulous about employing men of integrity where you must pay well so that they may not turn thieves, for there is ample field for villainy here." The *Betsy* was a small ship, only 65 feet long, with one deck, two masts and a woman figurehead, and apparently

The sea otter lazed on his back, flippers crossed over his chest.

was lost on a return trip to Boston. The 1802 Boston Ship Register is endorsed, "Vessel and papers destroyed by the natives on the Coast of Africa."

A New York ship, the 240-ton *Enterprise*, bound for Canton "with skins and dollars," followed the *Betsy* into San Diego Bay, in July of 1800, her captain, Ezekial Hubbard, putting forth the familiar plea of the need for bread and wood. The hospitable Spaniards by now were getting a little suspicious and Lt. Don Manuel Rodríguez, who was the presidio commander, required the *Enterprise* to anchor a league from the harbor and transact business by small boats, under the supposedly watchful eye of a guard at Ballast Point. Provisioning required six days; then the *Enterprise* sailed for Ensenada Bay, telling the same story there and getting help, and then repeating it at San Quintín, 200 miles south of San Diego, and at San José del Cabo, at the tip of the peninsula. The *Enterprise* arrived at Canton in such a leaky condition she had to be sold off.

Following the *Betsy* and the *Enterprise*, came the *Alexander*, the *Lelia Byrd* and the *O'Cain*, and all had vivid histories. The *Alexander*, a ship of 180 tons and 14 guns, and with a crew of 19, arrived in San Diego in 1803, and Capt. John Brown had a new story: His men were down with scurvy and needed time on shore to recuperate. Rodríguez was very sympathetic, permitted the *Alexander* to remain in the harbor, and provided food and supplies

OLD HAWAII was the Venice of the Pacific, the center of a vast sea trade from San Diego and other coast ports to China and around the world to Boston. American ships are shown at anchor at Hawaii in this old sketch.

as well. But, as duty was duty, he placed six soldiers on the ship to make sure nothing went wrong. The ailing men were kept at a safe distance from the presidio, but in spite of all the precautions, Rodríguez felt something was being put over on him, and he ordered a search of the ship. His officers found 491 otter furs, which they declared to be contraband and which were confiscated and stored in the presidio warehouse along with other seized furs. It seems that the soldiers also helped themselves to whatever they could slip away from the ship.

Capt. Brown was ordered to leave the port immediately, which he did, and put in at Ensenada on the pretext of needing more supplies but in reality to engage in further contraband. A few months later the *Alexander* turned up in San Francisco Bay, and Capt. Brown had another long story of needing wood and water. As nobody there was aware of her actions in the south, the *Alexander* was able to remain for seven days. She was back yet soon after, claiming to be in great distress because of troubles with Indians along the Northwest Coast. By this time, the Spaniards at San Francisco also had had enough of the *Alexander* and she was forced to leave. The officials at Monterey, however, were in ignorance as to the *Alexander's* tactics, and provided the ship with supplies as well as repairs. Capt. Brown hoisted anchor in the dead of night and sailed away without paying her bills. He had outfoxed the enemy.

Who owned all the furs confiscated at San Diego is not known for certain, but a corporal subsequently asked the governor to return to him 223 furs which he said he had merely pretended to sell to an American frigate, and a padre at San Luis Rey Mission asked for the return of 170 skins which he said mission Indians had sold to the Americans. They were not returned.

The *Alexander* had always seemed to be in trouble somewhere and in some way. On an earlier voyage to the Northwest Coast and China, her captain, Asa Dodge, after days of what was described as licentious behavior at the Sandwich Islands, had jumped overboard and been lost and, in another incident, the ship's powder magazine had exploded and killed 10 men. In the end, the 67-foot *Alexander* met the fate of so many of the proud adventurers of the seas. On her way home she was condemned at the Cape of Good Hope, as "unfit for sea," and sold off.

Now we come to the battle, the famous exchange between the American brig *Lelia Byrd* and the Spanish fort on Point Guijarros. It had taken more than five years to build and equip a fort near the base of Ballast Point, back almost against the foot of the Point Loma hills. It is assumed it was a three-sided open structure,

Spanish engravings on cannon El Júpiter, *cast in Manila in 1783, now on Presidio Hill.*

perhaps 75 to 100 feet in length overall, with its guns thus pointing through apertures south to the harbor entrance, straight ahead to the channel, and north to the customary anchorage between Ballast Point and what is now Shelter Island. It was built up of dirt, gravel and rocks and then faced with heavy timbers. It did seem to have an esplanade, at least around the base on which the guns were positioned. A flat boat was built to convey soldiers and supplies across the bay from the presidio. Behind the fort were some crude barracks and in a canyon a small dam was built as a reservoir to catch and store water. Various accounts tell of six to 12 guns. They weren't toys, as the *Lelia Byrd* discovered. They could blast heavy iron balls through the sides of ships, red-hot ones to set them afire, and balls chained together to foul the rigging. The only difficulty was that the enemy might shoot back.

The *Lelia Byrd* is described in customs house records as a "fast, Virginia-built brig of 175 tons," but little is known of her appearance. She was purchased at Hamburg, Germany, by Richard J. Cleveland and William Shaler, of Salem, and overhauled and refitted. They drew lots for positions, Cleveland becoming master and Shaler, supercargo, or business agent, and decided to enter the Northwest fur trade. They were adventurers as well as traders. At Valparaiso in May of 1802, they found a rival ship, the *Hazard*, and then went on to San Blas. There, and at *Las Tres Marías* Islands, they spent six months and, playing politics, managed to dispose of $10,000 worth of goods and buy 1600 otter skins. A rumor reached them of large numbers of otter skins at San Diego and they headed the *Lelia Byrd* north and passing the fort on Point Guijarros without as much as being hailed, anchored late in the day of March 17, 1803.

Next day, when Lt. Rodríguez with a guard of 12 men came on board, he heard the usual plea of the need of supplies, and promised three cattle, nine *arrobas* of flour, some salt and 24 chickens, for an assurance that the *Lelia Byrd* would leave the port promptly. Just to make sure it did not engage in illicit trade, Rodríguez put aboard five soldiers under Sgt. Joaquín Arce.

Capt. Cleveland insists that when Rodríguez came aboard he waited at the rail until his dragoons had lined up, with their hats in one hand and swords in the other, to form an honor guard through which he could pass to go aft.

"We had been told at San Blas that Don Manuel was an especially vain and pompous man; and indeed we found him so, for such a ridiculous display of a little brief authority and pompous parade, I never before witnessed. His dress and every movement envinced the most arrant coxcomb."

Cleveland tried to induce Rodríguez to sell the furs which had been confiscated from the *Alexander*, but met stern resistance. Cleveland was not to be defeated. He and his men inspected the fort and found eight brass nine-pounders mounted on carriages and a plentiful supply of ball, and "as the examination of the battery belonging to the most jealous and suspicious people on earth was a delicate business, we did not remain long." While ashore Cleveland learned that some of the soldiers had skins they were willing to sell, if they could do so without getting caught. That night, Cleveland sent two boats around the bay. One did return with some skins. The other boat was seized and the ship's mate and two sailors bound and placed under guard. The enraged Cleveland armed four of his men and went to the rescue. Apparently the captives were released without any shots being fired, but the situation was out of hand and sails were hoisted for a retreat past the guns of Fort Guijarros. Sgt. Arce and his guard were still aboard as helpless hostages.

Iron cannon El Capitán *cast in 1783 and now in Old Town Plaza.*

Cleveland's narrative of his experiences published as "A Narrative of Voyages and Commercial Enterprises," in 1824, reads as follows:

"Arriving safely on board, we perceived our men to be so indignant at the treatment of their shipmates, as to be ready for the fight, even had the odds been greater against us. We had, however, a disagreeable and very hazardous task to perform; a failure in which would be attended with ruin to us, besides subjecting us to the humiliating treatment of an incensed petty tyrant. Our position, at anchor was about a mile within the fort, of which mention has been made. It was necessary to pass within musketshot of this fort. With a strong wind, the quick passage of the vessel would render the danger trifling; but, unfortunately, we had now but the last expiring breath of the land breeze, sufficient only to give the ship steerage way, and an hour would elapse before we could presume on passing the fort; but no other alternative was left us, that did not present a more dreaded aspect.

"While making our preparations, we perceived that all was bustle and animation on shore; both horse and foot were flocking to the fort. Our six three pounders, which were all brought on the side of the ship bearing on the fort, and our fifteen men was all our force, with which to resist a battery of six nine pounders, and, at least an hundred men. As soon as our sails were loosed and we began to heave up the anchor, a gun without shot was discharged from the battery and the Spanish flag hoisted; perceiving no effect from this, they fired a shot ahead. By this time our anchor was up, all sail was set, and we were gradually approaching the fort. In the hope of preventing their firing, we caused the guard in their uniforms to stand along in the most exposed and conspicuous station; but it had no effect, not even when so near the fort, that they must have been heard imploring them to desist firing, and seen to fall with their faces to the deck, at every

Next Page, THE AMERICAN FUR SMUGGLER Lelia Byrd *slides past Fort Guijarros in an exchange of fire in one of two such battles as fought at San Diego. Nobody was hurt but the battle caused great excitement.*

renewed discharge of the cannon. We had been subjected to a cannonade of three quarters of an hour, without returning a shot and, fortunately, with injury only to our rigging and sails. When arrived abreast the fort, several shots struck our hull, one between wind and water, which was temporarily stopped by a wad of oakum. We now opened our fire, and, at the first broadside, saw numbers, probably of those who came to see the fun, scampering away up the hill at the back of the fort. Our second broadside seemed to have caused the complete abandonment of their guns, as none were fired afterwards; nor could we see any person in the fort, excepting a soldier who stood upon the ramparts, waving his hat, as if to desist firing."

Once out of the range of the fort's guns, the *Lelia Byrd* put the terrified Spanish guards ashore and restored their arms. The last heard of them they were shouting "*Vivan, vivan los Americanos*"!

Rodríguez' official version of the Battle of March 21 was slightly different. He claimed that the only reason for firing was to prevent the ship leaving with the captive Spaniards aboard, and when Sgt. Arce shouted that they were to be put ashore, the fort withheld its fire. However, when the *Lelia Byrd* drew abreast of the fort, and its guns opened up, the fire was returned but no damage was done to the fort or its defenders.

The *Lelia Byrd* sailed on south. At San Quintín Bay she was visited by Dominican friars from Baja California missions who, upon learning of the ship's arrival, had come to the bay by horse to pitch camp and engage in trading furs for European goods. Several days went by before any mention was made of the affair at San Diego, and then the subject was broached by a padre, with an air of innocence, who gave an accurate account of all that had happened. An unsealed letter written by the corporal of Fort Guijarros to a superior at Loreto had been passed down the line of missions and evidently had been read by everybody.

According to Cleveland, the corporal accused the commandant of enticing the *Lelia Byrd* into difficulties, then taking care not to enter the fort until the vessel was beyond cannon shot.

"He was profuse in his apologies to us. Our forbearance so long before returning the fire, our humanity and generosity to the guards, under such provocation, and our ceasing fire when they did, were considered by the corporal as acts of magnanimity which should recommend us to the kindness and hospitality of all good Spaniards."

The padres vied with each other to serve the *Lelia Byrd* and "they expressed great disgust with the character and conduct of Rodríguez and called him a poltroon who had subjected the Royal Flag of Spain to insult."

As for the embittered corporal, José Velásquez, who had written the letter, he was placed under arrest by Rodríguez, not for dereliction of duty, but on a charge of trading with the enemy. The

100

American goods found in his possession were seized and sold at auction for $212.

The *Lelia Byrd* had put into San Quintín Bay to repair damage, which consisted mostly of plugging up the holes in her side. Here, they found the *Alexander,* and after exchanging notes on their various encounters with the Spaniards, Cleveland and Shaler evidently continued their illusive wanderings and tradings up and down the coast, as a communication to the Viceroy recently found in Mexico reveals the *Lelia Byrd,* or *el pájaro,* the bird, as she was known to the Spaniards, had stopped at Monterey and dropped off a "black sailor" at his own request, and then stopped at San Buenaventura, to leave an Irish sailor who liked what he had seen of California. All ports were warned to watch out for her, but for the time being she disappeared.

Brig

The *Lelia Byrd* went on to Canton, where accumulated skins were sold and Cleveland left her to return to Boston on another vessel. Shaler, now in command, headed back for the West Coast and showed up at Guaymas in 1804. The port commandant, warily noting her 14 cannons but carrying out the orders he had received two years before, went aboard for an inspection. The crew took up their arms on the pretext their guns needed cleaning.

Shaler reported he had a cargo of Asian and European goods for trading along the Northwest Coast and had merely stopped at Guaymas for repairs. The port commandant was unable to verify any of the captain's statements, as all ship's papers were written in English, and she was allowed to depart. The commandant's report also gives us a little sidelight on life at sea in those times, in revealing the ship carried a woman and an Indian girl. The *Lelia Byrd* made two visits off San Diego, in the following year, but they passed without incident. Eventually she went back to the Hawaiian Islands, where Shaler sold her to the king. She wound up in the opium trade in the Orient and rotted away on Whampoa Beach.

Brigantine

Shaler, who later entered the United States Consular Service and served with distinction, produced an account of one of his journeys, as had so many others, and observed that "the conquest of this country would be absolutely nothing; it would fall without an effort to the most inconsiderable force." He said San Diego Bay was a safe anchorage for ships of any "burthen," but . . .

"There is a sorry battery of eight pounders at the entrance; at present it does not merit the least consideration as a fortification, but with a little expense might be made capable of defending this fine harbor. The presidio is about four miles distant from the anchorage. A considerable force would be necessary to hold this post, as a landing might be effected on the back of it, at the false port of San Diego (Mission Bay). The entrance of this

THE SHIPS that took the American flag over the Seven Seas sailed from New England ports. This is Crowninshield's Wharf in Salem in 1798. These small but sturdy vessels circled the globe, fighting storm, savages and death.

port is said to be too shoal for ships." As for the southern climate, he found it "particularly favorable to horses and mules, as they retain their strength and vigor till past 30 years." Shaler succumbed to cholera in 1833, at Havana, at the age of 55.

The *Hazard*, a large ship of Boston, with a crew of 50, and an armament of 22 cannon and 20 swivel guns, first appeared at San Francisco, at the same time as the *Alexander*, but badly riddled by bullets from an engagement against Indians in the Northwest, and in need of water and wood. Her difficulties must have been obvious, as she was given assistance, and then departed before the arrival of a belated Spanish order that she was to be seized before she and the *Alexander* could unite for an attack on Spanish presidios. As far as is known no such attack was contemplated. Capt. James Rowan took his vessel down the coast, at times giving his ship another name and repeating the woeful tale of disaster at the hands of Northwest Indians, and finally hauled up off San Diego. What happened here is not known, but if Capt. Rowan had any thought of dealing for the furs that had been confiscated from the *Alexander*, he was doomed to disappointment. The skins had rotted in the presidio warehouse, a loss of a fortune, and the now-thoroughly alerted Rodríguez bid the *Hazard* to be on her way.

It remained for Joseph O'Cain, who had been left at San Blas by the *Betsy*, to now put the sea otter trade on a more profitable basis. In command of the *O'Cain*, a ship of 280 tons which carried 18 guns, and was owned primarily by the Winship family of Boston, he sailed for Kodiak Island, in Alaskan waters, where he made a deal with the Russian, Alexander Baranov, the "Lord of the North Pacific," to supply him with Aleut hunters and their baidarkas, or canoes, and agreeing to share skins and profits. From there O'Cain proceeded directly to San Diego, in January of 1804, and when he was refused provisions, went on to San Quintín Bay, where he unfolded the usual story of having experienced terrible storms and heavy damage. While there his Aleut hunters fanned out over the sea and in a short time took 1100 sea otters. From the padres of Baja California they obtained 700 more. The Russian-American partnership became the new practice, and Yankee ships with as many as 100 Aleuts ravaged the otter herds of both Californias. By then the otters were beginning to show some signs of thinning out. In 1805, three ships left Boston for the Northwest fur trade and contract-hunting with the Russians. The *Peacock* was commanded by O'Cain's brother-in-law, Oliver Kimball, and the *O'Cain*, by Jonathan Winship. O'Cain himself was on another new vessel, the *Eclipse*. Rodríguez was ready for them. When the *Peacock* appeared off Los Angeles, Rodríguez sent soldiers up from San Diego and seized three of the crew at San Juan Capis-

THE FUR SHIPS of the early 1800's carried the American flag to all Pacific ports and then across the oceans to the Far East and around the Cape to New England. It was this kind of enterprise that built the United States.

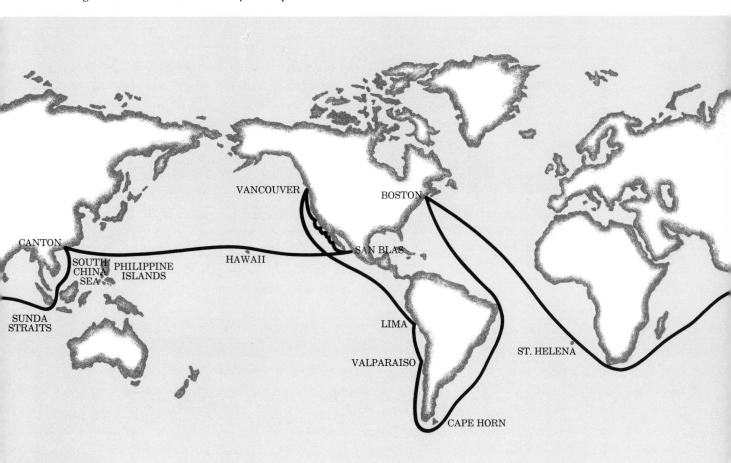

trano. The *Peacock* rushed down to San Diego, and though anchoring at a safe distance from the guns of Fort Guijarros, managed to get two letters ashore, one being a petition to the governor for release of the prisoners, and the other, instructing the prisoners to escape. When the letters were seized and opened, the *Peacock* gave up and went to Ensenada. The *O'Cain*, with 100 Aleut hunters, 12 native women and 50 baidarkas, began working the waters of Baja California, the ship innocently visiting the ports of Ensenada and San Quintín while the Aleuts secretly hunted from the off-shore islands. It took some time for the Spaniards to catch up with this one. The *Eclipse* with O'Cain began cruising the California coast and then, also anchoring just beyond the range of San Diego's battery, requested food and water, and as usual, met the customary rebuff. When the ship left, Rodríguez sent a guard under Corporal Juan Osuna all the way to Ensenada, just in case. O'Cain was reaching the end of his patience too, and with a force of his own of 15 men, he captured Osuna and his four soldiers and took them as prisoners aboard the *Eclipse*. He released two of them with a message to Rodríguez that unless the pilot of the *Peacock*, who had been seized at San Juan Capistrano, was released forthwith, the *Eclipse* would sail back to San Diego and bombard both the fort and the presidio to the humiliation of the Empire of Spain. It isn't too clear how it all came out, though there is indication all the prisoners, on both sides, were freed.

California waters were almost becoming American waters, and Spanish pueblos New England colonies. And the fighting ships of the expanding United States were making their strength felt in all parts of the world. They were punishing the pirate cutthroats of Morocco, Algiers, Tunis and Tripoli and assuring the freedom of the seas.

CHAPTER NINE

THE GOLDEN AGE

The golden age of the missions was at hand. The closing years of the 18th Century saw all but three of the 21 California missions built or started, with a now well-trod El Camino Real to link most of them a day's journey apart. Livestock by the thousands grazed over nearly a million acres. Orchards, vineyards and farm crops began to fill the valleys. Indians in increasing numbers learned to depend on the missions, to accept Christianity, and to slowly take up the rudiments of civilized living. A succession of sympathetic governors brought a period of cooperation between military and religious authority.

The kindly and orderly Fr. Lasuén, the president of the California missions, wrote in 1792, that at his request Antonio Domingo Henrique had arrived at the San Carlos Mission at Monterey and had "brought along his Indian wife from San Diego. At all the missions of the south as far as San Luis Obispo, he had made spinning wheels, warping frames, combs, looms, and all the utensils of the art save carding instruments. He has taught carding, spinning, and also the weaving of various woolen cloth, also of the Sayal Franciscano, of which they have already made clothing for some missionaries." Sayal Franciscano was a coarse woolen cloth.

At San Diego, Frs. Juan Mariner and Hilario Torrent, now in charge, reported that "three buildings have been enlarged; a portion

CIVILIZATION had laid its hand on this Diegueño Indian — and also had clothed him. This stone etching was made by an artist with American Boundary Expedition. Protection gone, he soon was to sink into degradation.

Candle rendering pot in San Luis Rey's soap and candle factory.

Irons were heated over charcoal by Indian women at the missions.

of the walls that guard the mission has been erected; a vineyard and a grove have been surrounded with a wall of adobe forming a circuit of 500 varas; and the fields have been prepared for planting." The wall was more than 1400 feet long.

A fresh spring was discovered not far from the mission and an irrigation ditch nearly 3500 feet long was constructed to bring the water to the fields. A mission school was opened in 1795. The year 1797 saw the baptism of 565 Indians and the mission population rose to 1405, thus becoming at that period the most populous mission in California. The figures were somewhat illusory, however, as the Diegueños were not a religious people and readily slipped back to their old ways. The Indian aversion to containment also was heightened by his fear of disease. White men's diseases, contracted from soldiers and settlers, were overwhelming to natives who had lived open and somewhat isolated lives. When diseases would spread to villages, and at times with appalling results, the Indians followed their time-honored practice of steaming themselves in their temescals, or hot-air baths, and then leaping into cold water. To those suffering such diseases as measles, this was fatal. But a complete return to native ways would not have been an answer. All over the continent the Indian was being pushed back or killed, no matter the resistance.

The French navigator, La Pérouse, on his visit to California had compared the mission establishments to the slave plantations of Santo Domingo. The winds of liberalism were blowing hard through French thinking and his was a casual glance at a complex system that had grown out of Spain's Laws of the Indies and by custom and necessity. The missions were an extension of Empire as well as of Christianity. The heart of the mission system in California went back to Fr. Serra's *Presentación* to the Viceroy in Mexico City in which he won reaffirmation of the Spanish doctrine that the missionary stood in relation to the Indian as a father to his child — "in loco parentis." The missionary had the responsibility for the Indian's conversion and education, his well-being and his discipline, and his preparation for freedom and citizenship.

The Indian joined the mission of his own free will. Once he was baptized — and he was fully advised of all its obligations — he no longer could wander the countryside as he wished but must reside at the mission, that is, in every circumstance where it was possible; accept his share of the work, and learn the ways of civilized man. If he fled, he would be brought back and punished. Two centuries of experience had taught both Spain and the missionaries that there was no other way. One of the reasons for the slow progress in development of the San Diego Mission was the necessity of allowing Christianized Indians to return periodically to their rancherias, or even to reside in them, because of poor crops due to lack of water. The Indians would revert quickly to their native state, and the work would have to be done all over again.

Fr. Lasuén wrote vividly of the trouble this caused at San Diego:

"At that mission they keep just enough Indians to justify the place being called a mission and to make it a refuge to which those who stay at their rancherias can have recourse in their needs. What good has been achieved and what progress made? O my venerable Fr. Guardian! What anxiety! What despondency! What sleepless nights! What anguish! What daily and nightly toiling on the part of the missionaries! What licentiousness! What a change in the neophytes from Christian civility to heathen barbarity! . . . There is no doubt that in all the pagan rancherias heathen practices prevail. Who will remove the obstacles the Christians encounter when they continue to live with their tribesmen at the very scenes of those heathen customs? And who will prevent them from joining their tribesmen or even from witnessing the orgies? Accustomed to their abominable feasts, and finding their recollections revived every hour, what place will they give to the catechism and to the obligations contracted in the Baptism they have received? They possess no energy to apply themselves to what is conducive to a rational, social, and civilized life. On the vigilance and incessant care of the missionaries it then depends whether or not the Indians observe what they have learned.

"Let it be sincerely borne in mind, however, that if at San Diego, as in Lower California, that method is employed, it is through dire necessity; for those sterile lands by no means produce the provisions necessary to support all the neophytes together. This impossibility compels the missionaries to permit the Christians to live scattered in their rancherias, obliged to visit the mission only from time to time. To let them live in this way is thought to be a smaller evil than to let them remain pagans. It is a necessary evil, but the result is disastrous."

There were no courts and no judges. California was a frontier, and justice in the mission domain was administered in large measure by the padres. What was right and what was wrong, and reward and punishment, had to be a matter of personal judgment. A form of Indian self-government was accomplished by the election of *alcaldes*, or constables, whose duty it was to bring before the padres the neophytes guilty of minor infractions and to administer the prescribed punishment. Major crimes, or crimes of blood, were punished by the military. The lash and the stocks were common in many parts of the civilized world in those years, as will be remembered from the experiences of English seamen under Capt. Vancouver.

Fr. Esteban Tapis, who succeeded Fr. Lasuén as president upon the latter's death in 1803, in response to formal questions put by the Viceroy in an *Interrogatorio*, described the Mission System of punishment:

"A man, boy or woman either runs away or does not return from the excursion until other neophytes are sent after him. When he is brought back to the mission, he is reproached for the transgression of not complying with the obligation of hearing holy Mass on a day of obligation. He is made to see that he has freely subjected himself to this and other Christian duties, and he is then warned that he will be chastised if he repeats the transgression. He again runs away, and is again brought back. Then he experiences the chastisement of the lash or the stocks. If this is insufficient, as is the case with some, seeing that a warning is useless, he is made to feel the shackles, which he wears for three days while he is kept at work. The same practice is observed with those who are caught in concubinage. With those who steal something of value, or who fight with the danger of doing harm, this order is not observed; for these are first chastised and then made to abhor theft or exhorted to keep the peace. It has been noticed that this is the most successful way of maintaining public and private tranquility.

"The stocks in the apartment of the girls and single women are older than the fathers who report on the mission. As a rule, the transgressions of the women are punished with one, two or three days in the stocks, according to the gravity of the offense; but if they are obstinate in their evil intercourse, or run away, they are chastised by the hand of another woman in the apartment of the women. Sometimes, though exceedingly seldom, the shackles are put on.

"Such are the chastisements which we inflict on the Indians in keeping with the judgment with which parents punish their own beloved children. We have begotten the neophytes for Christianity by means of our labors for them, and by means of Baptism in which they received the life of grace. We rear them by means of the Sacraments and by means of the instruction in the maxims of Christian morals. We therefore use the authority which Almighty God concedes to parents for the education of their children, now exhorting, now rebuking, now also chastising when necessity demands it. For these chastisements generally the assistance of the *comandante* or of the guard is not solicited. Yet it has always been asked when it appeared to us expedient. The Indians feel that they are never chastised without being well convinced of their guilt, and that, by the grace of God, they are never punished because of some ill will the missionary is supposed to have for one or the other. . . Hence it is that the neophytes accept with humility the Father as before."

At times there were accusations of excesses, and investigations were undertaken. Kindness and sacrifice were taken for granted. The life of the fathers was a hard one. Two of them worked at each mission among hundreds, even thousands of savages. Some of the padres paid with their lives, and willingly accepted martyrdom; a few others lost their minds; others became discouraged and returned to Mexico or Spain. Most of them kept on, and because of their vows of poverty, with no thought of reward on earth. They fought to avert the tragedy that finally and inevitably came to the Indians.

The mission lands, which eventually embraced most of the fertile coastal and upland valleys between San Diego and Sonoma, were not the property of the individual missionaries or the mission orders, or even of the church itself. The King of Spain took title

The carreta was familiar site on dusty trails of Old San Diego.

110

to all lands of California, upon settlement of San Diego in 1769, though this possession in effect was limited to the presidios and supporting lands, and the natives were recognized as the owners, under the King, of all the territory required for their existence. Towns and individuals were granted only usufructuary titles. The need of Indians for land to support themselves was expected to become less as they abandoned their wild ways and became more civilized, and this would permit a gradual increase in Spanish settlements.

As for the rest of California, and including all of the mission lands, the Spanish laws recognized the rights of the Indians to the soil of their fathers and protected the Indians against encroachment. The Laws of the Indies read: "We command that the residences and lands which may be granted to the Spaniards shall be given as not to prejudice the Indians, and that those which have been granted to their prejudice and injury, shall be returned to those to whom they may lawfully belong."

In time, and at the right moment of development, the missionaries were to turn the lands back to the Indians, and surrender the missions to the secular clergy, and move on to new frontiers. This point was never reached in California. The authority of Spain was waning, the empire was breaking up, and new forces were to be let loose.

Mission life was routine; order was brought out of a wilderness. In general, seven hours of the day were allotted to labor, with two hours of prayer daily and four or five on Sundays and on days of festivals. In the morning their food consisted of *atole* or a gruel of barley, wheat, or corn. At noon, they got *pozole*, which consisted of the same grains, only boiled. In the evening, it was the same food as in the morning, but in addition, every few days cattle were slaughtered to provide beef. Married couples and their small children were housed in the neophyte Indian village, in the vicinity of the mission; young girls, unmarried women and widows were given rooms or apartments of their own, as much as possible, and which were called *monjerios*. They were locked in at night, and this was consistent with Spanish customs of guarding the quarters of their young women even in their own homes. Their quarters grew into training schools where instructions in sewing, cooking and cleanliness were given by the wives of the Mexican carpenters and blacksmiths who had come to California to work at the mis-

This copper vessel is one of few relics found at Presidio site.

Next Page, THIS IS HOW MISSION SAN DIEGO appeared in the "Golden Age" of the missions. Gleaming white, it beckoned to the unbelieving Indian as well as to the weary traveler who rode dusty El Camino Real along coast.

111

D. Wayne Millsap

Mission millstones used in grinding grain and crushing olives.

This crude olive oil press was used at the San Diego Mission.

sions and begin new lives for themselves. In the late afternoons and evenings they could go to the village. While men and boys slept in their own quarters, they had considerable freedom and participated in church duties and, of course, in the trade and mechanics necessary to mission life. Many worked at the presidios, in construction or in private homes, and herding livestock and tending the fields of the *Nación*, or of the government.

The mission establishment was a world unto itself. It raised its own food, made its own clothing and many of its own tools, formed its own building materials, built its own waterworks, and operated its own little hospital and school; and its people were born, married and buried within its confines. By the turn of the century the San Diego Mission herds had grown to 7000 and its flocks to 6000. Annual harvests varied from 2500 to nearly 10,000 bushels, depending on weather. The Indians, with reluctance, were exchanging nakedness for covering. They were learning some Spanish and the padres some Mau, the language of the Diegueños.

Construction of new buildings proceeded apace. Adobe blocks and clay tiles were made by Indians from soil of the hills, and timber for roofs was hauled down from the high mountains by oxen. Lime kilns were built against the hillsides for mortar and plaster, and baking tiles. Fr. Esteban Tapis' report on labor done by California mission Indians said that, "Sixteen young men, and at times as many more middle-aged men, with two women to bring sand and straw, make 500 tiles a day. The troughs with clay are close by and are always filled." Wooden molds were used for making adobe blocks as well as tile. Tile was not made by forming clay around the thigh of an Indian, as sentimental tradition has it. They were shaped in that fashion so as to fit into each other. Important to the mission fathers were the vineyards and the olive orchards. Wine was a necessary part of religious ceremonies and from the olive came the oil for cooking. Grape cuttings were not sent into New California until 1779, and as late as 1781, Fr. Serra, in a letter to Fr. Lasuén, wrote that "I hope the maize is doing well, and that the vine shoots are living and bearing fruit, for this lack of wine for the Mass is becoming unbearable." By 1801, Lasuén was able to write that "The Missions of San Diego, San Juan Capistrano, San Gabriel, San Buenaventura, Santa Barbara and San Luis Obispo raise grapes and press some wine." Bancroft believes the padres' first grapes introduced into California were of south Spanish stock — first the reddish black grape of Los Angeles, rich in juice, and then the fruiter, bluish black Sonoma, which he said, yields a lighter wine. Other varieties were introduced as time

114

went on. The recollections of Carlos N. Hijar of California in 1834, give a description of old wine making:

"The wine of pastoral days was made after this manner: Suitable ground was selected, and a desvan or platform placed thereon. This was covered with clean hides, and the grapes piled upon it. Some well-washed Indians, having on only a *zapeta* (loin-cloth), the hair carefully tied up and hand covered with cloth wherewith to wipe away the perspiration, each having a stick to steady himself withal, were put to treading out the grape juice, which was caught in coras, or in leathern bags. These were emptied into a large wooden tub, where the liquid was kept two or three months, under cover of the grape skins to ferment. Such as did not flow off was put into wooden presses, and the juice into copper jars, and covered with a kind of hat. Through two or three inserted tubes heat was conveyed to the mass to aid evaporation and condensation. These jars served as a still for brandy. For white wine the first juice only was taken and stored."

An olive tree planted by the padres still lives in Mission Valley.

Olive seeds were brought into California before grape cuttings and by 1803, Lasuén reported that "in some missions they have begun to harvest olives; and at San Diego they have already made some very good olive oil." The olive press for the San Diego Mission is still in existence, at the Junípero Serra Museum. San Diego became a source of olive oil for most of the missions of the San Diego district.

The orange tree found its way from Spain to Mexico and then to San Diego.

It was a period of growth and prosperity that saw the beginning of a mission that became the largest and most beautiful of them all — San Luis Rey — The King of the Missions, east of Oceanside and a day's march, or 40 miles from San Diego. The need for a mission between San Diego and San Juan Capistrano had long been felt, and Lasuén personally explored the area and selected the site, rejecting one farther inland, at Pala, or Pale, as being too far from El Camino Real. The Pala site had been noted by Fr. Juan Mariner and Capt. Juan Pablo Grijalva on an exploratory trip in 1795, when they went up the San Diego River, and then through Sycamore Canyon to Santa María Valley, or Pamo Valley, and into what they named *El Valle de San José*, now known as Warner's Hot Springs. From there they went down the San Luis Rey River, and turned north through Santa Margarita and Las Flores to San Juan Capistrano. The site chosen for the new mission was on the north side of San Luis Rey River Valley which Fr. Juan Crespí had named *Cañada de* San Juan Capistrano when the Portolá Expedition to Monterey crossed it in 1769. Crespí had described it as an ideal location for a mission. To avoid confusion with San Juan Capistrano Mission, the new site was named Old Capistrano and the mission given the name of San Luis Rey de

Looking out over valley from bell tower of Mission San Luis Rey.

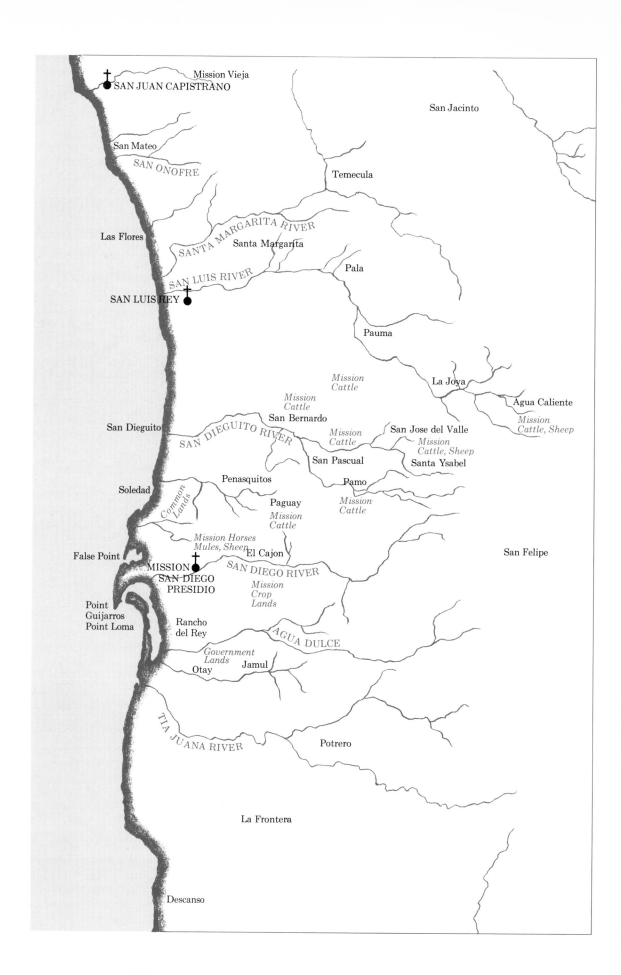

San Juan Capistrano
✝ SAN JUAN CAPISTRANO
Mission Vieja

San Jacinto

San Mateo

SAN ONOFRE

Temecula

Las Flores

SANTA MARGARITA RIVER

Santa Margarita

Pala

SAN LUIS RIVER
✝ SAN LUIS REY

Pauma

Mission Cattle

La Joya

Mission Cattle

San Bernardo

Agua Caliente

Mission Cattle, Sheep

San Dieguito

SAN DIEGUITO RIVER

Mission Cattle

San Jose del Valle

Mission Cattle, Sheep

San Pascual

Santa Ysabel

Penasquitos

Pamo

Soledad

Common Lands

Paguay

Mission Cattle

Mission Cattle

Mission Horses Mules, Sheep

El Cajon

False Point

✝ MISSION
SAN DIEGO
PRESIDIO

SAN DIEGO RIVER

San Felipe

Mission Crop Lands

Point
Guijarros
Point Loma

Rancho
del Rey

AGUA DULCE

Government Lands

Otay

Jamul

TIA JUANA RIVER

Potrero

La Frontera

Descanso

116

Francia, in honor of King Louis IX of France, as the Viceroy had commanded. It was the 18th mission in the California chain.

On the 13th of June, 1798, in the presence of soldiers from the Presidio of San Diego, and many Indian gentiles and neophytes, Lasuén conducted the ceremonies of founding a new mission and entrusted its completion to Fr. Antonio Peyri. No figure in California mission history lived in Indian heart and memory longer than Fr. Peyri. He remained with the King of the Missions until near its end, when, broken and in despair, he fled. This mission drew to it the Luiseño Indians of northern San Diego County, who were not Yumans as were the Diegueños, but belonged to the Shoshonean linguistic stock, and generally speaking they proved more adaptable and more religious. The Luiseños went to work with eagerness and by summer, 6000 adobe bricks had been made for a church which was completed in 1801-1802. In time it became the most populous mission in all of California.

There were now five missions in the San Diego District: San Diego, the "Mother Mission;" San Gabriel, San Juan Capistrano, San Luis Rey, and San Miguel which was about 55 miles below San Diego and under Dominican jurisdiction but dependent on San Diego for assistance and protection.

It was a tranquil period. The King's messengers continued their lonely journeys along El Camino Real, from Mexico to San Francisco and return, and the increasingly frequent appearances of American ships contributing the only excitement of the times. The warm sun of California was kind to the old soldiers, who after serving out their terms of duty, chose to settle down, many with Indian wives. Lt. Col. Don Diego de Borica, who was governor at the end of the first three decades of Spanish rule, wrote that it was a great country, with good bread and climate, with an astounding general fecundity, "both of rationals and irrationals. The climate is so good that all are getting to look like Englishmen."

Life was regulated by the sound of bells. They could be heard far up and down Mission Valley, calling the Indians to prayer and to work, and announcing the good or the bad tidings of the day. Ringing of the bells was an honor which the Indians loved, and a few of them were still ringing bells in abandoned chapels long after the mission period had come to a close.

In the early expeditions, bells came before food. The Serra-Portolá Expedition certainly carried a number of bells into Cali-

Original baptismal font of Fr. Peyri at Mission San Luis Rey.

TIJUANA

ROSARITO

DESCANSO

SAN MIGUEL MISSION

ENSENADA

Site of Mission San Miguel on Baja California Highway to Ensenada.

VAST AMOUNT OF LAND was needed to support mission establishments. This map shows the "frontier" of San Diego and the crop and grazing grounds of the mission. The great ranchos were formed out of former mission lands.

117

Historic mission bells disappeared from old Santa Ysabel chapel.

State's first pepper tree is seen through ruins at San Luis Rey.

fornia which had been taken from the old Jesuit missions of the peninsula. Two of three known to have been brought up in 1769 hung for years outside at Santa Ysabel but vanished in 1926. One bore the date of 1723, and the other that of 1767. The third bell still hangs at the San Diego Mission and bears a date of 1738. All missions at their founding were to have two bells, one presumably for devotions and the other for the day's routine, but all missions in time had as many as eight. The later bells were obtained in trade by way of American ships from Lima, Mexico, Boston and even from Russian sources. There were two types of bells: The devotional bells were large stationary ones which were rung by movement of the clapper, while smaller ones known as glad bells were suspended and designed to turn completely over. Their joyous ringing announced the comings and goings of padres and visitors and the events of the many festivals.

Edith Buckland Webb, describes the daily routine in her book, "Indian Life at the Old Missions":

"The Indians' day began at sunrise when the Angelus bell called them to prayers in the mission church. About an hour later another bell announced breakfast, whereupon each family sent to the community kitchen for its share of the food that had been prepared. After breakfast another ring of the bell sent all who were old enough and able to work to their appointed tasks. There were no laggards in this community. From the small boy who scared birds away from the orchard or straying animals from drying adobes to the little girl who helped prepare the wool for spinning, and the old woman who gathered wood for the kitchen fires, all who were able to work had some special task to perform. In the forenoon and again in midafternoon, one of the Padres gathered together all the children over five years of age and instructed them in the Doctrina. Following the morning period with the children, the Padre visited the fields and shops to see that no one was absent from work. Shortly after eleven o'clock the Padres had their noonday meal. From twelve until two o'clock the Indians ate their meal and enjoyed the inevitable siesta. Then back to work they went until about five o'clock, when it was time for prayers and devotions. At six o'clock came the ringing of the Angelus. Supper was then served. For the remainder of the evening until Poor Soul's bell was rung at eight o'clock, the Indians were free to do as they wished within certain limitations, of course. Thus it was, day after day, week after week, and year after year."

Not all went peacefully in the early years of the 1800's. At San Juan Mission, an Indian sent into the storehouse for fat, while carrying a lighted candle, took time out to amuse himself killing bats, and set the building afire, with a loss of 2500 bushels of wheat and six tons of tallow. The rains as always were undependable and something would have to be done about it. Another earthquake on May 25, 1803, damaged the San Diego Mission church. The next year, on April 26 at a ceremony conducted by Fr. Mariano Payeras, and with Commandant Rodríguez and his officers present, the bodies of Fr. Luis Jayme, the first Christian martyr of California; Fr. Juan Figuer, who died on Dec. 18, 1784, and Fr. Juan Mariner, who died on Jan 29, 1800, were taken from their old resting places and reburied in a common grave between the altars of the newer church. Another expedition was sent into the sierra to contact all Indian rancherias to establish more friendly relations so that fugitive Indians could be found and returned. Fr. José Bernardo Sánchez and *Alférez* José Joaquín Maitorena left San Diego on June 20, 1806, and visited all Indian settlements in a wide arc from San Luis Rey Mission to San Miguel Mission below the border. They returned on July 14 with two runaways.

Affairs at the presidio lapsed into routine. The 25 Catalán Volunteers were withdrawn, a light was placed on Point Guijarros to guide mariners, and the presidio was released from the obligation of the military protection of San Miguel. And it was just as well. A report said that of the six 6-pounders available for the protection of San Diego, five were now useless. The effective force at the presidio was about 80 men. The only fighting for a time was among themselves. In 1806 Rodríguez was recalled to Mexico, where he died in 1810, and Capt. Raimundo Carrillo was named to succeed him. Before he arrived Lts. Francisco María Ruiz and José de la Guerra y Noriega got into a dispute as to their respective authority. Ruiz knocked Guerra down and Guerra drew his sword. Fr. Sánchez interceded, bloodshed was averted, and peace was restored. A beginning toward a more civilized life was indicated by a notation that a sergeant was now teaching school at the presidio.

Considerable work was done in this period on trying to improve Fort Guijarros; numerous receipts found in Mexico City archives in 1961 testify to expenditures for nails and carpenters' work on the fort's esplanade and timber facing. The timbers had entirely rotted away in eight years. One receipt dated Oct. 9, 1808, was for work on *"Bastión Punta de Guijarros* named *San Joaquín,"* thus indicating for the first time that the fort had a formal name.

The earthquake of 1812 left these ruins at San Juan Capistrano.

The death of Rodríguez also had ended his role in a long dispute over some items missing from goods brought to San Diego for the presidio on the *Concepción* in 1800. Among them were four pairs of woolen socks and some cloth. The correspondence of Boards of Survey on who should be held responsible for the loss had covered a period of ten years. Poor Manuel, chasing up and down the beaches of Southern and Lower California, vainly trying to halt the rich fur smuggling, and subjected to ridicule and his loyalty and bravery questioned, was badgered constantly by the bureaucrats of Mexico City who insisted on knowing what had happened to the four pairs of socks.

Over the horizon the forces of change were gathering momentum. The United States bought from France the vast Louisiana Territory on the wide unprotected border of New Spain; the Lewis and Clark Expedition penetrated the northern wilderness to reach the Pacific at the mouth of the Columbia River, and the Pike Expedition conquered the Rocky Mountains. Napoleon turned on Spain and the Spanish Empire broke up. At 11 o'clock on the night of Sept. 16, 1810, in the little Mexican town of Dolores, Fr. Miguel Hidalgo walked out to the steps of his church and gave the cry of "Mexicans, viva Mexico!" A revolution that was to last more than a decade was under way.

Mission Dam, one of early structural marvels, is visible today.

California was far away and these events for a long time had little effect on the 40 Franciscan fathers whose converts now totaled 19,000. The Mission of San Diego was assuming its final appearance. The church which was restored in 1931 and stands today, was begun in 1808 and dedicated on Nov. 7, 1813. The mission buildings and walls formed a great square. Though the Southern California earthquake of 1801 had done some damage to the mission and presidio buildings, the great earthquake of 1812, which virtually wrecked the Mission of San Juan Capistrano and killed more than 40 persons, had little effect here.

This period saw the construction of one of the marvels of the mission era, the dam and aqueduct that brought a regular supply of water, at long last, to the orchards and fields. The project was begun in 1807, and probably was not finished until sometime in 1815 or 1816. The padres were too busy to keep detailed records. All of the missions had irrigation projects of one kind or another, some of them dating back to 1773. But none compared to the one at San Diego. With a skill born of necessity, they went to the head of Mission Gorge, through which the San Diego River plunges into Mission Valley, and on exposed bedrock built a dam of stone and cement and backed up a permanent reservoir of water. It was 244 feet long, 13 feet thick, 13 feet high and had a gate and spillway. The river ran the year around at this site, before it dropped through the canyon and in dry periods lost itself in the sands of Mission Valley. But the mission was six miles away, down an almost impenetrable rock canyon. The padres drew the water off on the right or north side, and ran it through an open tile aqueduct, by gravity flow, all the way down the canyon and then to the mission.

It was not until 1813, however, that the Frs. Sanchéz and Martín mentioned casually in a report, "We are working on an aqueduct, which is to bring water to the mission. We hope to succeed with the help of God." A year later they reported, "Work on the aqueduct is progressing; already as many as 6600 *varas* (3.8 miles) have been completed." And that constitutes most of the written history of the mission dam and aqueduct.

In 1867, Judge Benjamin Hayes inspected the old system and wrote the following description in his famous "Immigrant Notes":

Water was forced into dam's surge chamber to turn water wheel.

"Immediately on the right bank (going downstream), a few feet above the channel, commences the aqueduct by which water was drawn from this grand reservoir. It consists of a single tile about six inches at the bottom, resting upon small stones; on each side, a brick 18 inches square inclined outward, so as to make a surface of two feet of water, some 12 inches deep; these bricks lined on the inside with cement, and propped on the outside by small rocks solidly cemented. The aqueduct commenced at the dam and ran full three miles through a gorge the most difficult than can be conceived – keeping on the hillsides of the right bank of the river. Sometimes it crossed gulches from 10 to 15 feet wide. In such places a stone foundation was built up high enough to keep the level. The canal in general was simply of cobblestones and a narrow tile laid in cement in the bottom. In the gulches, the rock foundation has with time fallen down or been washed away. Such has been the strength of the cement, this brick canal holds together across the gulch as firmly as if cast iron pipe, and now and then portions of it hang to the rocky wall at the height often to 20 feet above the bed of the river. . ."

The dam itself impounded about 20-acre feet of water, which when carried down the gorge, was stored in a settling basin near the mission. The structure included a sand trap, to clear the water before it entered the flume, and a 4-inch penstock through which the water was forced by a pressure chamber apparently to turn the wheel of a grist mill.

Section of the aqueduct which carried water down Mission Gorge.

The eye can still follow the line of the aqueduct in certain places. It is difficult to estimate the cost in human toil. Hundreds of Indians must have struggled for years, under the sweating and tireless padres, and through the heat of summer, to carry tile and material for cement through a gorge almost impassable on foot. Engineers who saw the works in the early days were convinced that the fathers must have had the assistance of an engineer; but the padres had built such great works, with unskilled labor, throughout Mexico. It had to be done, and it was done. Once the aqueduct through the gorge was finished, they still had three miles more to go. The water had to be carried along and around the base of the curving hills in a dirt ditch just above the bed of the river, to reach the mission area. Floods and vandals eventually took their toll. Roaring flood waters washed away a 24-foot section of the dam. The flood of 1916 swept off much of what remained of the aqueduct, after many of the tiles already had been carried off for

An American, H. M. T. Powell, sketched Mission Las Flores in 1849.

Map shows location of Las Flores Mission site near Highway 101.

roofs, chimneys and hallways of pioneer homes. The struggle of the fathers to bring water to their crops and mission is in essence the story of San Diego.

The mission grazed its herds and raised its crops over a wide area of San Diego County. The presidio lands were close to the coast, embracing the region around the bay, and the principal common lands, or the lands on which the people as individuals could raise their own crops, were in Sorrento, or Soledad Valley. The government lands lay south of the presidio lands, embracing what is now National City and Chula Vista. In Spanish times this was known as *Rancho del Rey*, or the King's Ranch, and in Mexican days as *Rancho de la Nación*, or the national ranch. Here were grazed the stock of the military and the presidio. While the mission orchards were in the bed of the San Diego River, the larger crop acreage was in El Cajon Valley, which they knew as Santa Monica. Between the mission and Santa Monica, on the low hills and along the San Diego River below Mission Gorge, grazed the mission's horses, mules and some sheep. Cattle and sheep were grazed at *Valle de San José* and *El Agua Caliente*, now known as Warner's Ranch; cattle at San Bernardo Ranch, on the upper San Dieguito River; cattle in the Escondido area; sheep, horses and mules at Pamo, now known as Santa Maria Valley, site of Ramona; cattle at San Pasqual Valley and at Paguay, now known as Poway Valley.

The padres went on as if time were standing still. A second line of missions in the interior, to penetrate the sierra into which disgruntled converts and renegades were fleeing and stirring up trouble among mountain tribes, was considered and then abandoned. Instead, a number of the missions erected extensions, or *asistencias*, which in actuality became little missions. Three of these were in San Diego County. Two under the jurisdiction of Mission San Luis Rey were San Antonio de Pala, founded at Pala on upper San Luis Rey River in 1810, and Las Flores, established near the coast between Oceanside and San Clemente in 1823. The chapel at San Ysidro was established by the San Diego Mission in 1818. The padres traveled regularly to these chapels with the word of Christ.

The Diegueño Indians who had accepted Christianity were slowly changing, and a summary of their character and progress was prepared by Frs. Fernando Martín and José Sánchez at the San Diego Mission in 1812, in filling out a document called "*Respuesta*," or Answer, at the request of the Spanish Government. The two padres answered thusly:

The Indians did not seem eager to preserve the customs of their forefathers, and while they were adverse to labor and mechanical arts, they learned any task with facility; among the neophytes there was a good deal of fondness for Europeans and Americans, and no hatred or rancor was observed; there was no inclination to learn to read or write, but they could learn readily; the virtues of compassion, charity, and generosity were noticed especially in the women; there was much affection between man and wife, the parents loved their children, and suffered want themselves rather than let their children feel it; they trained their children and exhorted, reproved or punished them for doing a wrong, but this was not common to all of them. On the other hand, they were little trustworthy in their dealings and words; they were inclined to tell lies, for they dreaded chastisement; the dominant vices were impurity, stealing and murder. They were much inclined to pride and rancor; the men persecuted one another to death out of jealousy or for some other grievances; the women, when they were angered at their men, revenged themselves by committing suicide. The Indians had an idea of eternity, or reward and punishment, of a final judgment, or purgatory, hell and heaven, for some lived continent, others confessed during the year, many at Easter time, and at the hour of death all anxiously pleaded for the holy Sacraments. But in the same year, Fr. Pedro Panto died unexpectedly at the mission. It is believed his soup had been poisoned by an Indian cook, though this was never proved.

THE ROUNDUP, or la matanza, *was the big time of the year at all the missions. Here cattle stampede past San Gabriel Mission with* vaqueros *in pursuit. Young Californians liked to ride, but real work was not for them.*

The year 1812 was an important one in many ways. The United States was at war with England; conditions in Mexico, because of revolution, were extremely unsettled, and help for the missions, presidios and settlements in California began to dwindle. The territory was almost totally neglected. The military began to look to the unhappy missions for survival, demanding food, shoes, clothing and money; and the governor, at one point, instructed the San Diego Mission to send a dozen bottles of its famous wine to the Viceroy, for forwarding as a gift to King Fernando VII. For two hundred years New Spain had been governed for the benefit of Spain and the relatively few persons of Spanish blood who comprised a ruling or owning class. In all the years of Spanish rule only four viceroys had been born in America, and they were sons of Spanish officials. Of 602 captains-general, governors and presidents, only 14 were creoles. The Spanish colonial policy was one of fear and distrust of the colonists, and because of the great distances and difficulties of communication, even of the officials sent to rule over them. Creoles could aspire to little but mining and agriculture and were excluded generally from high office and commercial enterprises. The haughty Spaniards dismissed the native-born Americans as being indolent, fatally fond of extravagant display, and lacking in sustained energy. But the civil war dragged on, despite reverses and betrayals. Little of the details of all this reached San Diego though it seems the officers and the padres, who were mostly of Spanish birth, remained loyal to Spain.

THE RUSSIANS PREPARED for any Spanish, or English, threat with the erection of Fort Ross north of Bodega Bay. The Spaniards found they were too weak to do anything about challenging this Russian hold on California.

The presidio population grew to 130 males and 117 females, including children but not including 55 soldiers of the 100 scattered throughout the presidial district. In 1813, a few soldiers at the post, including Sgt. José María Pico, were accused of plotting or at least desiring a local revolt, and three of them eventually died in prison. At times they seemed more concerned about the Russians, who had moved down the coast and established Fort Ross above Bodega Bay, north of San Francisco. The Governor, Lt. Col. Pablo Vicente de Solá, of the regular Spanish Army, looked things over in 1817, and made a sad report. He saw no way of dislodging the Russian intruders, without bringing large forces into California; the troops already here were ineffective against an enemy armed with anything more than bows and arrows; the artillerymen were old and disabled; the cannons were defective, and ammunition lacking. He found the San Diego Presidio buildings in a so "fatally ruinous condition" he urged their removal to another site 300 yards farther south, but nothing was done. He warned also that the Anglo-Americans had been acquiring considerable knowledge of the territory and its lack of defenses.

One of the most curious — and for a time, most suspicious — visitors to the coast was Capt. James Smith Wilcocks, on the American ship *Traveller*, identified in Spanish reports as the *Caminante*. When his ship was sighted off Monterey, all guns were manned, soldiers marched to battle stations, and Gov. Solá himself donned his uniform and prepared for action. Ordered ashore, Capt. Wilcocks said he merely wanted to engage in trade. He was dressed in black with a swallowtail coat and tall fur hat. Thus there was every indication he was some kind of a spy. However, he managed to establish friendly relations and eventually, in September of 1817, picked up a cargo of grain at San Diego and carried it to Loreto, the first such shipment from this port. At Loreto his ship was seized by a Mexican treasury officer and stripped of valuables. It finally was released.

It remained for Frenchmen, however, to bring about a crisis in California. The revolution against Spain had swept South America, as well as Mexico, and foreign intervention was feared and expected everywhere. The American ship *Clarion* arrived at Santa Barbara and warned that two insurgent ships were being outfitted at the Hawaiian Islands for raids on the American coast. Gov. Solá sprang into action, if that is what it can be called. In the case of San Diego he ordered all articles of value, such as sacred church vessels and ornaments, taken to Pala; women and children were ordered to be ready to flee inland; all livestock, except horses fit for use, were to be driven inland; spikes where to be prepared in

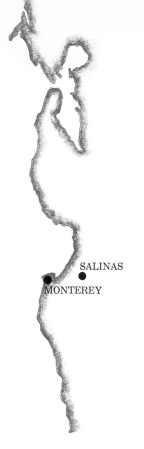

SALINAS
MONTEREY

Map shows Monterey and Salinas, to where Spanish force retreated.

case guns had to be spiked and abandoned; and all able bodied men were to hold themselves in readiness to meet the worst. Neophyte archers were ordered to presidios. Messengers to carry warnings were placed on the alert. Commandant Guerra at Santa Barbara pronounced in a letter that, "Under the protection of the God of battles I believe I can destroy all such villains as may have the rashness to set foot upon this soil." Well, nothing happened, for a time, and the guard was relaxed. But on the afternoon of Nov. 20, 1818, two vessels appeared off Monterey. They were the *Argentina*, carrying 38 heavy guns, commanded by Capt. Hippolyte de Bouchard, a Frenchman, and the *Santa Rosa*, with 26 guns, under a Lt. Peter Corney. They had sailed from Buenos Aires under the flag of another rebellious colony that had declared its independence from Spain, with the avowed purpose of stirring up trouble in California. The crew consisted of 366 men of many nationalities. One of these ships originally was American, and in all probability they were serving as privateers, perhaps financed in part by Americans sympathetic with the colonial rebellions against Spain. Corney himself was an American.

Exactly what happened in the early stages is confusing. After some shots were exchanged, and Bouchard had formally demanded the surrender of California, he put a large force of men ashore, led by Kanakas, or Hawaiians, armed with pikes, and a brief encounter was fought at Monterey, where Gov. Solá had assembled a force of 80 men. As Bouchard's men numbered into the hundreds, Solá retreated to the present area of Salinas, and waited the arrival of reinforcements from San Francisco and San Jose. With 200 men and a large force of Indians, the Spaniards marched back to Monterey, to find the town in ruins, and some of the buildings still burning, and the raiders and their ships gone.

Lt. Corney in his log reported regarding Monterey:

"It was well stocked with provisions and goods of every description, which we commenced sending on board the *Argentina*. The Sandwich Islanders, who were quite naked when they landed, were soon dressed in the Spanish fashion; and all the sailors were employed in searching houses for money and breaking and ruining everything."

They next plundered a ranch at Refugio, between Point Concepción and Santa Barbara, where they expected to find considerable wealth accumulated from smuggling, took on wood and water at Santa Cruz Island, and then cast anchor off Santa Barbara on Dec. 6, where some prisoners were exchanged with Spanish forces, to the great anger of Gov. Solá, when he learned of it, and then appeared off San Juan Capistrano on Dec. 14.

126

Up from San Diego for the defense of San Juan Capistrano came *Alférez* Santiago Argüello with 30 men. Lt. Corney tells the story:

"The Commodore sent his boat ashore to say, that if they would give us an immediate supply of provisions, we would spare their town; to which they replied we might land if we pleased and they would give us an immediate supply of powder and shot. The Commodore was very much incensed at this answer, and assembled all the officers to know what was best to be done."

The decision was made to land, pillage and sack the town. "We found it well stocked with everything but money and destroyed much wine and spirits and all the private property . . . next morning we punished about 20 men for getting drunk."

Despite his brave talk, Argüello had been unable to oppose the attack with 30 men, but now he was joined by soldiers from Santa Barbara and Los Angeles, under command of José de La Guerra, and a challenge was sent to Bouchard to land and fight. San Diego was made ready. But the ships disappeared. Had Bouchard succeeded in alienating California, it today might be an independent nation.

The soldiers went back to their customary duties. Lt. José María Estudillo, acting commandant of the Presidio at San Diego, had his hands full, as Indian runaways from San Diego and San Miguel in Baja California had joined in forays from San Diego to Santa Ana, stealing horses, cattle and mules, and selling them along the Colorado, and attacking ranchos, killing sheepherders and carrying off women.

Nature took a hand in affairs in 1820. The winter was a cold one, and there was considerable suffering. A comet was seen in the north. In January, an earthquake shook San Juan Capistrano. In San Diego, in September, it is said Mission Valley was flooded on a clear day from a cloudburst in the mountains. The last exploratory trip for new southwest mission sites, perhaps in the hope that if the present missions were secularized, new ones could be established in the interior, was undertaken by Frs. Mariano Payeras and José Sánchez in 1821. They went through El Cajon Valley to Santa Ysabel, and from there north by way of Pala and Temecula to San Jacinto and San Bernardino, before turning west to San Gabriel.

Ships came and went. A British whaler, the *Discovery*, put into port in August of 1820 and Lt. Ruiz, old, tired and suspected

Soldiers grumbled about getting paid. This is pay—next year.

Next page, THE MEXICAN FLAG replaces the Spanish and the shadow of ruin falls over the San Diego Presidio. It was 300 by 400. On the north was commandant's house; east, church and cemetery; south, guardhouse, gate, jail.

D. Wayne Millsap

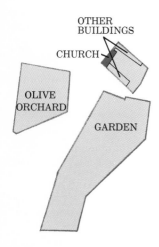

This drawing shows the layout of the mission, gardens, groves.

This outline of Presidio shows up on an old U.S. Topographical Map.

of alcoholism, was accused of allowing the ship's crew to take soundings in the bay. The American ship *Eagle* met a rebuff, when she arrived in 1821 and requested provisions. As far as the Spaniards were concerned, she was just another smuggler. That the padres were not above a little illicit trading was proved by the experiences of the *Eagle*. It was the *Eagle* which brought William Heath Davis, Sr., to California, and now under a new owner and new skipper, Eliab Grimes, she worked the coast out of sight of Spanish warships. The padres of San Luis Rey sent an agent to San Pedro to contact the *Eagle* and report they were ready to trade. The *Eagle* anchored off Las Flores Creek, and mission trading goods were brought down to the shore by *carretas*. Rough water prevented successful landings. The *Eagle* was forced to return to San Pedro, and the agent came up from San Luis Rey and purchased about a thousand dollars' worth of goods, mostly church ornaments, when trading was broken off in fear a chance investigator from San Diego might show up at any moment. In the next year, the *Eagle* attempted to seize a ship at Santa Barbara, in some dispute, and ran aground. The ship and her cargo were confiscated and sold at auction to the padres for $3,000.

The long struggle in Mexico was drawing to a conclusion. Spanish rule came to an end on Sept. 27, 1821. At San Diego, Frs. Martín and Sánchez, on Saturday, April 20, 1822, took the oath of independence from Spain and swore their allegiance to a new government in Mexico. They were required to submit a formal report as to mission lands and possessions. The property of the San Diego Mission, they reported, extended 13 leagues south, or about 40 miles, to El Rosario, in Baja California, east 17 leagues, or about 50 miles, to Santa Ysabel; north seven leagues, or about 20 miles, to *Cañada de San Bernardo*, or San Dieguito Valley, and was bounded on the west by the Imperial Presidio and settlements. This was a territory of 3000 square miles! The mission had 340 tame horses, seven droves of mares and burros, which with young numbered 504; 200 tame and untame mules, 8600 cattle and 19,000 sheep. There were 1686 Indians at the mission.

The military commanders in California took the oath on April 11 at a *junta* called at Monterey by Gov. Solá. San Diego forces were represented by Lt. José María Estudillo, who served as secretary of the meeting. The outcome of the revolution came like a blow. Fr. José Señán, president of the missions, wrote "May God have mercy on this province which seems at present to live between Scylla and Charybdis."

At first the military officials of California had refused to believe the reports of the success of the revolution and establishment of a new and independent imperial government. Gov. Solá, in fact, had written that he had received some documents from Mexico but they were "printed in a country of dreamers, since independence is a dream," and that since he, as well as others, were "aware that the immortal, incomparable Spanish nation has many and great resources with which to make herself respected," he "must look with contempt on such absurd views."

Some time was to pass before formal transfer ceremonies took place. Mexico City, distrustful of its province, and knowing the loyalty of the Franciscans to Spain, sent an agent, or *comisionado*, to California to extract oaths of allegiance and hasten a change in administration.

Chosen for the task was Agustín Fernández de San Vicente, *canónigo*, or canon, of the Durango Cathedral. He was jovial, pink-cheeked and indiscreet. The *San Carlos* brought him to Monterey, and sometime in late September or early October, the official ceremony was held, and then the canon started on a tour of provinces to repeat the performance. He mixed business with pleasure, being entertained en route with races, bullfights and games of all kinds. When it was learned he was approaching San Diego, it was suggested that he be given $2000 and a deck of cards. The point was well taken; official duties didn't interfere with his card playing there, and he wound up in a bitter dispute with Santiago Argüello over his gambling debts. Sometime between September and January, a formal ceremony also was held at San Diego.

When the hour came, and on the same day that the padres took a new oath of allegiance, the soldiers of the Presidio of San Diego lined up, and at the sound of drums and rifle shots, the red and gold flag of Spain, emblazoned with the lion of courage, was dipped and a homemade green, red and white flag of Mexico, with its native eagle, was hoisted aloft to the shouts of the people of *"Viva la independencia Mexicana!"* There was a flagpole. The ties of Old Spain were further cut the next day when the soldiers were ordered to chop off the queus which had been a mark of the royal forces. They didn't like it and neither did the women. To old soldiers it was a sad hour. Others saw an opportunity to get rich under a new regime; others saw the opportunity of seeking to avenge past wrongs. A few turned their eyes toward the prosperous missions and their plentiful lands.

Most of the white people in California were descendents of those who had come by way of the Anza trail, and out of them a kind of an aristocracy was beginning to form. The San Blas ships no longer came with regularity, and the Manila galleons, after more than a quarter of a thousand years, had ceased their lonely

Spanish dagger found in desert, evidently lost by early explorer.

journeys down the coast and passed San Diego in sailing the Great Circle Route between Manila and Acapulco.

San Diego had been under the Spanish flag for 280 years, since its discovery by Juan Rodríguez Cabrillo in 1542, and now it was all over.

Independence was not to bring any real benefits to most of the people of Mexico. New Spain had been divided between the Indian communities and the *haciendas*, and the fast-growing class of mixed people, or mestizos, was virtually dispossessed. Independence swept away the royal protection of the Indians and put an end to their special courts and the limits on their debts and labor. In the end the owners of the great *haciendas* got most of the former Indian lands and became more powerful than before. The *mestizos* remained as they had been — landless and dissatisfied. The removal of the Viceroy left a power vacuum that brought on another century of disorder and insurrection.

But the mark left by Spain on her long passage through the Western Hemisphere was a deep one. Spain left its language and its culture in a vast area from the United States-Mexican border to the tip of South America, and even in San Diego, the Hispanic influence still is reflected in its architecture, its place names and its way of life. America has been aptly called the step-daughter of Europe.

CHAPTER TEN

CAPT. DUHAUT-CILLY

These were the days of religious festivals, of cattle round-ups, of wild games on horseback, of bullfights and cock racing, of Indian laughter, and the excitement of the arrival and departure of ships from strange lands beyond the Pacific. The soldier never got paid, but who cared? He could dance with the commander's daughter. It was like a long and happy summer — and it couldn't last. As George Vancouver, the British navigator, had predicted, California and its riches were proving irresistible temptations to foreigners. And as Fr. Junípero Serra had feared, the vast mission holdings also were to prove irresistible temptations to the land seekers.

France, torn for so many years by revolution, feeble governments and European wars, never had been able to win a strong position in the Pacific. But in 1827, a group of French financiers fitted out a trading expedition under the command of *Capitaine* Auguste Bernard Duhaut-Cilly and sent it around the world and along the Pacific Coast. The expedition was a commercial failure, as much of the cargo had little interest to frontier people. But what he wrote about the Presidio of San Diego and Mission San Luis Rey has preserved a wistful picture of what life was like here so many years ago.

Things changed little in California in the early years of Mexican rule. The 21st and last mission was founded in 1823, at Sonoma,

THE CHURCH OF SAN LUIS REY MISSION today looks much as it did in Mexican days. Indians painted the six-foot thick walls and the tile pilars and arches, and worshiped humbly on their knees as there were no benches.

135

as San Francisco Solano, and it represented the northern-most Spanish-Mexican penetration. It had been planned to counter the Russian advances. More significant to the history of California were the arrivals of an American ship, the *Sachem*, of Boston, and the English ship, *John Begg*, both of which visited San Diego and picked up cargoes of hides, horns and tallow from the missions up and down the coast and began a trade that eventually shaped the future of San Diego and all California.

In the period from 1820 to the arrival of Duhaut-Cilly, at least 17 foreign vessels put into San Diego Bay, most of them primarily engaged in the fur trade, and others like the British whaler, *Discovery*, and the Russian brigantine, *Baikal*, stopping for repairs or provisions. One American captain, Benjamin Morrell, of the schooner *Tartar*, later put his experiences at San Diego into words, in "A Narrative of Four Voyages to the South Seas," and like the old seamen whose recollections of storms of old expand with the years, the San Diego of April 1825, grew mightily in memory:

Benjamin Morrell, who exaggerated San Diego experiences in 1825.

"The town of San Diego is four miles from the landing at the fort in a north-east direction. Its form is nearly circular and it is surrounded by a wall about 20 feet in height, which forms the backsides of the houses, the latter being erected against it; and fronting inwardly. There are about 250 houses erected in this manner from one to two stories high, built of freestone and neatly finished. There is also a large church, one nunnery, and a very neat little courthouse. This town contains about 1500 inhabitants, principally natives of the coast, and they appear to be a very agreeable, friendly kind of people."

While here the captain went on a hunting expedition in the back country and he has described how the party was attacked by wild Indians, he himself being shot through the thigh with an arrow. But he did not quail. He wrote that the chief of the attackers demanded the surrender of their weapons.

"We will perish first, I replied. But let us be politic. Demand honourable terms of capitulation, and gain us a moment's time for reflection. My companion did as I desired, in the savage's own dialect, and the answer was unconditional submission, or instant death. If we complied our lives would be spared. Should we resist, no quarter would be given. Having heard much of the treachery of this tribe, I resolved to place no confidence in the promises of their chief; but told my companions that we might better perish like men, with arms in our hands, than fall like cowards, by our own weapons, as we should be certain to do if we gave them up; that our first movement must be a desperate one; and that each man must bear in mind that he was contending for life and liberty."

A desperate battle supposedly ensued. Seventeen Indians were killed and four of Morrell's party wounded. The enemy was routed by gun and sword. It made good reading back in Boston.

When Duhaut-Cilly reached the California coast in the 370-ton

136

Le Heros, political affairs were in a generally unsettled state, but on his visits to many settlements and missions, he was able to fill 300 pages with detailed and beautiful descriptions of the life and times. At Santa Barbara, at the old mission, he found an enfeebled padre, alone at the time:

"I leaned toward him, and spoke loudly enough to overcome his deafness: 'I am a Frenchman. I come from Paris, and I can give you quite recent news from Spain.' Never did a talisman produce a more magical effect than these words, whose virtue I had already proved for drawing to myself the kindness and interest of the good fathers. The Spanish, in general, are extremely attached to their country; they love the ground, the customs, everything, even the errors of their government. I had no sooner pronounced these words than the old man, emerging from his lethargy, loaded me with compliments and such urgent questions that I could not find an instant reply. He recovered part of his past vigor, while speaking of his native land which he was to see no more."

There was much excitement at Santa Barbara when news came of the arrival of the new Mexican governor, Don José María Echeandía, who was to make his headquarters at San Diego. Duhaut-Cilly says:

"He was simply a colonel of artillery; but as he had the title and authority of commandant general, civil and military chief of the two Californias, he was given that of General in the country; and in addressing him, that of Your Lordship. He enjoyed the most extensive power, and he frequently made ill use of it. The frame of mind in which he found the Californians was well adapted to give him ideas of despotism which he had not, perhaps, brought from Mexico. Again, every one reared in Spanish habits and forms, loved the powers of the time, and to justify their regards, they willingly granted to them exaggerated qualifications; like the sculptor in the fable, they adored the work of their hands."

The *Heros* raised Point Loma on the 18th of April, and Duhaut-Cilly pronounced the harbor as, "certainly the finest in all California, and much preferable for the safety of vessels, to the immense harbor at San Francisco, whose great extent leaves it too much exposed to winds and waves."

The *Heros* worked into the channel, passed the heavy kelp beds which always were noted by all explorers and seamen, and anchored beyond Ballast Point.

"A rasant fort of 12 guns is built upon the point where this tongue of land joins Loma. On our approach, the Mexican flag was raised and enforced by a shot: at once we hoisted our own, paying the same respect. Every time we saw displayed the Mexican colors, they produced upon us a feeling of joy, and for a moment made our hearts beat. Some of us who had served under the empire took them always, at first glance, for those which had guided our steps to victory: the Mexican flag differs from the tricolor only in the part which is green instead of blue; the other parts are the same and similarly arranged."

A closer look took the edge off some of his enthusiasm.

French volume which told Europe about life in San Diego in 1827.

"Of all the places we had visited since our coming to California, excepting San Pedro, which is entirely deserted, the presidio at San Diego was the saddest. It is built upon the slope of a barren hill, and has no regular form: it is a collection of houses whose appearance is made still more gloomy by the dark color of the bricks, roughly made, of which they are built.

"It was however, at one time, the seat of government; a very mild climate, more favorable than Monterey to the disordered health of the commandant general, had perhaps induced him to prefer this place; some little charitable persons claimed the society of a lady at San Diego embellished, in his eyes, a spot so little attractive from its local features."

From Duhaut-Cilly we have a picture of changes on Presidio Hill. He said that on the sandy plain below the hill were scattered 30 to 40 houses of poor appearance, and some badly cultivated gardens. The settlers had begun to move down the hill, from the presidio around 1824. From a distance he could see the white mission far up the valley, and arranged to visit Frs. Vicente Oliva and Fernando Martín. Duhaut-Cilly seemingly was a fastidious man for those rough days, and he had little concept of frontier life. The padres at San Diego lived too close to the soil for him.

"The good fathers were about to dine, and they invited me to sit down with them. All they offered me was not presented in a manner to excite one's appetite; and as Fray Vicente vainly urged me to eat, Fray Fernando exclaimed: 'It is singular; it must be that the air at the mission is not kind to strangers: I never see one of them do honor to our table.' And while saying these words, he was arranging a salad of cold mutton, with onions, pimento and oil from the mission, the odor of which was nauseating; and having no knife, he tore this meat with his fingers and even with his teeth, mixing the whole by handfuls in a nicked plate, where were still seen some remnants of the supper of the evening before. Disgust alone could successfully resist a desire to laugh, which can be easily imagined; while my traveling companion, a young Californian, devoured, in a manner to please, everything placed before him. 'There is appetite for you,' said Fray Fernando."

Before leaving San Diego, on his first visit, he went hunting on Point Loma and was astonished at the abundance of small game and quail. He was told of organized hunts in which as many as 200 to 300 Indians, armed with curved throwing sticks, would form a line of battle, from the steep mountain bluff to the shore, and advancing abreast, drive rabbits and hares before them, forcing them into gullies or against walls or into impenetrable thickets, until they were terrorized.

"Some seek vainly to climb the wall on the right; others hurl themselves into the bay; there are some, and these are the only ones, to have any chance of safety, which attempt to run through the adverse front; it is a general massacre, a veritable Saint Bartholomew, in which many always perish before the remainder can pierce through the line of the Indians."

Duhaut-Cilly visited Mexican ports, and found agitation everywhere in the immense republic, and remarked that,

"It was not very difficult to see that in violently casting out of Mexico the wealthy Spaniards, or in having their heads fall, they had no other aim than to seize their fortunes. Modern consuls and tribunes banish beggars only from their tables and houses. The wealthy — cross the seas or die."

The *Heros* returned to San Diego on June 10, and Duhaut-Cilly decided to visit the Mission San Luis Rey "in view of making some trade with the president of that mission." San Luis Rey was at its height, or just passed it, with almost 3000 Indian neophytes, 1500 horses, 28,000 sheep, 22,000 cattle and all increasing by the thousands — far ahead of any other mission in California. Its lands extended 35 miles from north to south and 45 miles from east to west — a vast domain of more than 1500 square miles. It was a happy mission. At the presidio he joined up with a number of other persons who were making ready to go there for a double festival in honor of the consecration and of the patronal day of Padre Peyri.

A FRENCHMAN gives us the best picture of Mission San Luis Rey at its height. This sketch was found in the Duhaut-Cilly book recounting his experiences at the mission and in San Diego with French trading expedition.

Duhaut-Cilly's narrative reads as follows:

"To avoid the heat and to take advantage of a beautiful moonlight, we set out on the way, at 10:00 in the evening, at the moment when that luminary, in her third quarter, was rising behind the hills in the east. At the end of an hour, the road disappeared winding between two mountain chains. The moonlight was still cut off by the heights we had on our right, and darkness reigned in the depths of the valley. The trip was far from being as quiet as the one I had made lately, in quite similar circumstances when I went by night to the presidio of Mazatlán.

"The hope of the pleasure my companions of the road were promising themselves to enjoy at the feasts of San Luis had incited in them a liveliness which they fed still more by some glasses of brandy, every time they stopped to light a cigarita. The songs of the land were followed by quite scandalous little stories which each one related in turn; and if these anecdotes kept up the hilarity of the audience, the reputation of one's neighbor suffered cruel attacks from them. An unbounded carelessness was soon set up in the midst of this company; it was the moment for confidences; it was also that for jests which each one uttered without reserve."

The winter must have been a rainy one for though it was June they found the San Dieguito River rushing into the sea making, he said, a wild, rough bar, but the Californians "entered boldly and unhestitatingly into this torrent, and under pain of remaining alone I followed them." They barely made it, the current carrying them far below their starting point, almost sweeping them out to sea before the horses were able to vault to safety on the opposite side of the sandy valley.

Fr. Peyri's shaded old court had wells fed by a natural spring.

"Once more we turned inland, and after one and a half hour of travel, we descried before us, from the top of a slight eminence, the superb buildings of Mission San Luis Rey, whose brilliant whiteness was sent to us by the first light of day. At the distance we were from it, and by the uncertain light of dawn, this edifice, of a very beautiful pattern, supported upon many pillars, had the look of a palace; the architectural defects not being grasped at this distance, the eye seized only upon the elegant mass of this fine building. The verdant valley in which this mission is placed, already enlivened by great herds which could as yet be seen only as white and red spots, stretched to the north as far as the eye could reach, where the landscape was bounded by a group of high mountains whose outlines and summits were but softly made out through the light morning mists. Unconsciously I stopped my horse to examine alone, for a few minutes, the beauty of this sight; while my friends, the Californians, slight observers by nature, descended the hill; and I rejoined them at the end of a quarter of an hour, only at the moment I entered the mission."

Fr. Peyri welcomed them to the mission, served them chocolate and ordered beds prepared so they could rest until the dinner hour. Duhaut-Cilly wrote that the vast buildings of San Luis Rey were hardly sufficient to lodge the number of men and women who had gathered for the festivals.

"This construction forms an immense square of 500 feet on each side. The main front is a long peristyle borne upon 32 square pillars supporting

140

their full semi-circular arches. The building is, indeed, merely a ground floor; but its height, of fine proportion, gives it as much charm as dignity. It is covered with a flat tiled roof, around which, outside as well as within the square, is a terrace with a fine balustrade, which feigns still more height. Within is found a vast court, clean and well-leveled, around which pillars and arches, like those of the peristyle, make a long cloister, by which communication is had with all of the dependencies of the mission.

"To the right of the exterior facade is found the church with its bell tower surrounded by two rows of balconies. The front of this building is simple and without pillars, but the interior is rich and well decorated; a faucet gives a flow of water in the sacristy.

"The dwellings of the main facade are occupied by the padre and by strangers visiting the mission. Those of the court are used by the young girls who, till their marriage, do not live with the other Indians; there, also, are the storehouses for food, utensils, the workshops where are made the woolen and cotton stuffs for the Indians' clothes, and, lastly, the infirmary with its private chapel; for everything has been contrived for the convenience of the sick who could go to the church through the cloisters without failing to be under shelter; but this is a refinement. There is nothing more elegant than the pretty dome crowning this little temple, in which Fray Antonio has been pleased to make all his talent for decoration shine.

"In addition to the immense main building I have just described, there are two others much smaller, one of which is given up to the *mayordomos;* the other to the mission guard composed of a sergeant and 11 soldiers. This latter building has a flat roof and a dungeon with barbicans and loopholes.

"Two well-planted gardens furnish abundance of vegetables and fruits of all kinds. The large, comfortable stairway by which one descends into the one to the southeast, reminded me of those of the orangery at Versailles: not that their material was as valuable, or the architecture as splendid; but there was some relation in the arrangement, number, and dimensions of the steps. At the bottom of the stairs are two fine lavers in stucco; one of them is a pond where the Indian women bathe every morning; the other is used every Saturday for washing clothes. Some of this water is afterward distributed into the garden, where many channels maintain a permanent moisture and coolness. The second garden, situated in a higher place, can be watered only by artificial aid: a chain-pump, worked by two men, is used twice a day to accomplish this object. These gardens produce the best olives and the best wine in all California."

The ruins of the bathing and washing areas have been uncovered at the mission and may be seen just off the road on the river side.

"The dependencies of the mission are not limited to the various buildings composing it. Fray Antonio has had established, within a radius of 10 leagues, four ranchos, each one made up on an Indian village, a house for the *mayordomo* directing it, storehouses suitable for the harvests, and a very fine chapel. Every Sunday these administrators come to the mission to give account to the padre of the week's work and the condition of the rancho. Fray Antonio knew how to arouse among them a rivalry from which he reaped a great advantage for the general well-being of the mission. It is principally upon the lands of these ranchos that the great herds belonging to San Luis Rey are distributed."

On the evening of the 12th, volleys were fired to announce the festival of the following day. It began with a High Mass sung by

Fr. Peyri, whose memory still lives among Indians of San Diego.

Ruins of elaborate Indian laundry area at Mission San Luis Rey.

Water for laundry was filtered through charcoal in brick tunnel.

141

Indian musicians, and immediately afterward came the bullfights.

"This exercise offered nothing very remarkable; it took place in the inner court. Each rider proceeded to tease the bull, which rushed, with lowered head, now upon one, now upon another; but such is the agility of men and horses that they are almost never overtaken, though the bull's horn appears to touch them every instant.

The thoughtful, educated fathers had libraries in all missions.

"I was given a place at first with some persons on the terrace of the padre's house, overlooking the whole arena; but soon I, as also my companions in curiosity, were pursued by the Indian girls relegated to this spot from fear of accident. They were more than 200 in number, aged from 8 to 17; their dress was alike, composed of a red flannel petticoat and a white shirt. Their black hair, cut off to a length equal to half their height, floated over their shoulders. They came in a crowd to beg of us copper rings or pieces of money; and we amused ourselves at first by tossing them some *reals* (coins), that we might see them throw themselves one upon another and tumble in the most laughable manner; but gradually they grew bolder and so familiar that they ended by rushing upon us, and prepared to rummage in our pockets. Their bursts of laughter and their scoldings, which drowned the bull's bellowing, recalled to me the critical situation I found myself in one day on the island of Java, attacked, unarmed, by a troop of monkeys.

"We felt then that the moment was come to effect an honorable retreat; and to accomplish it we used strategy: we took all the small change remaining to us, and hurled it as far as we could; the swarm of girls left us instantly to run after the booty, and we profited by this short truce to escape. We went down to the padre's room, and sought protection behind a barricade built in front of his door."

Once back in the courtyard, they witnessed the continuation of a bullfight somewhat different from those in Spain, as death was not asked of the bull and, anyway, the fighting was being done by the young bloods — or the "people of reason" who were to become, in short time, the Dons of the great Ranchos. Duhaut-Cilly continues:

Restored kitchen shows how padres lived in Mission "Golden Age."

"The bull was not killed as in Spain. After it had been provoked, tired, teased for a half-hour, a small gate giving onto the plain was opened; no sooner had the animal seen this way of escape, than it made for it with all speed; the horsemen flew like arrows in its pursuit; the swiftest, upon reaching it, seized it by the tail; and, at the same instant, giving spurs to his horse, he overthrew the bull, sending it rolling in the dust; only after this humiliating outrage was it permitted to regain the pasturage in freedom. This exercise, demanding as much agility as firmness from the rider, is what is called in the country *colear el toro*."

The fiesta and its colorful sports events went on into the night, the laughter of the Indians mingling with the excited shouts of the young Californians. It was now time for cock racing, a sport less dangerous and to the Frenchman more interesting than bullfighting:

"Toward evening the *jinetes* (horsemen), having changed their horses began in front of the mission, the *carrera del gallo*. A cock is buried up to the neck in the ground; the riders place themselves 200 paces from it; and darting like an arrow, one hand on the saddle-bow, they lean over and carry it off by the head, as they pass. Their speed is so great that each one of them frequently races more than once before succeeding. But this is not all; if one of them seize the cock, all the rest rush upon him, to tear it from him; he tries to escape them by running away or turning this way or that; they intercept his course, press upon him; the horses mix together, crowd each other, rear upon their hind legs; the cock is torn in pieces, and some of the riders infallibly thrown down, becoming the butt for the laughter and jeers of their comrades and the fair spectators of this strife.

"These races ended with the game of the four corners, on horseback. The players were armed with long willow poles, with which they lashed each other unmercifully every time they met; and, to finish the game, the branches had to be broken up to the stump, which did not happen without some good whacks upon the head or face. The California girls seemed to take as much interest in these various races as the *hautes dames* of the fifteenth century were agitated in the brilliant tournaments, where their knights broke lances in their honor."

The Indians had their own games, too, and entered into them with an abandon and eagerness matching that of the "people of reason."

"While the *gente de razón* amused themselves thus variously, the Indians, on their part, betook themselves to their favorite games: the one seeming to please them the most consists in rolling an osier ring, three inches in diameter, and casting upon this ring, while rolling, two sticks four feet long, in order to stop it in its course. If one of the two sticks, or both together, go through the ring, or if the ring rests upon the two sticks, or upon only one of them, a certain number of points is counted, according to the amount of hazard. When a pair have played their game, two opponents begin again, and so alternately, until the match is finished.

"Other Indians, like the *Bas Bretons*, gathered into two large bands; each, provided with a stick in the shape of a bat, tried to push to a goal a wooden ball, while those of the opposing band strove to drag it in a contrary direction. This game appeared to attract both sexes alike. It happened, indeed, that the married women having challenged the single women, the latter lost the game. They came, crying, to complain to the padre, that the women, making an ill use of their strength, had taken unfair means to stop their arms as they were going to strike the ball. Fray Antonio, with a gravity worthy of the judgment of Solomon, made them give an exact account of the affair.

"During the explanation, the good missionary, his eyes half-closed, solemnly seated under the arched cloister, laid the index finger of his right hand upon his eyebrow, while the *medius* made a sort of square, passing under his nose: an attitude lending him an air of deep meditation. When the Indian girl had ended pleading her cause, he raised his head and declared the game void; but he could not help laughing in his sleeve, and he said to me in a low voice: '*Las pobrecitas! Es menester de hacer algo para ellas.*' (Poor young creatures! Something must be done for them.) 'It is by such means, and others like them, that I have succeeded in gaining the trust of these Indians.'"

It was a night to remember and Duhaut-Cilly was deeply moved by the scenes he had witnessed and the evident love that Indians held for Fr. Peyri and the understanding and gentleness with which he administered to their needs and their weaknesses:

Fr. Peyri's chasuble of hand-painted heavy silk of many colors.

"Truly, his mission was that, of all California, where these poor people were the best treated. Not only were they well fed and clothed; but still more, he gave them some money on feast days. Every Saturday he distributed soap among the women. On this occasion, all passed before him, and while two men took out of enormous baskets and gave to each one her share, the padre spoke to each in turn. He knew them all: he praised one, mildly reproached another; to this one a joke befitting the occasion, to that a fatherly reproof: all went away satisfied or touched.

"When night was come, I went with Fray Antonio to see the Indian dances, which appeared to me as interesting as they were strange. They were lighted by torches whose effect was to seem, by contrast, to spread a sad veil over the starry vault of the sky. A dozen men, having no other clothing than a cincture, the head adorned with tall feather plumes, danced with admirable rhythm. This pantomime always represented some scene, and was performed chiefly by striking the feet in time, and making, with eyes and arms, gestures of love, anger, fright, etc. The dancers held the head erect, the body arched, and the knees a little bent. Sweat, rolling down the entire body, reflected, as in a burnished mirror, the fire of the torches; and when it annoyed them, they scraped it off with a flat piece of wood which they held in their hand.

"The orchestra, arranged like a semi-circular amphitheatre, was composed of women, children and old men, behind whom one or two rows of amateurs could at least taste of this spectacle. The harmony of the songs governing the time was at once plaintive and wild: it seemed rather to act upon the nerves than upon the mind, like the varied notes from an Aeolian harp during a hurricane. From time to time the actors rested, and at the moment the song stopped, every one breathed at the same time into the air with a loud noise, either as a mark of applause or, as I was assured, to drive away the Evil Spirit; for, though all are Christians, they still keep many of their old beliefs, which the padres, from policy, pretend not to know.

"The next day, after the ceremonies and the procession of the consecration, the games began again in the same manner as the day before; but this time the bullfights were disturbed by an accident. One of the Indian girls, sporting upon the mission terrace, fell over the railing onto the pavement of the court, from a height of 20 feet, and broke her head."

The pulpit from which Fr. Peyri preached still in use at mission.

The time to leave was at hand. An interlude was over. Duhaut-Cilly returned to San Diego and learned that a seaman from his own ship had volunteered to join in a bullfight staged inside the presidio, but being nearsighted and failing to keep a respectful distance from the bull while it was being unleashed, he had been charged, thrown and knocked unconscious. He recovered, all right, but Duhaut-Cilly's report of the affair and the subsequent bullfight gives us an idea of the size of the presidio and the interior arrangements:

"This scene, begun in a tragic manner, was later enlivened by an odd incident. The church at the presidio, forming one of the sides of the interior court, is built upon the very steep slope of the hill, in such a way that one end of the roof rests upon the ground, while the other is raised nearly 40 feet above the soil. The bull, more ready for flight than combat, frightened by the cries of the spectators, and threatened by the noose, finding no outlet for escape, was driven into a corner near the spot where the roof of the church seems to join the mountain. There was no other retreat for it, and a spring of two feet in height put it upon the flattened roof of the chapel whence, continuing to go on, it might be predicted that it would have an abrupt introduction into the sanctuary, through the tiles where it thrust through now one leg, now the other. At last it reached, stumbling along in this fashion, the highest part of the roof, before recognizing the imminence of a danger which it then seemed to comprehend with a new terror. It tried, however, to turn about, in order to retrace its steps; but in this movement it slipped and fell into the court, with a heap of débris and in the middle of a cloud of dust. Can one conceive of the boisterous delight among the descendants of the Spanish roused by the cruel death of this poor animal?"

This early painting shows extensive San Juan Capistrano layout.

The *Heros* went back up the coast but was to visit San Diego a number of times. Duhaut-Cilly was to have the opportunity of adding a great deal more to the story of California and of the events at the little Presidio of San Diego.

Life flowed on with the passiveness of a quiet stream. There were still occasional troubles with unruly Indians but in a half century only two real actions had been fought with the foreigners they were supposed to keep away, and nobody really had been hurt. Soldiers had become messengers and stewards. Duhaut-Cilly wrote that military life among the California soldiers in no wise resembled that of a European soldier:

"They never drill; they are merely considered as mounting guard in the presidios and missions; their most frequent and regular duty is to serve as customs guards. Those entrusted with this care know how to take advantage of their position by favoring smuggling.

"These troops, although divided into artillery, cavalry and infantry, are alike mounted. Each soldier must have several horses which feed upon the government lands. These regiments have, correctly speaking, no uniform... These men occupy in society quite another rank than our European soldiers, and in this respect much more resemble the Turkish janissaries than any other body of troops. They have been seen to aspire to the hand of their commandant's daughter, and gain it. They are present at all the festivals given by their officers, return them courtesy for courtesy, and are their equal everywhere. They would receive a very large salary if they were paid what is owed them; but that has never happened to them, no more under the Spanish Government than under the Mexican, and there are some who are owed more than 20 years of their wages. They receive only their rations with tolerable regularity, and they are furnished clothing, from time to time, from the woolens, linens and shoes which are supplied by foreign ships for the amount of their customs duties."

As for the settlers of California, he found the men large and well formed, thick black beards disclosing their Spanish origin, "but they do not reap all the advantage from their figure; the custom of being always on horseback causes them to acquire an awkward shape. They are so little accustomed to make use of their legs that, in walking, they carry the entire weight of their body from one side to the other, as if they were lame."

The Californian, he wrote, was lazy, and the only work to which he would submit himself was taking care of the herds. He generally dined alone, served by his wife, sons and daughters. He was rarely seen without a cigar in his mouth. The young Californian could not shave, for the first time, without his father's consent, which often was not given before his 22nd birthday, the usual time for marriage. As for the women, he found them large and strong. "Some are seen with pretty faces, and which would pass for beautiful if they were less careless of their complexion, their hands and feet; they are usually sedate and modest."

Duhaut-Cilly's French gallantry deserted him when he came to describing the attire of California women. He described it simply as ludicrous.

"Their costume is a bizarre mixture of foreign and California fashions; it is, particularly, when they borrow something from the Mexican women that they become extravagant; for these Mexicans (those at least who were in California) are so laughably dressed that one should have a large portion of gravity to preserve any seriousness in the presence of their toilet."

He wrote that somehow the women had become convinced that pasteboard "melons" in which Parisian women carried their goods were the latest styles in hats, and had taken to wearing them and adding ribbons and feathers, to win the appellation from the men of Monterey as "melon heads."

The basic costume was composed of a petticoat, the upper part white, the rest red, and it hung from the hips on which it formed

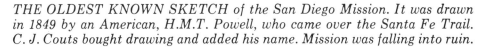

THE OLDEST KNOWN SKETCH of the San Diego Mission. It was drawn in 1849 by an American, H.M.T. Powell, who came over the Santa Fe Trail. C. J. Couts bought drawing and added his name. Mission was falling into ruin.

"a much puffed-out pad;" a white shirt of the same form as the man's; a *rebozo*, or muffler, of blue and white cotton, white stockings and black shoes. "In general, they have very beautiful hair which they allow to fall behind in a thick braid, as do the men." Evidently the queues had not all been cut when Mexico won its independence from Spain.

The men wore short trousers of wool or velvet, dark in color, ornamented at the knees with gold or silver lace. Below the trousers were large white drawers descending half way down the leg and covering part of white socks which always were worn loose. "The Californian who had on stockings well drawn up would excite a burst of sarcastic remarks." The outside waistcoat generally was of the same material as the trousers, had no collar, and was trimmed with piping and red ornaments. The coat, though it had metal buttons, was not made to be closed over the chest.

Around the waist they wore a red sash called a *faja*. Their shoes were buckskin fastened by lacing on the outside of the boot and heavily embroidered, the heel having an edging of fringed leather serving to bear the weight of huge spurs. When riding they wrapped their legs in *gamuzas*, or chaps of chamois leather and "the manner of rolling it about the calf of the leg is the touchstone of good Californian style. Woe to him whose *bota* would permit the shape of the leg to be made out. The young men the best dressed must appear to be supported upon two thick sausages, and as if to add to the illusion, the *bota* is made tight in the middle of the calf by a cord braided of gold and silk, the work of their lady-love." Hats were of felt, flat in shape and with wide brims. For protection from the cold they wore a cloak "which is nothing else than a piece of stuff with a hole for allowing the head to pass through, used in all Spanish colonies of America, and which is called, now *poncho*, now *manga*."

Though the costume had little appeal to Duhaut-Cilly he did acknowledge that it permitted perfect freedom to all movements of the body.

The chief fault among the men was gambling.

"Gambling occupies first place; they ruin themselves at it, and lose the inclination for work in this fatal occupation of nearly all their time. The most skillful player is he who cheats the most . . . If gambling ruins them, drunkenness degrades them still more; these two vices, here as with us, usually go hand in hand. They devote themselves to it, unbridled, unrestrained; thus, at their feasts, one sees almost nothing but brandy for all refreshment; and to arrange for a dance, which they call a *fandango*, though they were not acquainted with that dance, it needs but some gallons of this beverage and a few candles."

Most of the desirable land was still held by the missions, though some had been granted to individuals, for homes and ranchos, but was held without real title. The Californians, stirred by revolution and cries of Mexico for the Mexicans, were getting restless. Duhaut-Cilly knew the system could not last. The very wealth and prosperity of the missions were destined to bring their downfall.

On its final visit to the port of San Diego, the *Heros* anchored in its accustomed position, and then was ordered to go up farther, without any explanation being given. Three American ships were drawn up in echelons the whole length of the channel, with the three-master *Franklin* anchored five miles down the channel, the schooner-brig *Clio* in an intermediate position, and the brig *Andes*, the nearest to the *Heros*. The *Franklin* was a virtual captive of the Mexican government. In the jail at the presidio was an American trapper, or Mountain Man, named James Ohio Pattie, and six companions.

CHAPTER ELEVEN

D. Wayne Millsap

THE MOUNTAIN MEN

This was the era of the Mountain Men. They trapped, hunted, fought and explored their way across the Great Plains, found the passes through the Rocky Mountains, braved the vast western deserts, and, at last, broke through the high coastal barrier to reach the Pacific Ocean, to the astonishment of the little coastal settlements whose people still lived by the customs and traditions of Old Spain.

No stranger breed of men ever lived. Capt. B. L. E. Bonneville, a graduate of West Point who became a fur hunter, has memorialized the Mountain Men with this description of their costume and eccentricities:

"It is a matter of vanity and ambition with the free trapper to discard everything that may bear the stamp of civilized life, and to adopt the manners, habits, dress, gesture, and even walk of the Indian. You cannot pay a free trapper a greater compliment, than to persuade him that you have mistaken him for an Indian; and, in truth, the counterfeit is complete. His hair, suffered to attain a great length, is carefully combed out, and either left to fall carelessly over his shoulders, or plaited neatly and tied up in otter skins, or parti-colored ribbons. A hunting shirt of ruffled calico of bright dyes, or of ornamental leather, falls to his knees; below which, curiously fashioned leggins, ornamented with strings, fringes, and a profusion of hawks' bills, reach to a costly pair of moccasins, of the finest Indian fabric, richly embroidered with beads. A blanket of scarlet, or some other bright color, hangs from his shoulders, and is girt round his waist with a

WEARY AND WEATHERBEATEN, Jedediah S. Smith leads his Mountain Men across the Mojave Desert. This drawing captures the wild spirit of the trappers who broke the land trails to California for the later immigrants.

red sash, in which he bestows his pistols, knife, and the stem of his Indian pipe. His gun is lavishly decorated with brass tacks and vermilion, and provided with a fringed cover, occasionally of buckskin, ornamented here and there with a feather. His horse is caparisoned in the most dashing and fantastic style; the bridles and crupper are weightily embossed with beads and cocades; and head, mane, and tail are interwoven with an abundance of eagles' plumes, which flutter in the wind. To complete this grotesque equipment, the animal is bestreaked and bespotted with vermilion, or with white clay."

Sometimes you couldn't tell the Mountain Men from the Indians.

While other Americans in ships hunted the sea otter fur along the Pacific Coast, for the aristocrats of China, the Mountain Men sought the fur of the river beaver, for the hats of English gentlemen. As the rivers were trapped out, they moved farther and farther West, to the muddy but rich Colorado and then, once into California, to the San Joaquin Valley and the High Sierra. Behind them, eventually, came a trickle of traders and immigrants, then a flood of gold seekers and settlers. California was swept up into a whirl of change.

Two of them left records of their wanderings, in which San Diego played a part. They were Jedediah S. Smith and James Ohio Pattie. Smith put down his experiences as he went along, and though they were later burned in a fire, a copy had been made by a friend and started: "A Manuscript Journal of the Travels of Jedediah S. Smith thro' the Rocky Mountains and West of the same together with a description of the country and customs and manners of the Indians thro' which he travelled."

In a letter to a brother, Smith put down the personal creed of the Mountain Man:

"It is, that I may be able to help those who stand in need, that I face every danger — it is for this that I traverse the Mountains covered with eternal Snow — it is for this that I pass over the Sandy Plains, in heat of Summer, thirsting for water, and am well pleased if I can find a shade, instead of water, where I may cool my overheated Body — it is for this that I go for days without eating, & am pretty well satisfied if I can gather a few roots, a few Snails, or, much better Satisfied if we can affod our selves a piece of Horse Flesh, or fine Roasted Dog . . . "

A friend made this sketch after the death of Jedediah S. Smith.

Pattie has left us a "Personal Narrative during an Expedition from St. Louis, through The Vast Regions between that place and the Pacific Ocean, and thence back through the City of Mexico to Vera Cruz, during journeys of six years; in which he and his Father, who accompanied him, suffered unheard of Hardships and Dangers, had Various Conflicts with the Indians, and were made Captives in which Captivity his Father died; together with a description of the Country, and the Various Nations through which they passed." His father died when thrown into jail at San Diego, and lies buried somewhere on Presidio Hill. Actually, Pattie's story was put together by a fiction writer, Timothy Flint, of Cincinnati, who insisted he had kept to the facts though some of Pattie's experiences in San Diego hardly seem creditable. It doesn't seem that the Mexicans could have been that officious and suspicious.

The first to arrive at San Diego was Jedediah Smith. While most of the Mountain Men held that "God holds no man accountable after he crosses the Missouri River," Smith was very religious and always carried a Bible, which he read daily. He presented a grotesque appearance, having been attacked and mutilated by a grizzly bear which charged his horse. Smith, as well as the horse, were knocked to the ground, several of Smith's ribs were broken, and the bear took nearly all of Smith's head into his jaws. Half his scalp was laid bare, and one ear was left dangling by a string-like piece of skin. James Clyman, one of Smith's companions, volunteered to attempt to dress the wound and sew the scalp back together, with the sewing kit always carried by Mountain Men. Clyman later told the story:

The pistol of Jedediah S. Smith is preserved in the Serra Museum.

> "I put in my needle, stitching it through and through and over and over and laying the lacerated parts together as nice as I could with my hands. Water was found in about a mile, when we all moved down and camped . . . this gave us a lisson on the character of the grizzly Baare which we did not forget."

Smith trapped for a commercial organization in which he was a partner, and his expeditions were fairly large. The company that left the Bear River in northern Utah on Aug. 16, 1826, included 18 men and 50 horses, with the hope of crossing the deserts and attempting to reach the fresh, untrapped waters of California. Smith was convinced that lands beyond the Salt Lake were not as impassable as so many others believed them to be, and that there must be a river running west from the interior to the Pacific.

Family record giving birth date of Mountain Man Jedediah Smith.

From their winter quarters in Bear Valley, in the upper Wasatch Range, northeast of the Great Salt Lake and on the border of the present states of Utah and Idaho, they went directly south until they met the Sevier River. They followed its course down the Wasatch Range into southern Utah, and somewhere in the vicinity of the Sevier and Virgin Rivers they crossed the divide. Now, where was the great river, that was supposed to exist and flow to the Pacific? They followed the Virgin River southwest through the corner of Utah into southern Nevada, to its junction with the Colorado River, and followed its banks along the California-Arizona border, to the Mojave Desert.

Two runaway Indians from the San Gabriel Mission showed them the way across the desert and to the old Spanish settlements and the fabled California. Nothing could have been more astonishing to the padres than the appearance of the Mountain Men. A land route to California, which had been denied the Spaniards and then the Mexicans by the fierce Yuma Indians, now was held

A DESERT WILDERNESS was crossed on this route by Jedediah Smith, the Mountain Man who first broke the American overland trail to California. In San Diego, Smith was received with suspicion by the Mexican governor.

by the Americans. But the padres made them welcome and the trappers rested for two months, enjoying the warm climate and abundant food of the fertile San Gabriel Valley. They had little conception of the historic role they had played in opening an American overland way to a California so weakly held by Mexico. The Mexican officials, and in particular, Gov. Echeandía, however, were somewhat alarmed and suspicious, and required the Smith party to forfeit their weapons during their stay. And as they did not have proper Spanish papers, Smith was ordered to San Diego to explain his reasons for his illegal entry. At the presidio, he showed his American passport, surrendered a diary he had been keeping and said he had come as far only because he was in need of supplies; that his motives were strictly honorable, and merely sought permission, now that he was here, to return by another route, up the California coast to Oregon and to the Columbia River. To this last request, the governor said "no." He would have to leave the same way he had come into California.

Gov. Echeandía was suspicious and alert, and as he didn't believe that Smith and his men had walked a thousand miles just to look for furs, accused him of being a spy. This was Echeandía's favorite accusation. The captains of three American ships in the bay at the time, including William G. Dana, an uncle of Richard Henry Dana, later to etch his own name on the history of San Diego, all vouched for Smith, and when he was allowed to go free, one of them, Capt. William H. Cunningham, took him on the *Courier* to San Pedro, from where Smith made his way to San Gabriel.

When it came time to leave, one of Smith's men, John Wilson, refused to leave California. He was the first of many. Two others who had gotten into a fight at San Diego also gave Smith trouble. Jim Reed got drunk, abused an Indian convert, and Smith, according to the harsh law of the frontier, had him taken out and flogged. Dan Ferguson turned up missing. Once through Cajon Pass, and out of the possible sight of the Mexican guards, Smith swung north along the base of the mountains and then re-crossed them to reach the San Joaquin Valley. The trapping was wonderful.

Smith left most of his party in California, while he undertook a return journey, making the first crossing of the Sierra Nevada, experiencing terrible suffering in volcanic hills and in the alkali deserts in which they had to cover themselves with sand to escape death from the heat. Back at his headquarters, he organized a second expedition for California, and while crossing the Colorado River, they were attacked by the Mojave Indians. Ten of his men were killed, only seven of his party managing to escape to the opposite shore, where they barricaded themselves, and with butcher

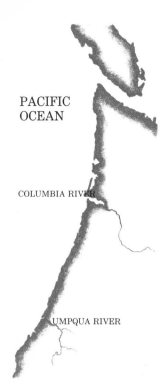

PACIFIC
OCEAN

COLUMBIA RIVER

UMPQUA RIVER

Map shows Umpqua River, where most of Smith trappers were slain.

knives tied to saplings, beat off an assault by 500 Indians. Under cover of darkness they slipped away.

In the Sacramento Valley they joined the men who had been left behind. Smith didn't want to give up the hope of finding the mythical San Buenaventura River which was supposed to flow from the Rocky Mountains all the way to the Pacific Ocean, and he continued trapping in the north. The Mexicans weren't happy to find him back in California. He was locked up at San José Mission and accused of claiming United States sovereignty over the valley where they had been camping. Though that charge was dismissed, Smith was removed to Monterey, jailed again, and taken before his old accuser, Gov. Echeandía, on a charge of having violated a pledge to leave California. One of the Smith's men, who had been wounded in the Colorado River fight, had been left behind in the south and wound up in the San Diego jail. He was released to rejoin Smith, and all agreed to leave California. The party of 20 started north and had an encounter with grizzly bears in which one man was seriously mauled, and Smith himself barely escaped with his life. On the way to Oregon they camped on the Umpqua River. While Smith and two companions scouted ahead upstream, Indians fell upon the camp, and in one minute slaughtered 14 men and one boy. Not a shot had been fired in defense. When Smith returned, he heard the sounds of Indian revelry, slipped up close and saw the mutilated bodies of his men, and the Indians dancing with the grizzly scalps. The three survivors melted into the woods and finally worked up to the protection of an English fort on the Columbia River.

It was the third massacre of a Smith party in five years. He never found the river for which he had searched so long. It never existed. It was Smith, though, who had firmly established the South Pass through the Rocky Mountains, which later became a virtual "Panama Canal" through which immigrant trains crossed from the Great Plains to the Western deserts and drove for California. Five years later, Smith met death when another expedition he was leading ran out of water in the Oklahoma country and he set out to see if he could find a stream or water hole. At the Cimarron River, he was surprised by a band of Comanche Indians, who frightened his horse by flashing mirrors and waving blankets. The horse veered and Smith was turned broadside to his attackers. They closed in on him, and though he managed to kill some of the Indians, he was lanced to death. This was on May 27, 1831.

After Jedediah Smith came others. Of some of the expeditions, such as that of Richard Campbell, little is known. After the American occupation of New Mexico, Lt. James H. Simpson, who was instructed to make a survey for a wagon route from New Mexico to San Diego or Los Angeles, reported that he talked with a Richard Campbell, at Santa Fe, who "informs me that in 1827, with a party of 35 men and a number of pack animals, he travelled from New Mexico to San Diego by way of Zuñi, and the Valley of the *Rio de Zuñi*, and found no difficulty the whole distance. He further states there is no question that a good wagon route was possible and wood, water and grass can be found in this direction, both to San Diego and the puebla de Los Angeles." Smith's narrative after his leaving San Diego and reaching the Northwest, has the following allusion: "In the meantime news came from the south that another party of Americans were near Too Larra Lake. I . . . was well convinced there were no Americans there . . ." Too Larra Lake was Tulare Lake in San Joaquin Valley.

As far as San Diego is concerned, the visit of James Ohio Pattie holds the most interest. He became well acquainted with San Diego's jail and experienced Echeandia's official displeasure. Strange winds blew through the hearts of Mountain Men. They were forever restless and forever seeking. The first of the Patties followed Daniel Boone into the Kentucky wilderness; his son, Sylvester, pushed his way into Missouri, and his son, James, joined his father in the long trail to the Colorado and Gila Rivers and to California. They trapped, and sometimes mined, up and down the continent, visiting the Grand Canyon and the Black Canyon, wandering as far north as the Yellowstone, and back to Santa Fe, and into Mexico. At Santa Fe, we pick up a journey of the Patties and six companions to the Gila River and then down the Colorado, in search of Spanish settlements which they believed existed at the mouth of the river, trapping and catching as many as 60 beavers a night, seeing animals resembling the African leopard, which presumably were jaguars, and keeping a close eye on the Yumas, the Cocopa and the Pima Indians. On Jan. 1, 1828, 100 miles below the confluence of the Colorado and the Gila, they ran into trouble. An Indian tribe showered them with arrows. They fired back and brought down six, and "the remainder fell flat, and began to dodge and skulk on all fours, as though the heavens had been loaded with thunder and mill stones, which were about to rain on them from the clouds . . . the fallen lay on the sandy beach."

The climate was getting hot and the beaver scarce, and no Spanish settlement, at which they hoped to sell the furs for foreign export, came into sight. The river began to betray them. They experienced the tidal bore, when the tide forces the sea up through the narrowing Gulf of California and against the pressure of the oncoming flow of the Colorado River. The terrifying effect, when the waters can rise or drop 40 feet, was first noted by Francisco de Ulloa who explored the Gulf in 1539.

"On the 18th, we first perceived that we had arrived on the back water of the tide; or rather we first attributed the deadness of the current to the entrance of some inundated river, swollen by the melting of the snow on the mountains. We puzzled our brains with some other theories, to account for the deadness of the current. This became so entirely still, that we began to rig our oars, concluding that instead of our hitherto easy progress of floating gently onward, we had henceforward to make our head-way down stream by dint of the machinery of our arms.

"We soon were thoroughly enlightened in regard to the slackness of the water. It began to run down again, and with the rapidity of six miles an hour; that is, double the ordinary current of the stream. We were all much surprised, for though I had seen the water of the Pacific at Ymus, (Guaymas) none of us had ever felt the influence of the tides, or been in a craft on the ocean waters before.

"We floated on, having had a beautiful evening's run, and did not come to land, until late; we then pitched our camp on a low point of land, unconscious, from our inexperience of the fact, that the water would return, and run up stream again. We made our canoes fast to some small trees, and all lay down to sleep, except my father, who took the first watch. He soon aroused us, and called on us all to prepare for a gust of wind, and a heavy rain, which he thought betokened by a rushing noise he heard. We realized in a few moments that it was the returning tide. Still, so strongly impressed were we, that a shower was approaching, that we made all the customary arrangements of preparation, by stretching our blankets to keep out the water from above. But our enemy assailed us from another quarter. Our camp was inundated from the river. We landsmen from the interior, and unaccustomed to such movements of the water, stood contemplating with astonishment the rush of the tide coming in from the sea, in conflict with the current of the river. At the point of conflict rose a high ridge of water, over which came the sea current, combing down like water over a milldam. We all sprang to our canoes, which the rush of the water had almost capsized, though we held the fasts with our hands. In 20 minutes the place where we lay asleep, and even our fire place was three feet under water, and our blankets were all afloat. We had some vague and general ideas of the nature of the tide, but its particular operations were as much unknown to us, as though we never had heard of it at all. In the consternation of our ignorance, we paddled our crafts, as well as we could, among the timber, not dreaming in the course of a few hours, the water would fall again. As it was, we gathered up our floating blankets, got into our canoes, and held fast to the brushes, until the water fell again, leaving us and our canoes high and dry. We were now assailed by a new alarm, lest the Indians, taking advantage of this new position in which we were placed, would attack and murder us."

In some apprehension they passed the night, and in the morning, with their spirits renewed and their clothes dried, they resumed their journey down the river, still expecting to find the Spanish settlements, until Jan. 28. When the tide ran out, the surf came up the river in a surging commotion.

"Here we were placed in a new position, not the least disheartening or trying, among the painful predicaments, in which fortune had placed us.

The beaver lured the first Americans across desert and mountains.

The fierce billows shut us in from below, the river current from above, and murderous savages upon either hand on the shore. We had a rich cargo of furs, a little independence for each one of us, could we have disposed of them as we had hoped, among the Spanish people, whom we expected to have found here. There were no such settlements. Every side on which we looked offered an array of danger, famine and death. In this predicament, what were furs to us? Our first thought was to commit our furs to the waters, and attempt to escape with our lives. Our second resolve was to ascend the river as far as we could, bury our furs, and start on foot for some settlement. We saw that the chances were greatly against us, that we should perish in the attempt; for the country yielded little to subsist on, and was full of Indians who are to the last degree savage and murderous, and whom nothing can subdue to kindness and friendship. We had no idea of ever putting ourselves in their power, as long as one of us could fire a pistol, or draw a knife.

"We now began to ascend with the tide, when it served us, and lay by when it ran down, until we arrived at the point where it ceased to flow. We then applied our oars, and with the help of setting-poles, and at times the aid of a cordelle, we stemmed the current at the rate of one, and sometimes two miles an hour, until the 10th of February, when we met a great rise of the river, and found the current so strong, that we had no power to stem it in any way. So we concluded to abandon our canoes, come to shore, bury our furs, and make our way across the peninsula to the coast of California, which we thought from the information of the Indians, could not be very distant."

Then began an epic journey across the wastes of Baja California, one that does not suffer in the telling. They worked their way through the river grass, weeds brush and vines of the river bottom, and came to the edge of a large salt plain.

"Here we struck a northwest course, and traveled the remainder of this hot and fatiguing day without finding any water. We began to suffer severely from thirst. The earth, also, was so loose and sandy, that at every step we sank to our ankles, the sun beaming down a fierce radiance the while; which made it seem as if the heavens and the earth were on fire. Our tongues became so parched, that not a particle of moisture flowed into our mouths. In this miserable and forlorn condition, abandoned by strength, courage and hope, we found some little alleviation of our misery, when the blaze of the sun was gone, and the cool night enabled us to throw down our weary and exhausted bodies under its dewy shade."

The morning brought no relief but in the afternoon they came in the sight of a little lake, and their joy knew no bounds. The water was too salty to drink, and in their sorrow and distress, they could look up to the high Sierra de Juarez Mountains, in north central Baja California, with their tantalizing snow-topped peaks glittering in the winter sun. They crossed the lake, probably one of the lower beds of the salt plain that farther north forms the Laguna Salada and which are filled periodically by tidal flow from the Gulf of California. Many American fliers have met death when forced down in this grim land.

Ascending some small hills they came upon an Indian encampment, made themselves sick drinking water, and were welcomed after assuring the Indians they were Christians and friendly Americans. One of them, however, to satisfy the curiosity of the Indians, especially of the women, had to strip himself so they could pinch and admire his white skin. The young girls had hair that reached almost to the ground. The chief agreed to supply guides to direct them to the Spanish settlements which, however, were not below them but to the west, on the coast, and beyond the mountains. They pushed on:

"What with the fierce sun and the scorching sand, and our extreme fatigue, the air seemed soon to have extracted every particle of moisture from our bodies. In this condition we marched on until nearly the middle of the day, without descrying any indication of water in any quarter. A small shrubby tree stood in our way, affording a tolerable shade. We laid ourselves down to get a few minutes rest. The Indians sternly beckoned us to be up and onward, now for the first time clearly explaining to us, that there was no water until we reached the mountains in view. This unseasonable and yet necessary information, extinguished the last remainder of our hope, and we openly expressed our fears that we should none of us ever reach it.

"We attempted to chew tobacco. It would raise no moisture. We took our bullets in our mouths, and moved them round to create a moisture, to relieve our parched throats. We had traveled but a little farther before our tongues had become so dry and swollen, that we could scarcely speak so as to be understood. In this extremity of nature, we should, perhaps, have sunk voluntarily, had not the relief been still in view on the sides of the snow covered mountains.

"Two of our companions here gave out, and lay down under the shade of a bush. Their tongues were so swollen, and their eyes so sunk in their heads, that they were a spectacle to behold. We were scarcely able, from the condition of our own mouth, to bid them an articulate farewell. We never expected to see them again, and none of us had much hope of ever reaching the mountain, which still raised its white summit at a great distance from us. It was with difficulty that we were enabled to advance one foot before the other. Our limbs, our powers, even our very resolutions seemed palsied. A circumstance that added to our distress, was the excessive and dazzling brightness of the sun's rays, so reflected in our eyes from the white sand that we were scarcely able to see our way before us, or in what direction to follow our guides. They, accustomed to go naked, and to traverse these burning deserts, and be unaffected by such trials, appeared to stand the heat and drought, like camels on the Arabian sands. They, however, tried by their looks and gestures to encourage us, and induce us to quicken our pace. But it was to no purpose. However, we still kept moving onward, and had gained a few miles more, when night brought us shelter at least from the insupportable radiance of the sun, and something of coolness and moisture."

At dark, camp was made, a fire lighted and shots fired to encourage the companions they had left behind. They answered and believing water had been found, pulled themselves ahead. They cursed with bitterness and said they wished they had been left behind to die in peace. With daylight, all crawled or dragged themselves onward until they sank into despair trying to climb a sandy hill.

"The sun was now so high, as to beam upon us with the same insufferable radiance of yesterday. The air which we inhaled, seemed to scald our lungs. We at length concluded to travel towards the north, to reach, if we might, some point where the hill was not so steep to ascend. At two in the afternoon we found a place that was neither so steep nor so high, and we determined here to attempt to cross the hill. With great exertions and infinite difficulty, a part of us gained the summit of the hill; but my father and another of our company, somewhat advanced in years, gave out below, though they made the most persevering efforts to reach the summit of the hill with the rest. Age had stiffened their joints, and laid its palsying hand upon their once active limbs, and vigorous frames. They could endure this dreadful journey no longer. They had become so exhausted by fruitless efforts to climb the hill, that they could no longer drag one foot after the other. They had each so completely abandoned the hope of ever reaching the water, or even gaining the summit of the hill, that they threw themselves on the ground, apparently convinced of their fate, and resigned to die."

There, Pattie left his father and another trapper by the name of Slover, and few of the party ever thought they would see them alive again. But water had to be found, or all would perish. Climbing a second sandy hill they beheld a stream. To them it seemed a miracle. Pattie rushed back to take water to his father.

"We found them in the same position in which we had left them, that is, stretched on the sand at full length, under the unclouded blaze of the sun, and both fast asleep; a sleep from which, but for our relief, I believe they would neither of them ever have awakened. Their lips were black, and

THESE DRAWINGS are from James Pattie's own narrative. In one, his father, Sylvester Pattie, and Isaac Slover are saved from death by thirst. In the other, the father, in exaggerated scene, is being buried at Presidio.

their parched mouths wide open. Their unmoving posture and their sunken eyes so resembled death, that I ran in a fright to my father, thinking him, for a moment, really dead. But he easily awakened, and drank the refreshing water."

Eight days later after crossing the summit of the mountains, they met some Christian Indians and learned that the Dominican Mission of Santa Catalina, on the headwaters of the San Quintín River, was only four days' march away. Pattie injured a foot, had to be temporarily left behind, then carried to the mission by Indians. Being foreigners, all were promptly thrown in the guardhouse by Mexican soldiers. They remained there a week and then were taken under guard, to a mission which Pattie identified as St. Sebastian. There was no mission by that name, so it must have been San Vicente, near the coast, southwest from Santa Catalina. Although still in custody, they were treated with courtesy while the sergeant got in touch with the post commander who was away at San Diego. Word finally came — Pattie's party was to be taken to the port of San Diego under guard. They went by way of Mission Santo Tomás, south of Ensenada, and San Miguel, 55 miles below San Diego, arriving at the presidio on March 26, 1828.

"In the evening we came in sight of San Diego, the place where we were bound. In this port was one merchant vessel, the ship *Franklin* of Boston."

They were asked to surrender their arms, as they were considered to be prisoners, and reluctantly obeying, were again, locked up, this time in the jailhouse on Presidio Hill. Hoping for a fair hearing, they gave themselves up to rest.

"We forgot our past troubles, opened our bosom to hope, and resigned ourselves to profound sleep. It is true, innumerable droves of fleas performed their evolutions, and bit all their pleasures upon our bodies. But so entire was our repose, that we scarcely turned for the night. No dreams of what was in reserve for us the following day floated across our minds; though in the morning my body was as spotted as though I have measles, and my shirt specked with innumerable stains of blood, let by the ingenious lancets of these same Spanish fleas."

Evidently San Diego was rife with suspicion and trouble. In the morning they were taken into the general's office, with their hats in hand, and Gov. Echeandía began an official interrogation of Pattie, who knew Spanish from his operations in New Mexico and Sonora.

"The first question was, who we were? We answered, Americans. He proceeded to ask us, how we came on the coast, what was our object, and had we a passport? In answer to these questions we again went over the story of our misfortunes. We then gave him the passport which we had received from the governor of Santa Fe. He examined this instrument, and with a sinister and malicious smile, observed that he believed nothing of all

Mission trail over which James Pattie, party were led to San Diego.

this, but considered us worse than thieves and murderers; in fact, that he held us to be spies for the old Spaniards, and that our business was to lurk about the country, that we might inspect the weak and defenseless points of the frontiers, and point them out to the Spaniards, in order that they might introduce their troops into the country; but that he would utterly detect us, and prevent our designs. This last remark he uttered with a look of vengeance; and then reperused the passport, which he tore in pieces, saying, it was no passport, but a vile forgery of our own contrivance."

Pattie was astounded. He insisted that all of them were full-blooded republicans and would rather die than be the spies and instruments of the Spanish King, or any other king. The general ordered them into silence, saying he didn't want to hear any long speeches, and, they didn't have valid papers of entry, they were going to stay in jail. Their guns were locked up, they were searched and their knives taken from them. They were ordered confined in separate cells, despite the pleading of father and son that they wanted to remain together.

"My prison was a cell eight or 10 feet square, with walls and floor of stone. A door with iron bars an inch square crossed over each other, like the bars of window sashes, and it grated on its iron hinges, as it opened to receive me. Over the external front of this prison was inscribed *Destinación de la Cattivo*. Our blankets were given us to lie upon. My father had a small package of medicines which he gave in charge to the sergeant, binding him on his word of honor not to part with it to any one. My door was locked, and I was left to reflect upon our position and my past misfortunes; and to survey the dreary walls of my prison. Here, I thought, was my everlasting abode. Liberty is dear to every one, but doubly dear to one, who had been from infancy accustomed to free range, and to be guided by his own will. Put a man, who has ranged the prairies, and exulted in the wilderness, as I have for years, in a prison, to let him have a full taste of the blessings of freedom, and the horror of shackles and confinement! I passed the remainder of the day in fierce walking backwards and forwards over my stone floor, with no object to contemplate, but my swarthy sentinel, through the grate. He seemed to be true to his office, and fitly selected for his business, for I thought I saw him look at me through the grate with the natural exulta-tion and joy of a bad and malicious heart in the view of misery.

"The church bell tolled eight in the morning. The drum rolled. A soldier came, and handed me in something to eat. It proved to be dried beans and corn cooked with rancid tallow! The contents were about a pint. I took it up, and brought it within the reach of my nostrils, and sat it down in unconquerable loathing. When the soldier returned in the evening to bring me more, I handed him my morning ration untasted and just as it was. He asked me in a gruff tone why I had not eaten it? I told him the smell of it was enough, and that I could not eat it. He threw the contents of the dish in my face, muttering something which amounted to saying, that it was good enough for such a brute as I was. To this I answered, that if being a brute gave claims upon that dish, I thought he had best eat it himself. On this he flung away in a passion, and returned no more that night, for which I was not sorry. Had the food even been fit to eat, my thoughts were too dark and my mind too much agitated to allow me appetite. In fact, I felt myself becoming sick."

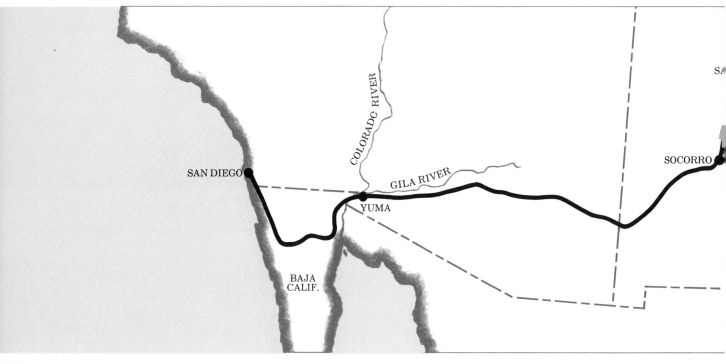

On the map: COLORADO RIVER, GILA RIVER, SAN DIEGO, YUMA, SOCORRO, BAJA CALIF., SA

MOUNTAIN MAN JAMES OHIO PATTIE and his party endured several trials in reaching San Diego by a long and torturous route from New Mexico and through Baja California. His narrative is famed in annals of exploration.

The sergeant of the post befriended Pattie as well as his father and brought him some palatable food. Soon he had regular visits, according to his story, from a woman of great personal beauty and of kind and affectionate nature, who promised to pray for him and to try and intercede on his behalf with the adamant general. Pattie identified her as a "Miss Peaks," and Bancroft thinks she may have been the sister of the friendly Sgt. Pico. The captain, of the American ship *Franklin* in the harbor, John Bradshaw, asked permission of the general to visit Pattie, and it was denied.

"But Captain Bradshaw, like a true hearted American, disregarded the little brief authority of this miserable republican despot, and fearless of danger and the consequences, came to see me without leave. When I spoke to him about our buried furs, he asked me about the chances and the means we had to bring them in? And whether we were disposed to make the effort, and if we succeeded, to sell them to him? The prisoners, as he separately applied to them, one and all assured him, that nothing would give them more pleasure. He assured us, that he would leave nothing in his power undone, in making efforts to deliver us from our confinement. We thanked him for this proffered friendship, and he departed."

Bradshaw attempted to have Pattie released temporarily as an interpreter, and also offered himself as a bond while Pattie returned to the Colorado River for the valuable furs, but all to no avail. It was jail and nothing else. A fortnight passed, and then Pattie received a note from his father, which was written in blood "drawn from his aged veins." The father feared that he was dying. Thus, as Pattie wrote, passed the days of agony and suspense. "But no grief arrests the flight of time, and the 24th of April came in which the sergeant visited me and in a manner of mingled kindness and firmness told me that my father was no more."

The funeral services were held the next day on Presidio Hill.

"At eight in the morning, a file of six soldiers appeared at the door of my prison. It was opened, and I once more breathed the fresh air! The earth and the sky seemed a new region. The glare of light dazzled my eyes, and dizzied my head. I reeled as I walked. A lieutenant conducted the ceremonies: and when I arrived at the grave he ordered the crowd to give way, that I might see the coffin that contained the remains of the brave hunter and ranger. The coffin was covered with black. No prayers were said. I had scarce time to draw a second breath, before the grave was half filled with earth. I was led back to my prison, the young lady walking by my side in tears."

His narrative has a scene of the burial ceremony, which greatly exaggerates the appearance of the presidio walls and buildings, and probably the dress of those attending. Presumably the father was buried in the little cemetery beside the church, as were the early Spaniards and Mexicans, though no actual graves ever have been found.

Though there were other American ships in the port at the time, on the 27th of June, Captain Bradshaw was accused of smuggling on the Baja California coast and in the Gulf of California, of transferring cargo from one ship to another illegally, touching at Santa Catalina without authority, refusing to show his papers, and, worst of all, of insolence to the governor. The padres were ordered not to have any business with him. The difficulties at the port called for an interpreter, and Pattie was taken from jail to read English documents which the general had received. A more friendly atmosphere gradually developed, and the general even took to saluting him, finally promising that if he could prove he wasn't a spy, he would be freed. A week of more disappointments went by, and when Pattie was called in again as an interpreter, he refused to serve, was whacked across the head with the general's sword, and locked up tightly once more. Eventually, he and the other prisoners won a little freedom, and the long summer passed. In September he was allowed to make arrangements to send his men to the river to retrieve their furs, but on condition he remain as a hostage. If the others did not return, he would be executed.

Pattie stayed behind, was accused of intrigue with Capt. Bradshaw and again threatened with death. There was some debate, he says, whether he would be burned. The ship *Franklin* finally escaped from detention, and while Pattie's narrative and Spanish and American documents do not all agree on what happened and when it happened, here is his version:

"A few days only elapsed before, the breeze serving, the Captain slipped anchor, and ran out of the port. He was compelled to perform this under a heavy shower of cannon balls poured forth from the fort, within two hundred yards of which he was obliged to pass. When he came opposite it, he hove to, and gave them a broadside in return, which frightened the poor engineers from their guns. His escape from the port was made without suffering any serious injury on his part. Their shots entered the hull of the vessel, and the sails were considerably cut by the grape. I was greatly rejoiced when I heard of their escape from these thieves. The general pretended great disgust at the cowardly conduct of the engineers, but, I believe, had he been there, he would have run too. I have no faith in the courage of these people, except where they have greatly the advantage, or can kill in the dark, without danger to themselves. This in my view is the amount of a Spaniard's bravery."

Air photo shows sailing ship anchorages off La Playa houses, in basin north of Ballast Point.

The second battle of San Diego apparently did more damage than the first one involving the *Lelia Byrd*. Duhaut-Cilly had been requested by the governor to provide a boat so he could put a guard on the *Franklin*, and while he stalled, the *Franklin* moved up nearer the port entrance, and on the morning of July 16, she slipped her anchor and sailed past Ballast Point, her crew hurling defiance at Fort Guijarros and shouting derision at the Mexican flag. The fort sent between 36 and 40 cannon balls her way. Once off the point, she fired a broadside of farewell and disappeared over the horizon. Duhaut-Cilly again met up with the *Franklin* in the Hawaiian Islands and learned that two holes had been driven through her hull, the rigging damaged, and Bradshaw himself slightly hurt.

Four of Pattie's men returned from the Colorado, two having deserted, but without furs — they had been spoiled by an overflow of the river, as Pattie had feared. Thus was lost a small fortune.

Americans were becoming nothing but trouble to the officious Echeandía. His troops had seized another American, Charles Lang, whom Pattie identified as James Lang, at Todos Santos Bay, with an organ and two trunks of dry goods, who claimed he had left the American ship *Alabama* with the intention of settling in California. Echeandía suspected they were smugglers and seized the goods. Pattie and Lang made some attempts to join up and escape in the brig which Lang said was in southern waters, but nothing came of them. The goods confiscated from Lang and the two companions and two Hawaiians who were with him, were sold at auction and Lang's case forwarded to Mexico City and then to a district judge at Guaymas for disposition. What eventually happened is not known.

The weeks and months rolled on, and until in December, a smallpox epidemic swept through the missions in Northern California, and according to Pattie's narrative, the key to freedom was at hand. He had in his possession a new vaccine, and upon his promise to vaccinate one and all, he was granted the freedom of the presidio. He claims that from the 18th of January, to the 16th of February, 1829, he vaccinated all the people belonging to the fort and the Indian inhabitants of the Mission San Diego. In return, the general gave them parole for a year, an introduction to all priests along the coast, and received a pledge to vaccinate all the inhabitants of the coast. From there Pattie and his men went to San Luis Rey Mission, where he suggests, he vaccinated 3904 Indians. Strangely, the records of the period are silent as to these incidents and to a widespread epidemic of smallpox, though an unusual number of deaths is reflected in mission reports in Northern California for that period. At San Francisco, Pattie wanted to settle up with the authorities, for his invaluable services, and finally he was handed a paper which read:

"I certify that James O. Pattie has vaccinated all the Indians and whites on this coast, and to recompense him for the same, I give the said James O. Pattie my obligation for 100 head of cattle, and land to pasture them; that is, 500 cows and 500 mules. This he is to receive after he becomes a Catholic, and a subject of this government. Given in the Mission of St. Francisco on the 8th of July, in the year 1829." — John Cabortes

Well, Pattie was outraged. He later turned up as a participant in California revolutions.

The first to follow the trappers were the traders. Out of the pioneering efforts of Pattie and Smith there developed a direct trade with New Mexico. New Mexicans first brought *sarapes* and *frazadas* for the Indians in exchange for beaver skins. In California the colorful blankets were traded to the natives for mules of a much larger and stronger breed than found in New Mexico and which were used on the Missouri and Santa Fe trails. Soon caravans of pack animals were making yearly trips to California, down the river routes, across the desert and up Cajon Pass to Los Angeles, from where agents would fan out over the province, from San Diego to San Francisco, trading the woolen fabrics of New Mexico for the silk and other goods brought in by sea from China.

CHAPTER TWELVE

THE HIDE DROGHERS

Hides of cattle began to replace furs of otters as the chief stock in trade of California. In fact, hides became known as California banknotes. The hide trade, for leather for the shoes of Europe and America, began to grow swiftly when the Mexicans wiped out many of the restrictions imposed on foreigners by Spain. For all practical purposes San Diego and Monterey became open ports. The British started the hide trade but the Boston men took over; everybody liked the Yankee traders. It was a turbulent period for California. The years of Spanish rule had generally been peaceful ones, as they had been over all of New Spain, but now unrest became rife. San Diego had been under military government since the founding of the first mission in California in 1769, but now there were feeble attempts at representative government in the spirit of republicanism that came over Mexico with the collapse of the empire that Gen. Agustín de Iturbide had sought to erect in the chaos of revolution. But there was more disorder than order, and Mexico itself was to know little but trouble and sorrow for almost a century.

In San Diego, the names associated with the first families of early California — the Picos, the Bandinis, the Estudillos, the Carrillos, the Argüellos and the Osunas, among others — began to appear in reports and correspondence. A colonization law passed by

FOR A LONG TIME THE UNITED STATES was known merely as "Boston" to the people of San Diego. From the Boston harbor of the 1800's sailed the fur and hide ships that transformed California into a New England "colony."

171

the Mexican Congress in 1824 favored the entry of foreign colonists though giving preference to Mexican citizens, and subsequent provisions opened the way for more land grants. Mission lands were not to be distributed, at the time, which in itself suggested an approaching end to the mission system and the land seizures that led to the great ranchos and the Days of the Dons which followed. By 1830 nearly 50 private ranchos had been granted to private individuals in California.

In 1820 the white population of the southern district, including the Presidio and Mission of San Diego, the Missions of San Luis Rey and San Juan Capistrano, but excluding the guard at San Gabriel Mission, was about 450 persons, a gain in a decade of only about 130 persons. The Pueblo of Los Angeles had about 650 white persons. The San Diego military force was about 100, including 23 invalids, of which 20 lived at Los Angeles or on private ranchos. By 1830 the white population had risen to about 520. Perhaps 400 white persons, 150 Indians, and two or three foreigners lived in the San Diego Presidio proper. Los Angeles had grown to about 1200.

The Bouchard scare of 1818, when the French captain sacked California, had brought about a belated effort to reinforce territorial defenses, and orders were sent to Guadalajara, San Blas and Sonora that two vessels were to be sent north with all the troops and ammunition they could carry. The first reinforcements of 100 arrived at Monterey on the transport *San Carlos* and the trading ship *Reina de Los Angeles* captained by one José Bandini. The name Bandini is of Italian origin though José Bandini was born in Andalusía, a province of Spain. José served the Mexican revolution well, and when peace came, he and a son, Juan, born in Lima, Perú, decided to settle in California, and came to San Diego and built a home, which became famous in the journals of the times and still stands in Old Town.

The second detachment, a company of 100 cavalry, part of the *Escuadrón de Mazatlán*, under Capt. Pablo de la Portilla and Lts. Juan María Ibarra and Narciso Fabregat and Ensign Ignacio Delgado, was ordered to San Diego, embarking on the ship *Cossack* on July 14, 1819. Winds carried the ship up into the gulf and they finally landed at San Luis Gonzaga Bay, in northern Baja California, and marched overland to San Diego, arriving Sept. 16.

Portilla's company was of high order, most of its men remaining here and contributing to development. The other detachment, an infantry company of San Blas under a Capt. José Antonio Navarette, was composed of criminals and vagabonds gathered from jails or by press gangs, and they were to prove a heavy burden

It was a long march from Gonzaga Bay to Presidio of San Diego.

on California. Pablo Vicente de Solá, who was governor at the time, had asked for a heavy artillery detachment, 400 carbines, 300 swords, and 15 or 20 cannon of large caliber, and money to repair the presidios and forts, so long neglected by Spain, but the *Reina* carried only five six-pounders and 10 four-pounders, and the *San Carlos*, 400 sabres and three flags. Solá described the sabre blades as "not fit for sickles." All the Mexicans had to fight were rebellious Indians.

Lt. Juan M. Ibarra led several engagements against rampaging Indians in April of 1826, losing three men but killing 28, at Santa Ysabel. He sent 20 pairs of ears and one prisoner back to the presidio, where the captured Indian was publicly shot on April 25. Ibarra used pagan and neophyte Indians in a second battle in San Felipe Valley, at about the same time, losing one Indian and having 14 others and one soldier wounded. Eighteen pairs of ears were taken.

In the same year a commission composed of Capt. Portilla, Lt. Romualdo Pacheco and Cadet Domingo Carrillo made a survey of the military situation and reported the presidio buildings in a "deplorable ruinous condition" and at least $40,000 was needed to repair them and the fort. Little assistance was forthcoming, but evidently, with tools and help borrowed from the mission, some work was done, at least at the fort, which was able to send a flurry of cannon balls at the *Franklin*, as will be remembered.

The Mexicans, in the flush of independence, drew up plans, more picturesque than practical, to assure the retention of California and to wrest all the trade in the vast Pacific from the Englishmen and the Americans, by revival of the old Philippine trade dominated for two and-a-half centuries by the Spanish Manila galleons. California was described as a paradise surely worth holding: "Fortunate the Californians in the midst of the promised land; happy the provinces that adjoin that land; lucky even the hemisphere that contains it."

To hold California, the Mexicans knew there would have to be a land connection, though the memory of the Yuma massacre was still alive, and attempts were made to re-open the Sonora route pioneered by Anza 49 years before. Capt. José Romero in 1823 was ordered to set out from Sonora with a force of 60 men to investigate the possibility of a mail service by way of the Colorado, but it wasn't until a year later that he got under way, not with 60 men, but 10. At the Colorado, the Indians agreed to help them cross the river on rafts. In mid-stream, they turned about and pushed the rafts back to shore, along with all the expedition's supplies and horses. Romero and his men were left practically naked and without food, and were forced to cross the desert and mountains to Mission Santa Catalina, over the same route taken later by the mountain trapper, Pattie.

A new path to San Diego and Los Angeles was marked out with the discovery of Warner's Pass by Santiago Argüello, while chasing Indian horse thieves in 1825. Argüello suggested that instead of following the old Anza route all the way across the Borrego Desert and up Coyote Canyon and over the San Carlos Pass, it would be better to go by way of the Fages' trail through the Carrizo Corridor and then turn off through San Felipe Valley and Warner's Hot Springs. The Mexican government sent Pacheco, who was a lieutenant of engineers, to investigate, and as a result, this became the official route for mail and was used by some immigrants from Sonora.

San Felipe Valley, the low-level route to San Diego, Los Angeles.

As with so many good intentions, the fine plans for California largely wound up in somebody's desk and were heard of no more. The "enemy" already had taken over considerably. His ships were everywhere. In 1825, for example, of the 47 vessels on the coast, 20 were American ships, eight English, two Russian, one Californian, one French, and only two Mexican. The nationality of eight is not known. In 1827 there were 33 ships on the coast, of which 12 were American, 10 English, three Russian, two French, and perhaps one German. Again, there were only three Mexican vessels.

How many Russian ships actually visited San Diego is difficult to determine. In 1825 three Russian ships, the *Baikal*, *Okhotsk* and *Kiakhta*, received permission to hunt for otter skins on equal shares between San Diego and San Quintín Bay, and records indicate that the *Baikal* went back and forth from Fort Ross to San Diego continuously between 1825 and 1830, and the *Okhotsk* between 1827 and 1829. A Hawaiian brig, the *Karimoku* gave considerable trouble. Capt. John Lawlor had a practice of hiding most of his cargo on some lonely section of the coast, or on one of the channel islands, and then putting into port with a small amount of goods, at a great saving in duties. When he arrived in San Diego in the autumn of 1828 he was accused of avoiding $1,000 in duties at San Pedro and touching at Santa Catalina despite warnings not to do so. The sails of his vessel were seized and held until he evidently worked out an arrangement for getting his goods and livestock off the island. Capt. William Cunningham of the American ship *Courier*, which made several visits here, and other sailing masters went so far as to erect

174

buildings on Santa Catalina, but they were forced to remove them.

With the reduction of the otter herds in the north, and the more liberal commercial policies that arose under the Mexican government, licensed hunting on a share basis, much of it in less-worked southern waters, was gradually replacing poaching. Many Americans who drifted into California, or deserted from ships, took to otter hunting, as did prominent Mexicans. The California-Russian contract with the *Baikal* was written by the Mexican fiscal agent at Monterey, and when the ship put into San Diego Harbor in 1826, Gov. Echeandía went aboard, and toasts were drunk in an

AN AMERICAN SAILOR, William Rich Hutton, made this sketch of life in California in the hide trade days. Hides are shown being dried for shipping at Monterey. Most of the hides were sent to San Diego, for transshipment.

175

TALLOW WAS A BY-PRODUCT of the California hide trade, and in this sketch by William Rich Hutton tallow is being rendered in iron kettles for sale to Russian traders. Tallow also was shipped to South American ports.

atmosphere of friendship and good cheer, until Echeandía discovered that a license to hunt had been granted by his old enemy, the fiscal agent. He cancelled it forthwith. In turn, Echeandía granted a new permit, though restrictive, which permitted the *Baikal* to hunt for otter in San Diego Bay, as well as along the coast from opposite San Luis Rey Mission to Todos Santos Bay. Aleuts from the *Baikal* in 20 canoes collected 468 furs in about less than three months. San Diego became a provisioning point for Russian operations in southern waters. A young seaman, Richard Henry Dana, Jr., later was to find evidence of their long stays in San Diego.

The growth of the hide and tallow trade was beginning to flood the California market with goods, and the fur men slowly gave way before a new trade, though furs were to make up parts of shipments from the coast for many years to come.

While Upper California was showing so much promise, despite official incompetence, Lower California was sliding backward down the path of history. The missionary movement had almost completely collapsed. By 1822, or near that time, 17 of the older mission establishments no longer even had resident priests. The native population, cruelly affected by disease and changes in ways of living, had declined in 150 years from about 40,000 at the time of the first white settlement to perhaps 5000. Few of the native Indians survive today. The revolution struck Baja California more directly than it did Upper California. Attacks by sea were carried out against the Pueblos of Loreto and San José del Cabo by ships of the English sea lord, Thomas Cochrane. Cochrane, who had fought the Spaniards in European waters, and participated in the revolutions in Perú and Chile, hoisted the flag of newly-independent Chile and, on the pretense that Baja California still belonged to Spain, sacked San José del Cabo on Feb. 17, 1822, even looting the church, and then sent one ship of war on up the gulf to Loreto, attacking it on March 4. The governor and the missionaries fled to Comondú, and Lt. José María Mata, with 16 men, was left to repulse the attackers, which he did after a time, and even recovered some of the booty.

Pearls were found in the Gulf, all the way from La Paz to Loreto.

One of the first foreigners to travel through Baja California, and to report on its progress, or lack of progress, was an Englishman, R.W.H. Hardy, sent to Mexico by the London Pearl Fishery Association to survey Baja California's pearl fishing which had been started so long before by Hernán Cortés, the Spanish conqueror of Mexico. He visited Loreto in 1825, found it a town of 250 persons, with the commandant able to muster a force of no more than six soldiers . . . "and their two cannon, with open breeches, so they might be expected to do equal execution, among friends in the rear and the enemy in front." As for the commandant, "he resides in the best house in the place, near the church, which was formerly celebrated for the richness of the Virgin's pearls; but in the visit paid by some Chilean or Colombian vessels . . . under pretense of making the colony free, the crew thought it their duty, it is said, to relieve the Virgin from her superfluous weight of pearls, and the church the greater part of its gold and silver."

He found that "the inhabitants of Loreto were of a dingy opaque olive-green which shows that there is no friendly mixture in the blood of the Spaniards and the Indians," . . . but in contrast, he said that in La Paz, "the inhabitants . . . are descendants chiefly of English, American and French sailors. There is an old seaman, married and living near it, who was with Lord Nelson in the ever-memorable battle of Trafalgar." The population was about 2000.

Aleuts in canoes, or baidarkas, were familiar sight off San Diego.

Pearl fishing along the gulf coast, and in particular from La Paz to Loreto, which once produced tremendous wealth, was dying; the beds were being fished out because no attention was being paid to the size of oysters taken. At Loreto, Hardy found six to eight boats engaged in pearl fishing, with the quantity procured annually by each of them between four and five pounds and worth perhaps $8000 to $10,000. A larger number of boats fished in the La Paz area.

It was Lt. Col. José María Echeandía, when he became Mexican governor of Lower as well as Upper California in 1825, who proceeded to establish a more representative government. Echeandía preferred the climate of San Diego, though some claimed it was not the climate he preferred but a woman of San Diego. There had been some territorial representation in the past but in 1826 Echeandía called a new election. On Feb. 18, 1827, five electors met at San Diego to choose not only *diputados* to reorganize the territorial *diputación* but also a *diputado* to the national congress. Ignacio López had been the first *partido* elector for the San Diego district, starting with 1822, and he had been succeeded by Carlos Castro. Agustín V. Zamorano, secretary to the governor, now was chosen elector for 1827-28, and in 1830 Juan María Osuna was elected. Juan Bandini succeeded Domingo Carrillo as *comisaro subalterno*, or revenue collector, in 1828, and José Antonio Estudillo became associate and treasurer of local funds.

Pablo Vicente de Solá, the last Spanish governor of California, was chosen to be the first congressman, but, in view of his background, this didn't seem very wise and the vote was reconsidered. Elected in his stead was Capt. José de la Guerra y Noriega, with Gervasio Argüello as substitute. Again the Californians seem to have acted without good judgment. Noriega had been born in Spain, though he was brought to Mexico as a child, and that was enough to make him undesirable in Mexico City and he was refused his seat in Congress. Argüello finally assumed the office.

At the meeting in San Diego, on Feb. 19, 1827, the *junta* of electors also chose seven *vocales*, or members, and three *suplentes*, or substitutes, for the territorial *diputación*, which convened at Monterey. In 1828 Echeandía summoned the *diputados* to San Diego but apparently most of the members didn't want to come and no meeting was held. They didn't seem to share Echeandía's local enthusiasms, whatever they were. Later in the year a meeting of the *junta* of electors was held here to reorganize the *diputación* by adding four more members. It convened at San Diego on Jan. 1, 1829, but proved unmanageable and was dismissed. Juan Bandini got in here too, as a *vocal*.

Trouble was in the air. Military officers also didn't seem to get along with each other, and Lt. José María Estudillo returned here from Monterey and in 1827 took command of the San Diego Presidio. He succeeded Capt. Francisco María Ruiz, who was 73

RANCHO
LOS
PENASQUITOS

Los Peñasquitos Rancho was the first granted in San Diego County.

years old and moved down from the presidio to Old Town where he planted one of the first orchards. Ruiz, born in Loreto, and a bachelor, also had been granted the first large private rancho within present San Diego County, a tract of 8486 acres which later became known as Los Peñasquitos Rancho, or small cliffs, occupying a narrow strip of valley running northeast from Sorrento to the Poway area. The grant was made in 1823 by Luis Antonio Argüello while serving as interim governor. The padres had protested strongly that the grant violated mission lands. The carving up had begun. In 1829, Jamul Rancho, 8926 acres lying between Jamul and Dulzura, was granted by Echeandía to Pío Píco, and Janal Rancho, 4436 acres, and the adjoining Otay Rancho, 6657 acres, east and southeast of Chula Vista, respectively, were granted to the Estudillo family. José María Estudillo became a captain in the same year, died in 1830, and was buried on Presidio Hill. He was the founder of a famous California family, which built the Old Town house now known as Ramona's Marriage Place.

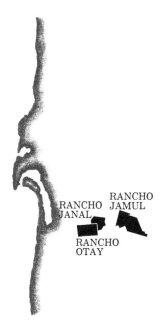

Map shows the location of three early ranchos in South Bay area.

Echeandía represented the long arm of the Mexican revolutionists and he attempted to move against all persons who had been born in Spain, or those who had not yet taken an oath of allegiance to the new Constitution. The padres had taken an oath of fealty to the republican government of Mexico, but they considered the new Constitution as anti-religious, and with some exceptions, one of them being Fr. Peyri at San Luis Rey, they refused to swear allegiance to any provisions which they believed to be against their religion or profession. Two of these were Frs. Fernando Martín and Vicente Pascual Oliva, of San Diego. The padres were still needed in California, however, as all feared the chaos that might follow if the padres were evicted, the mission system broken up too quickly, and the Indians released from any control. Echeandía issued a decree of partial emancipation for the mission Indians, permitting those at San Diego, for example, who had been Christians since childhood, or for 15 years, and those who were married and who had some means of livelihood, to leave the mission. He wanted the Indian communities to be organized into pueblos; the padres replaced with the secular clergy — as always was the long-range intention — and then parcel out the mission lands. This decree was issued on July 25, 1826.

The effect of this "emancipation" was described by an English sea captain, Frederich William Beechey, R.N., who visited California on HMS *Blossom*, in 1827 and 1828. In the latter year he wrote:

"In my former visit to this country, I remarked that the padres were much mortified at being desired to liberate from the missions all the Indians

179

who bore good characters, and who were acquainted with the art of tilling the ground. In consequence of these remonstrances, the government modified the order, and consented to make the experiment upon a few only at first, and desired that a certain number might be settled in the proposed manner. After a few months' trial much to his surprise, he found that these people who had been always accustomed to the care and discipline of school boys, finding themselves their own masters, indulged freely in all those excesses which it had been the endeavor of their tutors to repress, and that many having gambled away their clothes, implements, and even their lands, were compelled to beg or to plunder in order to support life. They at length became so obnoxious to the peaceable inhabitants, that the padres were requested to take some of them back to the missions, while others who had been guilty of misdemeanor, were loaded with shackles and put to work."

Accompanying Beechey was William Smyth, of the Royal Navy, an artist, who on this journey and subsequent visits to the Americas, made many water color sketches of early California life. He later became an admiral and a member of the Royal Geographic Society.

The view of the native, or of the adopted, Californian on the necessity of secularization was quite different from that of the missionaries, who labored until the end under the impression that they were obligated to hold the lands until the Indians were ready to receive them and care for themselves in a civilized state. But nobody could foresee when such a time ever would arrive.

The case of the Californians was best stated by José Bandini of San Diego, who in 1828 presented a detailed description of California in a report he made to the British vice consul at Tepic, for some reason or other, and on which he later expanded. Much of the material was used by his son, Juan, in his own political efforts.

Don José Bandini, founder of the prominent Old San Diego family.

José Bandini warned that "the missions have extended their holdings from one end of the territory to the other and have had a way of bounding one piece of property by the next, always opposing the private ownership of lands in between. They have unfeelingly appropriated the whole region, although for their planting and for the maintenance of their cattle they do not need all they possess. It is hoped that the new system of enlightment and the need for encouraging the resident *gente de razón* will compel the government to take adequate means to reconcile the interests of all."

He estimated there were about 5000 white people in California, most of them descendants of early settlers, and thus in 50 years a new generation had been formed, while, at the same time, deaths among the Indians were exceeding births by 10 per cent. As for the Californians, he reported they were robust, healthy and well built, and though they raised some cattle and vegetables, lacking privately-owned lands, their private enterprise was limited. He condemned his fellow citizens, as had visitors to California, and others still to arrive would do. "Most live in idleness. It is a rare person who is dedicated to increasing his fortune. They exert themselves only in dancing, horsemanship, and gambling, with which they fill their days. Most illnesses are unknown, and the freshness and the hardiness of the people demonstrate the beneficial effect of the climate." Ever gallant, as befitted a true Spanish son, he wrote that "the women in particular always have roses in their cheeks. These beautiful creatures are without doubt more active and industrious than the men."

He warned that unwise Mexican regulations would strangle trade, and that the port of San Diego should be left open, as the limiting of foreign trade to Monterey would ruin California. San Diego, he said, had a better port, a more powerful presidio, and a mission which needed the resources possible because of having to attend to frontier establishments. As places of residence, the presidios had outlived their usefulness and "it is certain that substantial towns will soon appear in California."

For all practical purposes, the port was open to foreign trade, as orders to close it in 1826 had not been carried out.

With time on their hands, the Californians were inclined to get themselves into trouble. The annals of the decade indicate that a woman charged with promiscuity had to stand with shaven head in church where all in the presidio could see her, and even a house of ill fame found mention. In 1826 a soldier, Victor Linares, shot his neighbor, Juan Germán, while on sentry duty, and a court-martial, after due deliberation, acquitted him on the grounds he had merely performed his duty. In 1828, five soldiers complained to Lt. Argüello of hunger and lack of clothing, and boldly requested some of their back pay. An angered Argüello started to put them in irons, but the adverse reaction of other troops caused him to slow down, and the appeal was taken to Echeandía. He promised to do something, and from all indications, all he did was to scatter the five to other presidios and stations. There were many small crimes of passion but one had a particular interest. In May of 1830 a civilian cut a soldier with a knife, escaped from the lockup, and sought refuge in the mission church. The right of church asylum again was an issue, as it was back in the early days of the presidio. Apparently the civilian lost the argument as he was sentenced to eight years in the chain gang. The majordomo, Hilario García, in November of the same year, was tried for cruelty to Indians, being charged with flogging a group of cattle thieves,

Artillery veterans milicianos manning Fort Guijarros in 1823.

and pulling one of them around by the hair until he died. The *fiscal*, Cadet Ignacio del Valle, insisted that García be sentenced to 10 years on the chain gang, but later his defender, Juan Bandini, branded the charges as Indian lies. In the end, García was sentenced to five years. The record also shows that an Indian was publicly executed in the presidio, on Oct. 30, 1824, before a great crowd, but nobody, apparently, thought to put down the reason.

The new Mexican government didn't help matters by increasing the number of convicts being sent to California. A small number had arrived in 1825, and then orders were issued that convicted criminals from all parts of the republic were to be sent to California, and within a year more than 100 had been sentenced to go and work on the presidios. Echeandía protested somewhat feebly, and asked that at least "useful convicts" be sent. In 1830, the *Maria Ester* brought 80 convicts from Acapulco, but they were not allowed to land at San Diego, because of the absence of the governor, and they were unloaded at Santa Barbara. Thirty of the worst were promptly trans-shipped to Santa Cruz Island, supplied with some cattle and fish hooks, and left to their own fate. Soon reduced to virtual nakedness, they built rafts and floated back to the mainland. A good many of them became law-abiding citizens. Six months after the first group had arrived, the *Leonor* under the command of Capt. Henry D. Fitch, a Massachusetts-born captain, brought 50 more and left 23 of them at San Diego. It seems, however, that by paying a $3-head tax they gained their liberty. The issue of the convicts was the start of the bitter feelings that arose between Californians and Mexicans.

The padres of Upper California still were carrying on pretty much as usual. The missions had become great commercial institutions which supported the life of the country. And the hide trade was turning San Diego into a cosmopolitan settlement. The firm of McCullough, Hartnell & Co., which sent the vessel *John Begg* to San Diego for hides in 1823, became the first mercantile house in California. An Englishman, John Begg, had established himself at Lima, Perú, and developed an extensive trade in South American hides, and then with the easing of restrictions against foreigners trading in California, joined with William Petty Hartnell, another Englishman, and Hugh McCullough, a Scotsman, in entering the California market. Hartnell and McCullough were aboard the *John Begg* and got official permission from the governor to make contracts with the various missions for hides and tallow. Some of their dozen ships sailed direct from California to England and others began trading from Monterey to San Diego, to Lima and Santiago, and then around the Horn, up the South American Coast to

San Gabriel furnaces 12 feet deep used in making soap, candles.

Chemical vats used in tanning processes at San Juan Capistrano.

Montevideo and Rio de Janeiro, and then across the Atlantic to Liverpool.

There were hides for the English market and tallow for South America, as well as other miscellaneous products, such as soap, horse hair, horns, hemp, beef in brine, suet, and at times, wheat. For the missions, in exchange, came the products of civilization, such as clothing, farming implements, musical instruments of all kinds, kitchen utensils, a variety of food products to relieve the monotony of daily life, such as coffee, tea, cocoa, sugar, and rice,

THE ENGLISH DEVELOPED the hide trade along South American coasts. They won the race to California and were the first to put a commercial agent into San Diego. This map shows the route of the John Begg Co. of England.

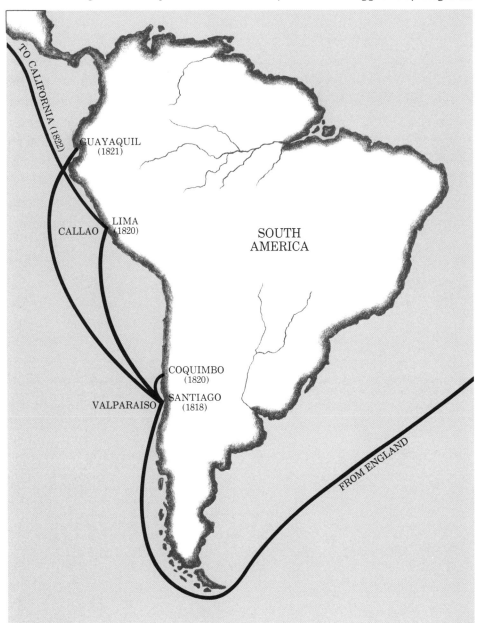

and the gold and silver threads so desired for embroidery and ornaments, and needles and buttons.

Cattle were multiplying by the thousands and they dotted the hills and upper valleys from the Mexican border to Sonoma County. The cattle were the fattest during the summer months of July, August and September, and the roundup, called the *matanza*, was held at every mission, with the *vaquero* lassoing the cattle with their *reatas* and Indians doing the butchering. The hides were removed for trading, the best meat cut into strips and dried or jerked, and the remainder left for the coyotes. San Diego became the chief center of the hide trade and all Boston firms eventually maintained depots here on a sandy shelf of Point Loma which now is the site of the Naval Fuel Depot. The drying, curing and storing of hides required a warm port, free from rain and heavy surf, and with not too much fog, and the loading was easier and faster in calm, protected waters. This was the only port which met all requirements.

The busiest time of the year at all the missions was during *la matanza*. The work had to be done quickly, and usually with heavy waste, because of the lack of refrigeration. Mission ranchos were the scene of feverish activity with scores and sometimes hundreds of Indians employed in a variety of tasks. The stench of rotting carcasses, or that from the burning of piles of unwanted meat, would hang over the valleys and hills for days.

Fats were piled into *carretas* to be taken to the mission for making tallow and soap. The tongues were saved for smoking and storing. At the end of the day the ox heads were placed in holes in the ground, covered with hot stones, and left to roast all night, for a favorite breakfast.

The hides removed by skinners would be staked out on the ground to dry, to prevent shrinking, then, folded lengthwise, packed and carted to the mission tannery. All of the missions had elaborate brick vat systems for the curing and tanning of hides, with use of brine, lime and oak bark; and while some had vat systems for rendering tallow, others melted it in iron kettles placed over huge brick furnaces. Some of the leather would go for shoes, saddles, beds, *reatas*, and rawhide thongs for tying building planks, and scores of other uses. Hides of sheep went for leather jackets for the soldiers. Most of the ox hides, however, would be stored for the merchants of England and America. When the ships arrived, long lines of Indians, pack mules and *carretas* loaded with hides and *botas*, or bags, of tallow would wind their way down Mission Valley across the dry river bed and the silt plain between Old Town and Point Loma, and along the base of the point to La Playa.

Before being loaded aboard ship, the hides would have to be softened by soaking in salt water and brine, scraped, stretched again, dried, and then beaten to remove all dust. Packed on ship they would be taken thousands of miles to London or Boston, and often the same hide came back to San Diego in the shape of fancy shoes. When the hot, trying season was over, there was the *fiesta*, and hundreds of candles made from tallow twinkled from mission windows and arches in the late summer evening of a mellow countryside.

The company's schooner, *Young Tartar* sailed up and down the coast, collecting hides and goods at various depots, and then reloading them onto larger vessels at San Diego and Monterey, for the long run to England. The *Young Tartar* was wrecked on a San Diego beach in 1826. The McCullough and Hartnell firm

HIDES OF CATTLE WERE COLLECTED from missions and private ranchos throughout California, and then taken to depots for loading on ships, to be run to Boston or to be stored in barns at San Diego for larger shipments.

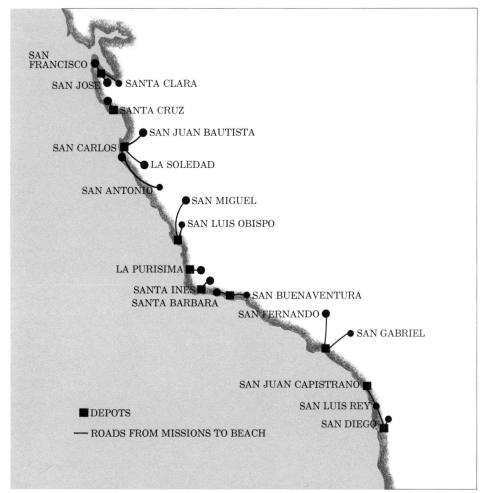

SAN FRANCISCO

SAN JOSE ● ● SANTA CLARA

■ SANTA CRUZ

● SAN JUAN BAUTISTA

SAN CARLOS ■

● LA SOLEDAD

SAN ANTONIO ●

● SAN MIGUEL

● SAN LUIS OBISPO

LA PURISIMA ■ ●

SANTA INES ■ ● ● ● SAN BUENAVENTURA
SANTA BARBARA

SAN FERNANDO ●

● SAN GABRIEL

SAN JUAN CAPISTRANO ■

SAN LUIS REY ●

SAN DIEGO ● ■

■ DEPOTS

— ROADS FROM MISSIONS TO BEACH

broke up in 1828, but Hartnell remained in California, and became a respected, but sometimes tragic figure, in the state's pioneer history.

The missionaries at San Diego liked Hartnell, a Protestant, though they seemed to be more canny than their brothers in the north, preferring not to tie up on long contracts, as the Americans indicated they were willing to offer more for hides than would the Britishers. Though the local customs officers welcomed the English firm, calling it "Macala y Arnel," and offered land for a store and warehouse, and young Hartnell always stayed at the famed Bandini home when in San Diego — where something always was going on — he preferred Monterey, being so unkind as to describe San Diego as "the Devil's hole." Juan Bandini had married Dolores Estudillo, the daughter of Capt. Estudillo, and they were raising a family that became known the land over for the beauty of its women and the graciousness of its hospitality. Monterey proved to be bad for Hartnell, personally. It was the same old story of wine, women, and debts. Worse, however, in the eyes of the padres, was the discovery that he had been consorting in the privacy of his library with the works of Voltaire. He was rescued from his Godless ways by the friendly but concerned padres, undergoing baptism and writing that at last grace had been granted him "to know the right path."

A month after Hartnell and McCullough had first arrived in California, one William Alden Gale, an American engaged in the otter and seal trade along the coast, returned to Boston and persuaded the shipping firm of Bryant and Sturgis to enter the California hide trade. That brought the ship *Sachem* to San Diego on two voyages, with Gale as supercargo, to start another long association by sea between San Diego on the West Coast and Boston on the East Coast. Thus it was, too, that in 1828, the ship *Brookline*, outfitted by Bryant and Sturgis, sailed from Boston harbor with a young man named Alfred Robinson aboard her as a clerk.

CHAPTER THIRTEEN

ALFRED ROBINSON

It was a beautiful July morning in Boston in 1828, and the ship *Brookline* slipped quietly down the bay with a light wind from the southwest. Alfred Robinson, a sensitive and adventurous youth, wrote in his notebook that the breeze soon freshened, "and the sight of friends who had accompanied us to the wharf, the buildings, the steeples, and the neighboring hills of Boston, all gradually grew fainter and fainter, 'till like a dream they passed away'." Ahead of them was a journey of 15,000 miles. Their destination was California. They would arrive at the hour of momentous change.

For three months the *Brookline* pursued her peaceful way down the coast of North America and South America, and then rounded the Horn and opened up upon the Pacific, the great South Sea. The scene changed quickly, and we learn from Robinson of the terrors of the sea in the days of sail.

"Thick clouds appear in the horizon, whose quick advance and fearful aspect betoken the coming storm! The ship is prepared to meet its fury — sail after sail is taken in, till from a top-gallant studding sail, and running before the wind, she is lying to, reduced to a close-reefed main-topsail, and mizzen staysail. The storm at length comes — cloud after cloud adds new fury to its blasts — the sea rises, and in its way would seem to engulf all before it — one vast surge comes aboard with heavy crash, and sweeps the deck of boats and spars, the bulwarks, and all that meets its course. The climate changes also; and cold, snow and hail are added to the terrors that

MORE EXCITING to San Diegans than revolutions was the elopement of Capt. Henry D. Fitch, an American, and Doña Josefa Carrillo, a Spanish beauty. They were married in Valparaiso but met plenty of trouble on return.

surround us. At length, however, the storm abates; sail is made, and we are again in apparent security; but soon it returns with redoubled fury; and the ship is again lying like a log upon the oceans. Thus we proceed, gale succeeding gale! One storm only ceasing, to give place to another — our good ship making but little progress, until, at last, enabled to take a northerly course, and the wind proving favorable we rapidly leave these tempestuous latitudes. A few days of prosperous gales bring us to anchor in the pleasant bay of Valparaiso."

After three days of rest and provisioning, the *Brookline* again sailed north for California. On the night of Feb. 15, 1829, as she was being towed into the port of Monterey, by long boat, there was a flash of fire from shore and a ball of iron shot across the bow. The anchor was dropped in a hurry, and soon Mexican customs officials came out in small boats, and when they identified the vessel and learned it came for legitimate trade and not for smuggling, everybody was happy. The affair of the ship *Franklin*, which had escaped under fire while being detained on suspicion

THIS IS ALFRED ROBINSON'S own sketch of the ship Brookline *which brought him to San Diego. It was a pioneer ship in the hide trade and for many years was a familiar sight in the old sail anchorage just off La Playa.*

of smuggling at San Diego, had made the Mexicans wary of ships slipping along the coast in the darkness. They did find, however, that all ports with the exception of San Diego and Monterey, which were fortified, were closed to foreign ships, and as this threatened the success of their hide trading venture, William Gale, the supercargo, decided to appeal to the governor at San Diego, but failing to gain satisfaction by courier, had the *Brookline* put to sea for the run down the coast. They arrived, completed somewhat successful arrangements, though as far as Gale was concerned the general's license to trade was "opening the door just enough to catch my fingers and jamb them," and made preparations for a long stay. But San Diego, he commented, was "the center of hell for strangers." They anchored as did all ships of the time, in the deep water north of Ballast Point and within easy reach of the sandy shore of La Playa, which was to become known as "Hide Park."

"The long boat was hoisted out," Robinson wrote, "the ship moored, spars were landed, royal yards and masts, and top-gallant yards were sent down, and these and all other surplus rubbish about the decks sent on shore and deposited. Lumber was discharged, and the carpenter commenced building a large house for the storage of hides, which, when finished, served as a place of accommodation for the lighter part of our cargo while under the examination and care of the custom-house officers; for the government as yet had not deemed it important to erect an '*Aduana*' in this port."

While all this was in progress, Gale and Robinson visited the Presidio. Horses were sent down to them by Don Manuel Domingues, a brother-in-law of Gale. Robinson writes:

"I was unable myself to comprehend the use and necessity of all the trappings connected with the saddle-gear, which appeared to me cumbrous and useless in the extreme; but my companion, who was an old cruiser in these parts, was well acquainted with their convenience and necessity; so with his experience as a guide, we galloped off on our excursion."

The way, he wrote, was barren of interest until they came suddenly to an almost perpendicular descent of some 30 or 40 feet into a deep and broad ravine, where formerly the river had flowed, but its bed was new filled with bushes and shrubs.

"Previous to this we passed a small shanty in an unfinished state, which had been erected some time before as a Custom-House, but owing to its incapacity and situation had been abandoned. We saw also the commencement of a new Presidio, that, on account of the difficulty of procuring water, had also never been completed. These two monuments of the imprudence and want of foresight of the Governor, served as very good evidence to me of the want of sagacity and energy of the government.

"A short ride further brought us to the house of our friend Don Manuel. We rode into the '*patio*' or court-yard, where a servant took the horses. At the threshold of his door we were met by Don Manuel, who embraced

191

us cordially and presented us to the family, his mother, wife, and sister. This was to be our home during the ship's detention, and though its coarse mud walls and damp ground floor did not altogether coincide with the idea I had previously formed of it, yet if their walls were cold and their floors damp, their hearts were warm, and the abundance of their luxurious entertainment more than compensated for any disappointment."

Robinson found Gov. Echeandía not at all the person described by the trapper, Pattie, but his real troubles were still ahead of him.

Alfred Robinson, in later years, after experiences in San Diego.

"After dinner we called upon the General Don José María de Echeandía, a tall, gaunt personage, who received us with true Spanish dignity and politeness. His house was located in the center of a large square of buildings occupied by his officers, and so elevated as to overlook them all, and command a view of the sea. On the right hand was a small Gothic chapel, with its cemetery, and immediately in front, close to the principal entrance, was the guard-room, where the soldiers were amusing themselves; some seated on the ground playing cards and smoking, while others were dancing to the music of the guitar; the whole was surrounded by a high wall, originally intended as a defense against the Indians. At the gate stood a sentinel, with slouched hat and blanket thrown over one shoulder, his old Spanish musket resting on the other; his pantaloons were buttoned and ornamented at the knee, below which, his legs were protected by leggins of dressed deer-skin, secured with spangled garters.

"On the lawn beneath the hill on which the Presidio is built stood about 30 houses of rude appearance, mostly occupied by retired veterans, not so well constructed in respect either to beauty or stability as the houses at Monterey, with the exception of that belonging to our 'Administrador,' Don Juan Bandini, whose mansion, then in an unfinished state, bade fair, when completed, to surpass any other in the country."

He found the climate milder than any other port on the coast, rabbit and quail plentiful, and the plains and ponds crowded with ducks and geese. The ship was made ready for business, and the goods and products of New England shops and factories put on display.

Journal of Alfred Robinson and of his life in Mexican San Diego.

"Visitors were numerous, both male and female, who came on board to purchase. Amongst others, the reverend Padre Antonio Peyri, of the Mission of St. Luis Rey, had expressed a wish to visit his many friends on shipboard, for besides our own, there were two other vessels then in port; the English brig *Vulture* . . . and the Mexican brig *María Ester*, from Acapulco. The good old priest was accordingly invited, and the last day of his visit was to be passed with us; other friends came also, and dinner was prepared for the occasion. As the old gentleman was held in universal respect upon the coast, not only as founder of the Mission over which he presided, but also as a man of great mental energy and capacity; high in favor with the government for these qualities, and being dearly loved by the people for the extreme benevolence of his disposition, we prepared to receive him with 'all honors.' Accordingly, as the reverend padre descended the gangway, we thundered forth a salute, and proceeded to show him the different parts of the vessel. Particularly did we call his attention to our traderoom, which had been fitted up with shelves and counters, resembling in appearance a country variety store. The amount of his purchases testified how vastly he had been pleased.

"On the following morning he departed, and when the boat had reached a short distance from the ship, the men laid upon their oars whilst our guns sounded a parting salute. As the smoke cleared off, I beheld the old man standing in the boat, and gazing towards us with apparent delight, and I thought I could perceive by the glistening of his eye, that future patronage would be the result of this reception."

The arrival of more and more American ships, and the continual encroachment of American trappers, were straws in the wind. The routes mapped out by Jedediah Smith and James Ohio Pattie were becoming well known. David Jackson with a party of nine hired men and a Negro slave left Santa Fe in late August of 1831 to purchase mules in California, and going by way of Tucson and the Gila River, reached San Diego in November. After buying mules throughout the southern territory they left in February on the return journey. One of the hired men stayed behind. He was J. J. Warner. The route by which they passed through San Diego County led across San José Valley, which later was to bear his name.

In Washington, the capital of the expanding United States, the idea of possessing California, or at least part of it, was beginning to take form. During the Administration of President Jackson there were some discussions with Mexico, and the secretary of state wrote to the chargé d'affaires in Mexico that "the port of San Francisco would be a most desirable place of resort for our numerous vessels engaged in the whaling business in the Pacific" and he was instructed to sound out the possibilities of acquiring at least the upper part of California as far south as Monterey. The British were to hear about the suggestion and in later years got busy influencing Mexico against it. In San Diego, the fiestas and the gambling continued to fill the days, as usual, as they always had, until one day, on Nov. 12, 1833, there was a shower of meteors. The people looked up from their tables and their games and then rushed to the presidio chapel and the mission. Perhaps it wasn't too late after all. Nothing more happened, at least not just then. The military, almost destitute, had more personal problems to try them. *Alférez* Salazar reported he would be unable to go to Monterey, as assigned, as he lacked a shirt and jacket, and his poor cloak did not cover the frightful condition of his trousers.

Education had become a matter of public concern, and Echeandía, in a report in 1829, said education had been "paralyzed" until he took action in 1826-27 and had schools established, the one at San Diego having 18 students. Juan Bandini urged that the supreme government send teachers for a small college of grammar and philosophy. Though the white population of California was about

5000, Californians had little knowledge of the rest of the world, and even the United States generally was referred to as "Boston" and American ships as "Boston ships."

Robinson gives us some detail of one of the romances of early California. This was the elopement of Capt. Henry D. Fitch and Doña Josefa, daughter of Joaquín Carrillo, of San Diego. Capt. Fitch was a young American sailor whose name has been connected with several ships sailing under different flags up and down the California and Mexican coasts. He first arrived at San Diego in 1826, and by the following year he had given her a written promise of marriage. As he was not a Catholic, and marriages between Catholics and Protestants were not receiving official and necessary sanction, he was baptized on April 14, 1829, by the Dominican Padre Méndez of the presidio chapel, who promised to conduct the marriage ceremony. Some secrecy had to be maintained. At the last moment, with her family and guests assembled in the Carrillo home, the bride's uncle, Domingo Carrillo, backed out, and the friar's courage failed him. Even Doña Josefa's tears failed to move him. But she had courage, if the padre didn't. That night, without her parents' knowledge, her cousin Pío Pico, took her on his horse and carried her down to a boat which took her out to the *Vulture*, the vessel which Robinson mentioned was in port upon his arrival, and put her aboard and in the arms of Capt. Fitch. By morning the *Vulture* was far down the coast. They were married in Valparaiso on July 3.

The town was shocked, the parents grieved, the officials frustrated. A year and a half later Fitch returned to San Diego as captain of the *Leonor*, with his wife and infant son aboard. He refused to appear before Padre Sánchez, of San Gabriel Mission, vicar and ecclesiastical judge of the territory, merely sending his marriage certificate, and sailing up the coast to Monterey. There, his arrest was ordered by Echeandía. He was confined and his bride put away for safekeeping in a "respectable" home. In time, both were allowed to go to San Gabriel, where they were confined again, though separately, and were subjected to repeated interrogations before an ecclesiastical court. Many witnesses were examined both at San Gabriel and San Diego. The court argued that the marriage was null and void because they had not obtained a dispensation from the bishop at Valparaiso, and anyway, the marriage license certificate was torn and blotted, included no statement of the city or church where the ceremony was performed, and had not been properly legalized.

At last the vicar rendered his decision on Dec. 28. He ruled that the charges had not been substantiated, the marriage was not null

Henry Delano Fitch, American who eloped with Doña Josefa Carrillo.

194

but valid; that both parties should be set at liberty; that on the following Sunday they should receive the Sacraments that ought to have preceded the marriage, and must present themselves in church with lighted candles in their hands to hear High Mass for three *dias festivos*, and recite together for 30 days one third of the rosary of the Holy Virgin.

Furthermore, the vicar decided "considering the great scandal which Don Enrique has caused in this province, I condemn him to give as penance and reparation a bell of at least 50 pounds in weight for the church at Los Angeles, which barely has a borrowed one."

The crisis over, all in San Diego breathed easier. Now they could get on with such relatively unimportant things as fiestas and revolutions. The *Brookline* went up and down the coast, discharging at San Diego the hides and tallow collected from port to port, and then time was taken out to participate in the blessing of the house of *Señor* Juan Bandini. Gen. Echeandía, his officers, and many friends and their families were present, the ceremony commencing at noon when the chaplain proceeded through the different apartments sprinkling holy water upon the walls.

The following is Robinson's description of the music and dances which followed:

"This concluded, we sat down to an excellent dinner, consisting of all the luxuries the place afforded, provided in Don Juan's best style. As soon as the cloth was removed, the guitar and violin were put in requisition, and a dance began. It lasted, however, but a little while, for it was necessary for them to spare their exertions for the evening *fandango*. So *poco a poco*, all gradually retired to their homes.

"At an early hour the different passages leading to the houses were enlivened with men, women, and children, hurrying to the dance; for on such occasions it was customary for everybody to attend without waiting for the formality of an invitation. A crowd of *leperos* was collected about the door when we arrived, now and then giving its shouts of approbation to the performances within, and it was with some difficulty we forced our entrance. Two persons were upon the floor dancing 'el jarabe.' They kept time to the music, by drumming with their feet, on the heel and toe system, with such precision, that the sound struck harmoniously upon the ear, and the admirable execution would not have done injustice to a pair of drumsticks in the hands of an able professor. The attitude of the female dancer was erect, with her head a little inclined to the right shoulder, as she modestly cast her eyes to the floor, whilst her hands gracefully held the skirts of her dress, suspending it above the ankle so as to expose to the company the execution of her feet. Her partner, who might have been one of the interlopers at the door, was under full speed of locomotion, and rattled away with his feet with wonderful dexterity. His arms were thrown carelessly behind his back, and secured, as they crossed, the points of his *sarape*, that still held its place upon his shoulder. Neither had he doffed his 'sombrero,' but just as he stood when gazing from the crowd, he had placed himself upon the floor.

The Bandini house in its early days had only one story, of adobe.

Early American sketch of fandango done from memory of Mexicans.

"The conclusion of this performance gave us an opportunity to edge our way along towards the extremity of the room, where a door communicated with an inner apartment. Here we placed ourselves, to witness in a more favorable position the amusements of the evening. The room was about 50 feet in length, and 20 wide, modestly furnished, and its sides crowded with smiling faces. Upon the floor were accommodated the children and Indian girls, who, close under the vigilance of their parents and mistresses, took part in the scene. The musicians again commencing a lively tune, one of the managers approached the nearest female, and, clapping his hands in accompaniment to the music, succeeded in bringing her into the center of the room. Here she remained awhile, gently tapping with her feet upon the floor, and then giving two or three whirls, skipped away to her seat. Another was clapped out, and another, till the manager has passed the compliment throughout the room. This is called a *son*, and there is a custom among the men, when a dancer proves particularly attractive to any one, to place his hat upon her head, while she stands thus in the middle of the room, which she retains until redeemed by its owner, with some trifling present. During the performance of the dances, three or four male voices occasionally take part in the music, and towards the end of the evening, from repeated applications of *aguardiente*, they become quite boisterous and discordant.

"The waltz was now introduced, and 10 or a dozen couples whirled gaily around the room, and heightened the charms of the dance by the introduction of numerous and interesting figures. Between the dances, refreshments were handed to the ladies, whilst in an adjoining apartment, a table was prepared for the males, who partook without ceremony. The most interesting of all their dances is the *contra danza*, and this, also, may be considered the most graceful. Its figures are intricate, and in connection with the waltz, form a charming combination. These *fandangos* usually hold out till daylight, and at intervals the people at the door are permitted to introduce their *jarabes* and *jotas*."

This is how patio of Estudillo house looked in Robinson's days.

In time Robinson moved in with the Estudillo family, which he said, "consisted of the old lady Domínguez, Don José Antonio Estudillo, his wife, Doña Victoria, with two children, and three servants, and it was nearly time for the religious festival of *"la Noche Buena."*

Don José Antonio called for the customary exhibition of the "pastores." There were rehearsals night and day and at last Christmas arrived. Robinson gives us the first written description of a Christmas scene in the Presidio of Old San Diego:

"At an early hour illuminations commenced, fireworks were set off, and all was rejoicing. The church bells rang merrily, and long before the time of Mass the pathways leading to the Presidio were enlivened by crowds hurrying to devotion. I accompanied Don José Antonio, who procured for me a stand where I could see distinctly everything that took place. The Mass commenced, Padre Vicente de Oliva officiated, and at the conclusion of the mysterious '*sacrificio*' he produced a small image representing the infant Saviour, which he held in his hands for all who chose to approach and kiss. After this, the tinkling of the guitar was heard without, the body of the church was cleared, and immediately commenced the harmonious sounds of a choir of voices. The characters entered in procession, adorned with appropriate costume, and bearing banners. There were six females representing shepherdesses, three men and a boy. One of the men personated Lucifer, one a hermit, and the other Bartolo, a lazy vagabond, whilst the boy represented the archangel Gabriel. The story of their performance is partially drawn from the Bible, and commences with the angel's appearance to the shepherds, his account of the birth of our Saviour, and exhortation to them to repair to the scene of the manger. Lucifer appears among them, and endeavors to prevent the prosecution of their journey. His influence and temptations are about to succeed, when Gabriel again appears and frustrates their effect. A dialogue is then carried on of considerable length relative to the attributes of the Deity, which ends in the submission of Satan. The whole is interspersed with songs and incidents that seem better adapted to the stage than the church. For several days this theatrical representation is exhibited at the principal houses, and the performers at the conclusion of the play are entertained with refreshments."

San Diego was a tranquil land, but dissatisfaction and dissension had been getting out of hand in the north. In 1828 a revolt of sorts had taken place in Monterey, some ungrateful soldiers marching out of the presidio and declaring, as it were, a strike, not for more pay but just for any kind of pay. Lt. Romualdo Pacheco had persuaded them to return, and imprisoned some of their leaders. Later in the same year, two soldiers disclosed a plot to rise against the governor and seize Monterey Presidio. Their leader was a convict-rancher named Joaquín Solís, who in view of his service in the war of independence, had been given a comparatively light sentence of banishment to California for some crime or other. But it wasn't until late in 1829, on the night of Nov. 12-13, that

FIESTAS AND GAY BALLS enlivened existence in New Spain, even in remote outposts such as San Diego. William H. Meyers, a gunner on an American ship, painted this ball scene while on trading trip in West Indies.

197

a real revolt took place. The soldiers at Monterey seized the presidio without opposition, many joining up, others however, preferring neutrality to battle. The insurgents proceeded to the homes of the officers, captured them and locked them up. As their leader was only a corporal, the command was offered to Solís, the ex-convict who nominated himself as commandant-general of California. He got the support of Monterey and most of the north.

Solís evidently had more ambitious plans than merely seeking a redress of grievances, and he drew up a proclamation against Echeandía which was read, by the way, in the presence of the American hide merchants, Hartnell and McCullough, to put California in the hands of a temporary governor. Solís then went to San Francisco, where he was received with a military salute, and picking up additional troops, marched with about 100 to Santa Barbara to face the enemy, the forces of Gen. Echeandía.

At San Diego, Echeandía had heard of the revolt on Nov. 25, and after getting a vote of confidence from his officers at the presidio, issued a warning to Solís and followers to lay down their arms, or they would be considered traitors and accomplices of the Spanish invaders then at Veracruz. But war it was. As Robinson described the scene at the Presidio of San Diego, "old rusty guns were repaired, hacked swords were sharpened, crude lances made, and all the force that could be mustered was soon on its way to meet the enemy." Echeandía and his army left San Diego on Dec. 1, and reached Santa Barbara on the 15th. A revolt at the presidio there was put down, and it was made ready for a defense.

What really happened at Santa Barbara we don't know in full. Echeandía gave his own version of what happened in January of 1830 in a report to the Mexican minister of war:

"On the 13th the rebels came in sight of the *divisioncita* of government troops, and from that time by their movements and frivolous correspondence endeavored to gain a victory; but knowing the uselessness of their resources and the danger of being cut off on their retreat, they fled precipitately at dusk on the 15th in different directions, spiking their cannon, and losing 26 men who have accepted the *indulto*."

Solís' version of the events at Santa Barbara went this way:

"Having taken a position between the presidio and mission, I found it impossible to enter either one or the other, the first because it was fortified, the second because of the walls pierced with loop-holes for musket-fire, and of all the people within, so that I knew we were going to lose, and this was the motive for not exposing the troops by entering."

He added that as a force of 150 men had been assembled to execute a surprise attack on him, and seeing himself without means of defense for want of munitions, "I determined to spike the can-

non, and retire with my army to fortify myself at Monterey —
lo que verifiqué al momento."

Dr. Stephen Anderson, who was on hand to render medical
assistance, in a letter wrote that "You would have laughed had
you been there . . . the two parties were within sight of each other
for nearly two days, and exchanged shots, but at such a distance
that there was no chance of my assistance being needed." The only
casualty of record was a horse.

Still in Northern California, James O. Pattie, the American fur
trapper, became aroused by the insurgents' intention of compelling
all Americans and Englishmen to swear allegiance to the government or leave California. He wrote in his diary that he dispatched
a runner with two good horses to warn Echeandía of the approach
of Solís, and also that the news of the outcome of the battle was
received with great rejoicing in Monterey, where praise was heaped
on Solís for being able to execute a judicious retreat.

*American seamen loved
the province's women
and its revolutions.*

"The name and fame of Gen. Solís was exalted to the skies. All the florid
comparisons, usual upon such occasion, were put in requisition, and all the
changes were sung upon his various characteristics, wit, honor and courage.
The point was carried so far as to bring him within some degrees of relationship to a supernatural being. Then the unbounded skill he displayed in
marshaling his force, and his extreme care to prevent the useless waste of
his men's lives were expatiated upon, and placed in the strongest light.
The climax of his excellence was his having retreated without the loss of
a man."

Pattie now claims that an American named John Roger Cooper,
a former sea captain who had settled down as a merchant, broke
out a barrel of rum and while the admirers of Gen. Solís rendered
themselves *hors de combat*, rallied all foreigners, including Scots,
Irish, English, Dutch and Americans, amounting to 39 men and,
convincing the rest of the inhabitants that Solís was not a hero
but an enemy, made ready for a battle of their own. When Solís'
retreating army arrived, most of his men, seeing presidio cannons
turned in their direction, surrendered. Solís and six mounted
officers fled. They were pursued, a short fight took place and one
man was killed, according to Pattie's narration, and Solís offered
his sword in surrender. The rebels were placed in irons and locked
up. Pattie informed Gen. Echeandía of the victory, accomplished
under the American flag, and that the enemy was his to dispose
of as he saw fit. Such records as are available do not bear out all
of Pattie's details of the events at Monterey, but its recapture
was effected with the help of foreign residents.

Investigations were conducted, and when it was found difficult
to make a case against many of the soldiers who had merely
wanted action on getting their pay, Echeandía seized on a charge

*Hunting the big grizzly
bear was a favorite but
dangerous sport.*

the men had talked about raising the Spanish flag once again over California. In the end, 15 prisoners were loaded onto the American bark *Volunteer* to be delivered to San Blas, where they were kept in chains for months but some made their way back to California. The soldiers from San Diego marched back home, the presidio sprang back to life, and for a time things went on as usual. But not for long. The Mexican government also had had enough of Gen. Echeandía and a successor, Manuel Victoria, arrived at San Diego overland from Loreto in December of 1830. He found that Echeandía, instead of being present to turn over the government, had slipped away to Monterey where he issued a proclamation, without any legal authority whatsoever, that amounted to a virtual confiscation of the property of the California missions. The decree of secularization was issued by Echeandía on Jan. 6, 1831, just three weeks before Victoria was able to arrive in Monterey and assume formal command. Upon learning of the decree while at Santa Barbara on his way north, Victoria was able to prevent its publication in the south, and took immediate steps to prevent its being put into effect in the north, and reported it to Mexico. This aroused the animosity of a group of young Californians, who long had coveted the mission lands and who, perhaps rightly, felt that the mission system was holding back the growth and development of California. Echeandía made it clear he would lead any revolt.

Victoria moved fast, and often illegally, to establish his authority and banish his enemies. Abel Stearns, American-born but a naturalized citizen of Mexico and a resident of California since 1829, was ordered to leave the country. He sailed from Monterey but either got off at San Diego or near the frontier in Baja California. José Antonio Carrillo was taken into custody on a charge of fraud and eventually sent to San Diego and banished to San Vicente in Baja California. José María Padrés was sent to San Blas.

They didn't stay away very long. Pío Pico in his own history said that in November his brother-in-law, José J. Ortega, rushed down from Monterey to warn him that Victoria planned to come south and hang both Pico and Juan Bandini. Pico was a senior *vocal* of the *diputación*, or assembly, and Bandini was a *diputado suplente*, or alternate, to Congress. Pico summoned José Carrillo, also a brother-in-law, to return to the province, and a secret meeting was held at Pico's ranch at Jamul. In the dead of night Pico and Carrillo slipped into Old Town and met with Bandini. Whether Victoria really had any intention of hanging anybody or whether it was a manufactured excuse for revolt, is not known. But an insurrection was decided upon, and the next two weeks

Pío Pico, one of the men who played big role in state's politics.

were spent in seeking out sympathizers, both in San Diego and Los Angeles. Those joining the plot in Los Angeles were fearful of meeting Victoria and his soldiers in a frontal attack and suggested they wait until Victoria had passed Los Angeles, and then he could be attacked from the rear while massed Diegueño Indians were thrown against him from the front.

On Nov. 29, 1831, Pico, Bandini and Carrillo issued a *pronunciamiento* of their grievances, and that night, with a party of 12 or 14 plotters, seized the presidio and garrison of San Diego. Among them were Ignacio, Juan and José López; Stearns, Juan María Marrón, Andrés and Antonio Ibarra; Dámaso and Gervasio Alipás, Juan Osuna and Silverio Rios. The 30 soldiers at the presidio offered no resistance. Pico said that he was given the task of taking Capt. Argüello into custody. Pico went to Argüello's house, found him playing cards with his wife and Lt. Ignacio del Valle, begged their pardon for the intrusion, drew his pistols, and requested that the two officers accompany him to the presidio guardhouse.

Santiago Argüello, soldier, revolutionist and political leader.

Bandini said he had been made responsible for the arrest of Capt. Portilla. But from all evidence Capt. Portilla was, if not a willing and secret participant, at least a willing captive. In the aftermath, Capts. Portilla and Argüello, and Lts. José María Ramírez, del Valle and Juan José Rocha, signed an addition to the *pronunciamiento* in which they charged Victoria with abridging the federal constitution. The acts of all these officers were acts of treason, and they subjected themselves to execution, by the firing squad or by hanging.

A Frenchman in San Diego at the time, Juan de la Cruz Montblanc, in a written report later in Mexico stated that Echeandía had remained in the background while the garrison was seized, and then stepped forward to accept the leadership of the revolt, ordered Portilla and the officers to obey him, had the flag raised in the presidio plaza and a cannon salute fired. The Frenchman also reported, though verbally, that five foreign vessels, which were to have sailed before the insurrection, remained in the Port of San Diego, and it was his belief that the captains had pledged assistance, if necessary, to the plotters. Foreigners more and more were beginning to play influential roles in California politics.

The *pronunciamiento*, which had been written by Bandini, proclaimed that ... "let the rights of the citizen be born anew; let liberty spring up from the ashes of oppression, and perish the despotism that has suffocated our security." In all probability what the conspirators really had in mind for the future was an independent California, under their leadership.

The Army of San Diego, under command of Portilla, marched north to meet the Army of Gen. Victoria. At Los Angeles, they were welcomed with enthusiasm, the political prisoners were freed, and now a citizen army of about 150 strong marched out to confront Victoria's force of about 30 men of the San Blas and Mazatlán companies, at Cahuenga Pass.

Bandini, Pico and Carrillo, the instigators of the revolt, were far removed from the scene of action. The facts of the subsequent battle are obscure. Victoria held the enemy in contempt and calling upon Portilla to surrender, ordered his men to fire, perhaps over the heads of the opposition, to let them know he meant business. Portilla fled. Others held their ground. José María Avila, with the Army of San Diego, and Capt. Romualdo Pacheco, aide to Victoria, clashed on horseback, with drawn swords and lances. As the horses swung around, and away, Pacheco received a bullet in the back which pierced his heart and he fell dead. Things happened fast in the next few minutes, and Victoria himself went down with several severe lance wounds. Avila was unhorsed and killed. The encounter was over as quickly as it had begun. The wounded Victoria was taken by his men to San Gabriel, where he resigned as governor of California, then went to San Luis Rey for further rest, and finally to San Diego. There he boarded the *Pocahontas*, which had been chartered by Bandini to take him back to Mexico.

He was joined by Fr. Peyri of San Luis Rey. Peyri was through with California. He long had sought his passport, on account of age and despair at the onrushing fate of the mission he had built and so loved, and finally being granted the privilege of retirement, he slipped away at night to board the *Pocahontas*. The Indians to whom he had been a practical as well as spiritual father learned of his flight and 500 of them went to San Diego, to plead with him to return, but the ship sailed on Jan. 17, 1832. His work of 33 years at San Luis Rey had come to a close.

One of the last persons to talk with Fr. Peyri and record his feelings was Robinson, only a few days before his departure, and

"the tears of regret coursed down the cheek of the good old friar, as he recalled to mind the once happy state of California. His great penetration of mind led him to foresee the result of the new theory of liberty and equality, among a people where anarchy and confusion so generally prevailed, and who, at the time, were totally unprepared for, and incapable of self-government. He chose rather retirement in poverty, than to witness the destruction and ravage that from this time ensued."

Alexander Forbes, an Englishman who visited the two Californias and published a history of them in London in 1839, wrote that he had the pleasure of seeing Fr. Peyri on his way to Mexico,

202

and that he was of prepossessing appearance, and looked like a robust man of 50 though he was then 67 years of age.

"In his grey Franciscan habit, which he always wore, with his jolly figure, bald head, and white locks, he looked the very beau ideal of a friar of olden time. This worthy man having entered the cloisters of a convent, may be considered dead to the world. But he will live long in the memory of the inhabitants of California. . ."

But there was no peace for the good padre. He returned to Spain and there found so much strife he was unable even to visit his native town. From Spain it is learned that he had brought two young Indian neophytes with him from California and placed them in the Propaganda College in Rome, the city in which he himself finally died, regretting that he had ever left his mission and his "children."

The two Luiseño boys were Pablo Tac and Agapito Amamix. Agapito died in Rome in 1837. Pablo Tac began his studies in Latin grammar, and while still a boy between 12 and 14 years of age, produced what may have been the first literary work by a native California Indian. His sketch of the Luiseño Indians, their customs and life at Mission San Luis Rey, has been preserved. He also produced an incomplete dictionary of 1200 words, studied rhetoric, the humanities and philosophy, before dying a few weeks before his 20th birthday.

At San Blas, Victoria wrote to Mexican officials warning of the plans of Echeandía and the *diputación* and declaring that they could only bring ruin to the missions and all of California, and that he feared an attempt would be made to separate the territory from Mexico.

At Monterey, the triumphant Echeandía convoked the state assembly and Pío Pico was elected temporary governor and Echeandía military commander. They soon fell out and Pico took himself out of the picture. Rule of the state was divided, Echeandía taking the south and Capt. Agustín V. Zamorano the north. Echeandía, though he was aware that Mexico was sending up a new governor, issued another *reglamento* on the missions and emancipation of the Indians, this one affecting only those in the south, San Diego, San Luis Rey, San Juan Capistrano, and San Gabriel. Indians were enticed from their work; many at distant points revolted, and robberies and murders became common. Robinson wrote that at San Pedro he learned the Missions San Juan Capistrano and San Luis Rey were being drained of their richest possessions:

"Daily reports were received of robberies and murders, committed by the Indians at St. Diego, who were in a wretched state. At the Mission below that place, which is called St. Miguel, they revolted and attempted to kill the priest, but he defended himself within his house, with the assistance of two soldiers, and finally drove them off . . . stabbings were frequent at St. Juan and St. Luis; and the drunken Indian, as he staggered along from his scene of debauch, ejaculated, 'Soy libre!' I am free."

Frs. Martín and Oliva at Mission San Diego, in reply to Echeandía's *reglamento*, wrote that

"We shall not oppose nor do we oppose whatever Your Honor may determine, for we continue here at this mission only for the spiritual welfare of these people. Since May 20 of this year, the neophytes of this mission have already managed their temporalities without any meddling in their affairs on our part. If at any time anything has been said about the damage which the little remaining property is suffering, it was done because the waste in the management is notorious. Only the wine cellar has not been turned over to the Indians, because this has been regarded as not conducive to their corporal and spiritual welfare."

By the year 1832 the regular annual reports on the state of the mission ceased. The last report signed by Fr. Fernando Martín on Dec. 31, 1832, listed a total of 6522 baptisms since the founding of the mission in 1769. There had been 1803 marriages and 4332 deaths recorded. At the end of the year 1832 there were 1455 neophytes at the mission, 4500 head of cattle, 13,250 sheep, 150 goats, 220 horses and 80 mules. Fr. Martín, who finally took the oath of allegiance to the republican constitution of Mexico, one of the few friars who did so, served all of his time in California at the San Diego Mission, arriving in 1811 and dying here in 1838.

The ranchos, which in Spanish times played only a small role in development of the province, now began to assume a greater importance. The San Blas ships no longer came regularly, and private agriculture and stock raising increased steadily. The Mexican period saw the granting of many ranchos, and the hide trade was to make many of the owners wealthy. In 1831 the San Dieguito Rancho, now known as Rancho Santa Fe, comprising 8824 acres, was granted provisionally to the Silva family but Juan María Osuna took possession in 1836. The Santa María Rancho, or Pamo Valley, 17,708 acres, was granted provisionally to a Mexican soldier, Narciso Botello, but eventually passed to José Joaquín Ortega. San José del Valle, or Warner's Ranch, 26,688 acres, was taken over as a grazing ground in 1834 by the brother of Capt. Pablo de la Portilla, and was granted to him two years later.

The new commandant general and inspector, and *jefe superior político*, was Brevet Brigadier-General José Figueroa, who had been commandant general of Sonora and Sinaloa for five or six years and thus somewhat conversant with the continuing troubles in California. He was given detailed instructions on the encourage-

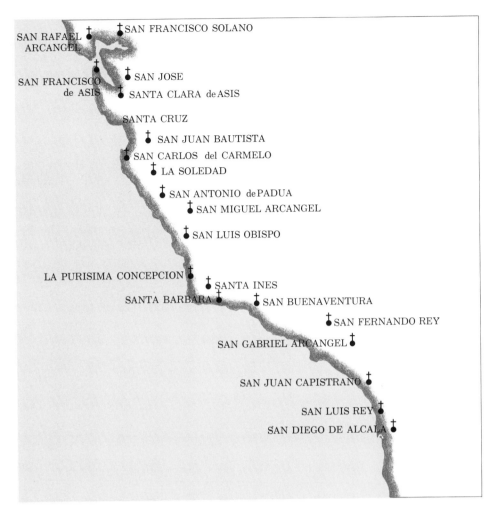

SAN RAFAEL ✝
ARCANGEL ●

✝ SAN FRANCISCO SOLANO

SAN FRANCISCO ●
de ASIS

● SAN JOSE

✝ SANTA CLARA de ASIS

SANTA CRUZ

✝ SAN JUAN BAUTISTA

✝ SAN CARLOS del CARMELO
✝ LA SOLEDAD

✝ SAN ANTONIO de PADUA
✝ SAN MIGUEL ARCANGEL

✝ SAN LUIS OBISPO

LA PURISIMA CONCEPCION ●
✝ SANTA INES
SANTA BARBARA ●
✝ SAN BUENAVENTURA

✝ SAN FERNANDO REY

SAN GABRIEL ARCANGEL ●

✝ SAN JUAN CAPISTRANO ●

SAN LUIS REY ● ✝
SAN DIEGO DE ALCALA ●

THE MISSIONS REACHED THEIR PEAK between 1823 and 1830, and then their decline set in. The 21 establishments, with their vast lands, herds and rich crops and gardens, were prizes eagerly sought by a new generation.

ment of trade, colonization and distribution of lands both to citizens and foreigners, and in particular, in regard to the secularization of the missions, which in effect abrogated all that Echeandía had done but yet called for study with a view to a change in the system. To enforce his orders he was given a command of 75 officers and men lately released from prison for revolutionary attempts. They sailed on the *Catalina*, and at Cape San Lucas, the soldiers revolted and with the aid of the sailors, seized the ship, all the arms and money, and sailed away to the mainland to join a new uprising under Gen. Santa Ana. The *Catalina* later was returned to La Paz and Figueroa and his men finally made their way to Monterey, arriving in January of 1833. He took quick command of affairs; members of the rebellious factions eventually were granted amnesty, and Echeandía himself, after bringing Figueroa up to date on the missions and secularization, boarded the *Catalina* at San Diego and sailed for Mexico.

205

Robinson thought less of Echeandía even than did Pattie, the trapper: "What a scourge he had been to California! What an instigator of vice! 'Hombre de vicio,' as he was called. The seeds of dishonor sown by him will never be extirpated so long as there remains a mission to rob, or a treasury to plunder." But Echeandía settled down in his old profession of engineer and apparently lived out a peaceful life.

As for the American, Pattie, he finally abandoned California to its fate, for the time being, and went to Mexico to seek satisfaction for his services to California, but had to borrow money to get back to the United States. When aging, though still restless, he is believed to have taken to the trails once more, during the gold rush. A companion later recorded that "this man left my camp in the Sierra Nevada Mountains, amidst the deep snows of the terrible winter of 1849-50.... I suppose he perished in the deep snows, or was killed by Indians."

Big schemes were still in the air. In Mexico City, José María Hijar, a wealthy Mexican, and José María Padrés, who had been ousted from California by Victoria, joined with the territory's new congressman, Juan Bandini of San Diego, to promote a plan of colonization which certainly had as its base the confiscation of mission lands. Largely through their influence the Mexican Congress passed the Secularization Law of Aug. 17, 1833, converting the missions to parish churches. Padrés was named *ayudante inspector* of California, ranking second only to Figueroa, and Hijar, *jefe político* and director of colonization. The colonization program was well organized and financed, and the colonists, mostly tradesmen and professional people of good quality, were to receive certain sums of money, free passage, some tools and livestock and farms from public lands. There were about 250 of them, including women and children, and they sailed in two vessels, the *Natalia*, and the *Morelos*, from San Blas, encountering storms and sickness. The *Natalia* put into San Diego, at the request of Bandini, and the colonists were divided temporarily between San Gabriel and San Luis Rey Missions, eventually making their way to Monterey, traveling from mission to mission. The other ship made it directly to Monterey. The *Natalia*, which some believe to have been the same vessel on which Napoleon escaped from Elba, went on the beach near Monterey and broke up.

Though he was instrumental in obtaining passage of the law on secularization, Bandini failed in an effort to have the Congress close the port of Monterey to foreign ships in favor of San Diego. He did, however, win appointment as inspector of California customs houses. His authority was not recognized in Monterey and he had to content himself with conducting San Diego as an open port, regardless of the Congress. Bandini soon fell into disgrace, as an investigation revealed he had brought more than $2,000 in goods into California aboard the *Natalia* and had neglected to declare them or pay duties. Despite Bandini's protests that such a charge was absurd, and all had been according to law, he was fined $700, the goods were confiscated, and he was suspended from office. Bandini's outrage lasted for years.

The colonization scheme ran into delay when Gen. Santa Ana took command in Mexico City, revoked Hijar's political authority, and Figueroa decided to wait for more instructions before going further than he already had with the secularization. The Californians, too, became somewhat disenchanted with Padrés when they learned he had brought along 21 Mexicans to serve as administrators of the missions, posts which the Californians obviously had desired for themselves. They had not long to wait, however. Figueroa decided to go ahead and in conjunction with the California *diputación* published official regulations for secularization. The decree was to affect only 10 missions at first, with half of the property to be turned over to the Indians, and the rest administered for the benefit of the church and the public good. Figueroa appointed 10 administrators. Six more missions were to be secularized in 1835 and the remaining five in the following year. But the Californians had no intention of turning mission lands over to the Indians, and in effect the decree shunted them to a few locations, deprived them of voices in all affairs, and required that "the emancipated will be obliged to aid in the common work which in the judgment of the *jefe político* may be deemed necessary for the cultivation of the vineyards, gardens, and fields remaining for the present undisturbed." The padres were to stay on as parish priests, and while they declined the title, they remained to do what they could for the Indians, though they no longer had authority over them. A subsequent Mexican law, passed by the Congress in April of 1834, insisted that secularization should go into effect within four months.

Figueroa toured the state to explain the blessings of liberty to the Indians. At San Diego Mission only two heads of families out of the 59 considered ready for freedom, asked for emancipation, and 14 living in the San Dieguito area. On Sept. 20, 1834, Mission San Diego was transferred by inventory from Fr. Fernando Martín to Juan José Rocha, newly appointed commissioner, and in April of the next year Joaquín Ortega became administrator, to be paid from income from farm products which the Indians were expected

Juan Bandini, plotter, merchant, host, famed in city's history, shown with daughter, Ysidora.

to produce the same as before. The accounts of San Luis Rey were turned over to Capt. Pablo de la Portilla by Fr. Buenaventura Fortuni. San Luis Rey still had the largest population of all the missions, and was the only one to show a gain from 1831 to 1834. There were 2844 neophytes. Large livestock, however, had declined sharply, from more than 27,000 to 13,000. Secularization brought chaos. Portilla wrote:

"The Indians absolutely refused to obey orders . . . they would listen to no reason. It was impossible to make them understand or appreciate the advantage of industry and obedience . . . they all with one voice cried out, 'We are free . . . we do not choose to work!' . . . The intentions of the government were doubtless praiseworthy; 'liberty throughout the world,' ought to be the way of every good citizen. But the Indians of California did not possess the qualifications for Liberty; and it was necessary for their preservation that something should be done to protect them against themselves."

After being secularized the missions were to be pueblos. By the end of 1835, the 16 missions had been secularized and lands and goods divided, as planned, and it was then that the Mexican Congress passed a new law virtually repealing secularization. Nobody in California paid any attention to it. Robinson, as witness to these events, wrote that many of the Spanish and Mexican families "that were poor soon became wealthy, and possessors of farms, which they stocked with cattle."

The mission establishments never became Indian pueblos, or towns, as long anticipated under Spanish laws and Mexican promises. As far as is known, only three Indian towns composed of ex-neophytes actually were organized in San Diego County, in San Dieguito Valley, at San Pascual and at Las Flores.

CHAPTER FOURTEEN

Thursday Aug. 14th 1834. Went on board brig "Pilgrim", lying at Central Wharf. Towards night, being nearly ready for sea, the vessel hauled out into the stream, & came to anchor. ——

Friday Aug. 15th. 34. Took on board gunpowder, had a fine breeze but did not set sail. ——

Saturday Aug. 16th 34. At 10. A. M. Wind E. N. E. took a pilot on board, weighed anchor, & set sail; but the wind coming round dead East, came to anchor in the Roads. At 10. P. M. at a light breeze springing up from the South ard & Westward, got under weigh, & stood out to sea. ——

Sunday Aug. 17th 34. Were out of sight of the land. At night all hands called aft, & the sea watch set. The crew consists of Fr. A. Thompson, Captain; Andrew B. Amerzene, chief mate; Geo. Forster 2nd Mate; 5 able seamen, 4 hands, Steward, Cook, & Carpenter. This vessel is about two hundred tons burthen & owned by Messrs. Bryant, Sturgis, & Co. Boston. ——

Tuesday Aug. 19th. Came into the Gulf Stream. In the evening wind, and a heavy sea. Double reefed the topsails. ——

Wednesday Aug. 29th. Fine weather returned with the morning. About o'clk P. M. two sails hove in sight; they passed to leeward, out of reach

RICHARD HENRY DANA

The most historically famous ship of the California hide trade arrived at San Diego in 1835. This was the little Boston brig *Pilgrim*, and aboard her was Richard Henry Dana, Jr. The presidio of Spanish times was crumbling away, a system of priestly rule was disappearing and San Diego itself was changing into a cosmopolitan port in which the flags of a dozen countries snapped in the breeze and the words and music of people collected from the docks of the world livened the days in old La Playa. The bells of the adobe mission church were being stilled but through the morning fog the bells of the ships of the hide and fur trade could be heard across the bay in the little town struggling to keep alive at the foot of Presidio Hill.

Dana was 19 years old, the son of a prominent Cambridge, Mass., family and a descendant of a signer of the Declaration of Independence. He had developed a serious eye trouble as the result of an attack of measles, and unable to continue his studies at Harvard University, chose to undertake, in the lingering tradition of the times, a voyage "before the mast" before settling down to a career. The sea quickly restored his full vision, and by the end of the long cruise, a rather prudish youth had become a vigorous, healthy, yet still-sensitive man who wrote a book, "Two Years Before the Mast," which thrilled a generation, unintentionally brought about

THIS IS THE ORIGINAL LOG, or journal, kept by Richard Henry Dana Jr., and from which he later wrote his classic, "Two Years Before the Mast." It is preserved in the Massachusetts Historical Society Museum of Boston.

changes in the conditions for seamen aboard ships around the world, and has been in print continuously since 1840.

Dana was not a reformer, and though shocked at the injustice of floggings he witnessed aboard the *Pilgrim*, he himself blamed much of the troubles at sea on the sailors themselves, describing many of them as blasphemous and abandoned men. Despite the hardships and cruelties experienced on long voyages in cramped quarters on rat-infested wooden ships, Dana knew that "there is a witchery in the sea, its songs and stories, and in the mere sight of a ship, and the sailor's dress, especially to a young mind, which has done more to man navies, and fill merchantmen, than all the press gangs of Europe."

When he left Boston he thought he would be away for 18 months, but soon learned that it would be at least two years before he would see again his home and family. Hides were getting somewhat scarce on the coast, and his firm, Bryant, Sturgis & Co., the pioneer in the Boston trade, intended to use the *Pilgrim* as a tender. The *California*, another company ship, already was at San Diego preparing to sail for Boston with a full cargo of hides, and she would be followed on the coast by another large ship, which the *Pilgrim* would help load with 40,000 hides before she could take on her own cargo and start the long and hazardous return journey.

Not much larger than the older privateering fur ships, the *Pilgrim* was an 180-ton vessel of only 86 feet seven inches in length and about 21 feet six inches in beam, and carried a crew of 15 men.

The *Pilgrim* cruised down the coast toward San Diego which Dana learned had become the depot for the vessels engaged in the hide trade, each one having built a large house of rough boards in which they stowed the hides as fast as they collected them in trips up and down the coast, and when they had procured a full cargo, spent a few weeks here taking it in, smoking ship, laying in food and water, and making other preparations for the long voyage home.

The bay was approached at sunset on March 13, and Dana noted in his journal that "we had a large and well-wooded headland directly before us." This description of Point Loma has led to continual debate as to whether the Point actually was wooded at the time of Dana's visit, or that some trees still existed from a warmer, wetter era.

"There was no town in sight, but on the smooth sandy beach, abreast, and within a cable's length of which three vessels lay moored, were four large houses, built of rough boards and looking like the great barns in which ice is stored on the borders of the large ponds near Boston, with piles of hides standing round them, and men in red shirts and large straw hats walking in and out of the doors. These were the hide houses. Of the vessels: one, a short clumsy little hermaphrodite brig, we recognized as our old acquaintance, the *Loriotte*;

another, with sharp bows and raking masts, newly-painted and tarred, and glittering in the morning sun, with the blood-red banner and cross of St. George at her peak, was the handsome *Ayacucho*. The third was a large ship, with topgallant-masts housed and sails unbent, and looking as rusty and worn as two years 'hide-drodging' could make her. This was the *Lagoda*."

As the *Pilgrim* drew nearer to them in the anchorage north of Ballast Point, she dropped anchor. It failed to hold and she drifted

THE BRIG PILGRIM *had a lot of sea running in front of her when she sailed from Boston for San Diego and other California ports. This map shows the 15,000-mile route sailed by Richard Henry Dana Jr., to West Coast.*

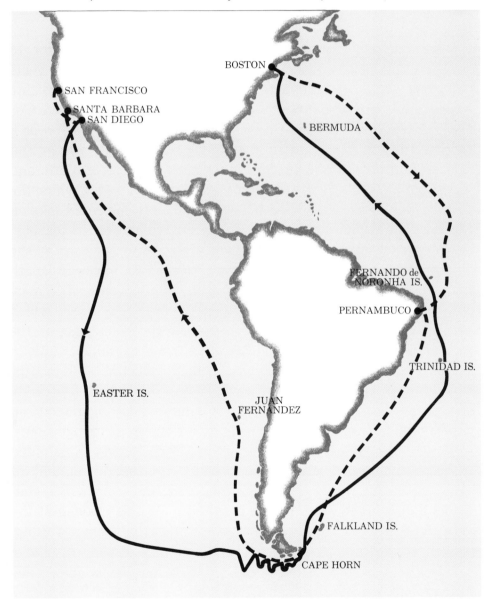

Next page, THE LITTLE BRIG PILGRIM *bucks a heavy sea on its way to California. The* Pilgrim *brought Richard Henry Dana Jr. to San Diego where he put down the story of hide trade at La Playa that has lived for generations.*

into the *Lagoda*. Several hours of work were required to get her clear and finally brought to a safe anchor opposite the company's hide house which had been built with the arrival of the *Brookline*, which had brought Alfred Robinson to California. Given leave, Dana and a companion, dressed in the traditional white duck trousers, blue jacket and straw hat, headed for the town's grog shop, to demonstrate that despite education and family background, he was a true shipmate ashore as well as aboard ship.

As for the grog shop,

"This was a small adobe building of only one room, in which were liquors, 'dry goods.' West India goods, shoes, bread, fruits, and everything, which is vendible in California. It was kept by a Yankee, a one-eyed man, who belonged formerly to Fall River, came out to the Pacific in a whale-ship, left her at the Sandwich Islands, and came to California and set up a *pulperia*."

Richard Henry Dana, Jr., as sketched from daguerrotype of 1840.

Sailors from each of the ships in the bay took turns in buying rounds of drinks, as custom required, and finally, Dana and his companion having manfully acquitted themselves of all obligations, slipped out and mounted rented horses to see the country. Horses were cheap and the rental charge was for the saddle. They rode around the bay to see the San Diego that was entering a period of decline. The civil population as well as the military force had decreased considerably and would continue to do so for a number of years. Fort Guijarros which had fired so bravely on heavily-gunned and blockade-running American smugglers already had been abandoned.

Dana wrote:

"The first place we went to was the old ruinous presidio, which stands on a rising ground near the village, which it overlooks. It is built in the form of an open square, like all the other presidios, and was in a ruinous state, with the exception of one side, in which the commandant lived, with his family. There were only two guns, one of which was spiked, and the other had no carriage. Twelve half-clothed and half-starved-looking fellows composed the garrison; and they, it was said, had not a musket apiece. The small settlement lay directly below the fort, composed of about 40 dark brown looking huts, or houses, and three or four larger ones white-washed, which belonged to the *gente de razón*. This town is not more than half as large as Monterey or Santa Barbara, and has little or no business."

The adobe blocks of crumbling walls were being used in building the newer houses of Old Town. Leaving the presidio behind, and riding up the sandy bottom of the San Diego River Bed, through grass grown green and rank, and around bushes and thickets, they saw ahead the white walls of the mission, and fording the small stream that was running, came directly upon it.

"The mission is built of adobe and plaster. There was something decidedly striking in its appearance: a number of irregular buildings, connected with one another, and disposed in the form of a hollow square, with a church at one end, rising above the rest, with a tower containing five belfries, in each of which hung a large bell, and with very large rusty iron crosses at the tops. Just outside of the buildings, and under the walls, stood 20 or 30 small huts, built of straw and of the branches of trees grouped together, in which a few Indians lived, under the protection and in the service of the mission.

"Entering a gateway, we drove into the open square, in which the stillness of death reigned. On one side was the church; on another, a range of high buildings with grated windows, a third was a range of smaller buildings, or offices, and the fourth seemed to be little more than a high connecting wall. Not a living creature could we see. We rode twice round the square, in the hope of waking up some one; and in one circuit saw a tall monk, with shaven head, sandals, and the dress of the Grey Friars, pass rapidly through a gallery, but he disappeared without noticing us. After two circuits we stopped our horses, and at last a man showed himself in front of one of the small buildings. We rode up to him, and found him dressed in the common dress of the country, with a silver chain round his neck, supporting a large bunch of keys. From this, we took him to be the steward of the mission, and, addressing him as 'Majordomo,' received a low bow and an invitation to walk into his room. Making our horses fast, we went in. It was a plain room, containing a table, three or four chairs, a small picture or two of some saint, or a miracle, or martyrdom, and a few dishes and glasses.

"'*Hay alguna cosa de comer?*' said I, from my grammar. '*Si Señor!*' said he. '*Que gusta usted?*' Mentioning *frijoles*, which I knew they must have, if they had nothing else, and beef and bread, with a hint for wine, if they had any, he went off to another building across the court, and returned in a few minutes with a couple of Indian boys bearing dishes and a decanter of wine. The dishes contained baked meats, *frijoles* stewed with peppers and onions, boiled eggs, and California flour baked into a kind of macaroni. These, together with the wine, made the most sumptuous meal we had eaten since we left Boston; and, compared with the fare we had lived upon for seven months, it was a regal banquet. After despatching it, we took out some money and asked him how much we were to pay. He shook his head, and crossed himself, saying that it was charity — that the Lord gave it to us. Knowing the amount of this to be that he did not sell, but was willing to receive a present, we gave him 10 or 12 *reals*, which he pocketed with admirable nonchalance, saying, '*Dios se lo pague.*' Taking leave of him, we rode out to the Indians' huts. The little children were running about among the huts, stark naked, and the men wore not much more; but the women had generally coarse gowns of a sort of tow cloth. The men are employed, most of the time, in tending the cattle of the mission, and in working in the garden, which is a very large one, including several acres, and filled, it is said, with the best fruits of the climate."

Going through the little settlement at the foot of Presidio Hill, on their way back to the ship, they found Indian boys and girls engaged in a ball game, amid the clapping and screaming of their elders; sailors reeling about town, or being thrown from vicious horses to the delight of the Mexicans from whom they had obtained them, and a half dozen Sandwich-Islanders dashing about at full gallop "hallooing and laughing like so many wild men." Beacon Hill in Boston was never like that. Aboard ship, with daylight, came the cry of "all hands ahoy" and shore clothes were laid aside for the taking out and landing of the 3500 hides collected

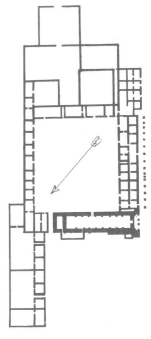

This is layout of San Diego Mission as made by U.S. Surveyors.

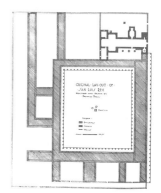

Original layout of San Luis Rey Mission as determined by ruins.

217

along the coast. There would be no time to think of home until the house had been filled to its capacity of 40,000 hides.

"The hides, as they come rough and uncured from the vessels, are piled up outside of the houses, whence they are taken and carried through a regular process of pickling, drying and cleaning, and stowed away in the house, ready to be put on board. This process is necessary in order that they may keep during a long voyage and in warm latitudes."

As soon as the hides were landed, the captain intended to leave two or three of the crew and an officer on shore, to take charge of curing the hides, and fill out the crew with Sandwich-Islanders. There was a considerable colony of them at La Playa, as it was the habit of ships' captains to use them as extra crew members in trade between the Hawaiian Islands and California. But he could not get any Sandwich-Islanders to go, although he offered them $15 a month, for the report of the flogging had got among them, and he was called "*aole maikai*" (no good), and that was an end of the business. They were, however, willing to work on shore, and four of them were hired and put to curing the hides.

Model of Pilgrim *which brought Richard Henry Dana to San Diego.*

When unloaded, the *Pilgrim* made another journey up the coast for more hides, returning early in May, to find the harbor deserted, all the hide houses but that of Bryant, Sturgis & Co. closed up, and between a dozen or 20 more Sandwich-Islanders living on the beach, "keeping up a grand carnival." They made their home in a large oven which had been built on the beach by the Russians for baking bread. It had a door on one side and a vent-hole in the top, and while it could hold eight or 10 men fairly comfortably was crowded with all of the Hawaiian natives, who lived in happy idleness, drinking, singing and playing cards, and cutting up a bullock once a week for food. The captain of the *Pilgrim* tried to hire some of them, but as long as the money from their previous hide work lasted, "it was like throwing pearls before the swine."

After the *Pilgrim's* cargo of hides and tallow had been discharged, some of the Hawaiians, their money gone, were ready to resume work, and this time Dana was left on the beach in charge of hide-curing. His quarters were in the large hide house itself. Dana grew very attached to the Hawaiians, finding them interesting, intelligent and kind-hearted, with their winsome and carefree ways and such odd names as Ban-yan, Fore-top, Rope-yarn, Pelican, or Mr. Bingham, which had been given to them by sailors. They all had a great desire to see the United States but were afraid of rounding Cape Horn as they suffered much from the cold.

There was time for rest and relaxation, too, and Dana, one Sunday, after writing letters to be sent home aboard the *Lagoda*, watched the *Ayacucho* drop her foretopsail, which was a signal for her sailing and the crew heaving at the windlass.

"I listened to the musical notes of a Sandwich-Islander named Mahanna who 'sang out' for them. Sailors, when heaving at a windlass, in order that they may heave together, always have one to sing out, which is done in high and long-drawn notes, varying with the motion of the windlass. This requires a clear voice, strong lungs, and much practice, to be done well. This fellow had a very peculiar wild sort of note, breaking occasionally into a falsetto. The sailors thought that it was too high, and not enough of the boatswain hoarseness about it; but to me it had a great charm. The harbour was perfectly still, and his voice rang among the hills as though it could have been heard for miles. Towards sundown, a good breeze having sprung up, the *Ayacucho* got under way, and with her long sharp head cutting elegantly through the water on a taut bowline, she stood directly out of the harbour, and bore away to the southward. She was bound to Callao, and thence to the Sandwich Islands, and expected to be on the coast again in eight or 10 months."

As the months went by the ships came and went and the hide houses began to fill up. The crews of vessels depositing their hides at San Diego came ashore in the evenings.

Bark

"Spanish was the common ground upon which we all met; for everyone knew more or less of that. We had now, out of 40 or 50 representatives from almost every nation under the sun — two Englishmen, three Yankees, two Scotchmen, two Welshmen, one Irishman, three Frenchmen (two of whom were Normans, one from Gascony), one Dutchman, one Austrian, two or three Spaniards (from old Spain), and half a dozen Spanish-Americans and half-breeds, two native Indians from Chile, one Negro, one mulatto, about 20 Italians, from all parts of Italy, as many more Sandwich-Islanders, one Tahitian, and one Kanaka from the Marquesas Islands.

"The night before the vessels were ready to sail, all the Europeans united and had an entertainment at the *Rosa's* hide-house, and we had songs of every nation and tongue. A German gave us '*Ach! mein lieber Augustin!*' the three Frenchmen roared through the Marseillaise Hymn; the English and Scotchman gave us 'Rule, Britannia,' and 'Wha'll be King but Charlie?'; the Italians and Spaniards screamed through some national affairs, for which I was none the wiser; and we three Yankees made an attempt at the 'Star Spangled Banner!' After these national tributes had been paid, the Austrian gave us a little pretty love-song, and the Frenchmen sang a spirited thing — '*Sentinelle! O prenez garde á vous!*' and then followed the *mélange* which might have been expected. When I left them, the *aguardiente* and *annisou* were pretty well in their heads, they were all singing and talking at once, and their peculiar national oaths were getting as plenty as pronouns."

Barkentine

The *Alert*, also owned by Bryant, Sturgis & Co., and on which Dana was to return to Boston, arrived and brought welcome mail and newspapers, and for Dana, in addition, a supply of duck to make some new clothes, and flannel shirts and shoes. Thus the long summer and autumn passed, and then spring came again. The *California* long since had sailed with a full cargo and was on her way back. Nearly 40,000 more hides were stacked at La Playa ready for loading. Dana had gone aboard the *Alert* on her coastal cruises and in March she returned to San Diego. "This was our last port. Here we were to discharge everything from the ship, clean her out, smoke her, take in our hides, wood, and water and set sail for Boston." Early the next morning came the cry "all hands ahoy" for the heaving out of ballast. Dana said that a regulation of the port forbade any ballast to be thrown overboard, and accordingly the long boat was lined with rough boards and brought aside the gangway, but where one tubfull of ballast went into the boat, 20 went overboard — if nobody from the presidio was watching. This saved more than a week of rowing and unloading at Ballast Point, and "this is one of those petty frauds which many vessels practice in ports of inferior foreign nations, and which are lost sight of among the deeds of greater weight which are hardly less common."

The connection between San Diego and Boston has led to stories of the paving of Boston streets with cobblestones taken from Ballast Point as ballast. To be sure, old streets of Boston were paved with cobblestones though this was started back in the late 1600's. Most of the old stones have been covered over, though some still are to be seen around Louisburg Square on Beacon Hill. A loaded ship would not need more ballast, but many a ship over the years had to make it back with a disappointing cargo. The *Alert* was made ready, and the bottom of the hold covered over with dried brush for dunnage, and with everything leveled off, the operation of taking on hides began, a task that required from two to six weeks.

The little *Pilgrim*, still cruising the coast and picking up hides, returned to San Diego and "it was a sad sight for her crew to see us getting ready to go off the coast, while they, who had been longer on the coast than the *Alert*, were condemned to another year's hard service." The *California*, too, was back in San Diego, discharging hides for storing to make up another cargo. The time came for Dana to say goodbye to San Diego.

"This promised to be our last day in California. Our 40,000 hides and 30,000 horns, besides several barrels of otter and beaver skins, were all stowed below, and the hatches were caulked down ... All our spare spars were taken on board and lashed, our water-casks secured, and our livestock, consisting of four bullocks, a dozen sheep, a dozen or more pigs, and three or four dozens of poultry were all stowed away in their different quarters."

Here Dana, in his narrative, inserted a paragraph to the effect that the ship had also taken aboard a small quantity of gold dust, which Mexicans or Indians had brought down from the interior. "It was not uncommon," he wrote, "for our ships to bring a little, as I have since learned from the owners. I had heard rumors of gold discoveries, but they attracted little or no attention, and were not followed up." The Gold Rush to California was 14 years away.

The hide trade was to go on for many years, though like everything else in California at the time, conditions were uncertain and troublesome. Five Boston companies engaged in the hide trade during the 20 years of its existence, McCullough, Hartnell and Company, which soon withdrew; Bryant, Sturgis & Company, J. B. Eaton and Company, Appleton and Company, and B. T. Reed. William Heath Davis, Jr., another of the Boston men, who arrived on the bark *Louis* in 1831 and remained to write his famous book, "Seventy-five Years in California," estimated that more than a million and a quarter hides were shipped out of California during the years of the hide trade, and 13 ships alone, including the *Pilgrim*, the *Alert*, the *California* and the *Lagoda*, took out more than 300,000 in the five years from 1831 to 1836. Hides sold for $2 each and Bryant, Sturgis & Co. bought and exported 500,000 in 20 years. Alfred Robinson tells how he often had $200,000 to $300,000 in goods entrusted to the missions.

The hide houses on La Playa built of rough boards bought from Boston, were given the names of ships in the trade, and from the recollections of pioneers in the area it was established that the hide houses were named as the California, the Admittance, the Sterling and the Tasso. The first American flag raised on California soil probably was the one that flew over the *Brookline's* house which became known as the California. And the sight of the Mexican flag never kept the Americans in the harbor from celebrating the Fourth of July by burning powder on the decks of the ships.

The hoisting of the flag, made aboard ship out of shirt cloth, was described in later years in the Boston Advertiser by Capt. James P. Arther, who was the first mate of the *Brookline* when the first hide house was built in 1829. The Advertiser commented that "these men raised our national ensign, not in bravado, nor for war and conquest, but as honest men to show they were American citizens . . . and while the act cannot be regarded as in the light of a claim to sovereignty, it is still interesting as a fact, and as an unconscious indication of manifest destiny."

The advent of secularization had brought on an increase in the slaughter of cattle though nowhere in the amount so often cited. At their height all of the missions never had more than 200,000 head on the ranges. Over a period of 20 years the missions had been drained of a million dollars in cash and goods to support the military, and the indolent, and now, facing ruin, the herds of cattle were reduced, the hides and tallow sold, and the carcasses left to bleach on the dry hills. Juan Bandini later said that 2000 cattle

Map of La Playa showing location of the four big hide houses, shacks.

were killed in one day at a single mission, but did not identify the mission, and José Antonio Estudillo was to add that after a time nothing but hides were saved. Pío Pico in his historical notes said that in 1833 he was working at Rancho San José, which belonged to Mission San Luis Rey, and was slaughtering cattle for half shares with the mission. The mission in 1832 had 27,500 cattle.

"My contract with the fathers had no limit. I was to kill as many head of cattle as I could but to turn over half the hides. I brought 10 cowboys and 30 Indians on foot from the Missions of San Luis Rey and San Diego, with more than 300 horses. I first slaughtered 2500 head at the Coyote Rancho. Then I moved to that of San José Rancho and killed about the same number."

Thus 5000 were killed in one period at San Luis Rey and perhaps another 5000 at San Gabriel. There are no records of any other large scale slaughtering for hides.

The territorial assembly had moved to prevent any indiscriminate cutting down of herds, and in reply to their warning, Fr. Vicente Pascual Oliva at San Luis Rey reported that only old, wild and unbranded cattle were being killed, out of the necessity for clothing, and to settle the debts of the mission with the Ameri-

THIS IS ANOTHER OF THE SKETCHES of California life drawn by an officer of the Royal Navy, William Smyth. It was called the California mode of catching cattle. It also reveals many details of the dress of the times.

can traders, as he was bound and pledged to the amount of $16,000 and had no other way to raise money except through the sale of hides. The contractors often killed more than they reported to the missions and slipped the hides off for private sale.

The slaughter of stock was not new to California, however. Wild horses especially often ravaged the grasslands and their numbers had to be cut down by drastic measures, or the cattle and sheep would starve. In 1808 more than 7200 horses were killed in the Santa Barbara area and at Monterey in 1810, 3200 were slaughtered. Horses were shipped directly from San Diego to the Hawaiian Islands, and sometimes to Baja California, and stories persist that in times of drought, in the days of the great ranchos, wild horses were rounded up and driven over the cliffs of Torrey Pines. One report has it that several hundred cattle once were killed near San Francisco merely for hides in which to pack bread sold to the Russians.

All this left Dana with some unhappy impressions of Californians. As had so many others who visited these shores, he found the men thriftless, proud and extravagant, the women possessing a good deal of beauty but little education and protected by the ready weapons of fathers and brothers, but "the very men who would lay down their lives to avenge the dishonor of their own family would risk the same lives to complete the dishonour of another." Murders committed by white settlers were seldom punished; in case of crimes of Indians, justice, or rather vengeance, was swift. A white man who had run away with another's wife, and then murdered him to boot, was pointed out to Dana on the streets of San Diego; but an Indian who had killed another in hot blood, over the fatal stabbing of a horse he was riding, was taken out and shot. Dana's eyes could not fail to see the sadness brought on the country by secularization of the missions:

"Ever since the independence of Mexico, the missions had been going down; until at last, a law was passed, stripping them of all their possessions, and confining the priests to their spiritual duties, at the same time declaring all the Indians free and independent *Rancheros*. The change in the condition of the Indians was, as may be supposed, only nominal; they are virtually serfs, as much as they ever were. But in the missions the change was complete. The priests have now no power, except in their religious character, and the great possessions of the missions are given over to be preyed upon by the harpies of the civil power, who are sent there in the capacity of *administradores*, to settle up the concerns; and who usually end, in a few years, by making themselves fortunes, and leaving their stewardships worse than they found them.

"The dynasty of the priests was much more acceptable to the people of the country, and, indeed, to every one concerned with the country, by trade or otherwise, than that of the *administradores*. The priests were connected permanently to one mission, and felt the necessity of keeping up its credit. Accordingly the debts of the missions were regularly paid, and the people were, in the main, well treated, and attached to those who had spent their whole lives among them. But the *administradores* are strangers sent from Mexico, having no interest in the country, not identified in any way with their charge, and, for the most part, men of desperate fortunes — broken-down politicians and soldiers — whose only object is to retrieve their condition in as short a time as possible. The change had been made but a few years before our arrival upon the coast, yet, in that short time, the trade was much diminished, credit impaired, and the venerable missions were going rapidly to decay."

Dana was in error in believing the administrators had been sent up from Mexico; the Californians had succeeded in taking things over themselves, and he did not fully understand the historical Spanish role of the frontier missions. To an idealistic youth from Boston, whose ancestor had signed the Declaration of Independence, on principle and justice, the California revolutions were selfish and petty affairs.

"They are got up by men at the foot of the ladder . . . the only object, of course, is the loaves and fishes; and instead of caucusing, paragraphing, libelling, feasting, promising, and lying, they take muskets and bayonets, and, seizing upon the presidio and custom-house, divide the spoils, and declare a new dynasty. As for justice they know little but will and fear."

The situation hardly could have been otherwise, however. San Diego was a long way from Mexico City, and Mexico was in the agony of her own search for stability and freedom.

From Dana we also get a passing glimpse of Juan Bandini, now in reduced circumstances as a result of his troubles at San Diego. The *Alert* took him from Monterey to Santa Barabara, as a non-

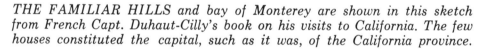

THE FAMILIAR HILLS and bay of Monterey are shown in this sketch from French Capt. Duhaut-Cilly's book on his visits to California. The few houses constituted the capital, such as it was, of the California province.

paying passenger, and to Dana he was a typical example of the decadent aristocrat of California, indolent and poor but proud:

"He had a slight and elegant figure, moved gracefully, danced and waltzed beautifully, spoke good Castilian, with a pleasant and refined voice and accent, and had throughout the bearing of a man of birth and figure. Yet here he was, with his passage given him, for he had no means of paying for it, and living on the charity of our agent. He was polite to every one, spoke to the sailors, and gave four reals — I dare say the last he had in his pocket — to the steward who waited upon him."

It was all hard for Dana to understand.

"Such are the people who inhabit a country embracing four or five hundred miles of sea-coast, with several good harbours, with fine forests in the north; the waters filled with fish, and the plains covered with thousands of herds of cattle; blessed with a climate, than which there can be no better in the world; free from all manner of diseases, whether epidemic or endemic; and with a soil in which corn yields from seventy to eighty-fold. In the hands of an enterprising people, what a country this might be! we are ready to say. Yet how long would a people remain so, in such a country? The Americans (as those from the United States are called) and Englishmen who are fast filling up the principal towns, and getting the trade into their hands, are indeed more industrious and effective than the Mexicans; yet their children are brought up Mexicans in most respects, and if the 'California fever' spares the first generation, it is likely to attack the second."

The "California fever" was laziness, a native disease which even to this day is hard to resist.

The tip of Point Loma disappeared below the horizon as the *Alert's* sails filled with the prevailing wind on the long run down the coast. In the south, it ran into a series of violent storms and was almost crushed by the weight of ice that formed on her decks, spars and lines. One evening, Dana wrote, "The captain called all hands aft, and told them that not a man was to leave the deck that night; that the ship was in the greatest danger, any cake of ice might knock a hole in her, or she might run on an island and go to pieces. No one could tell whether she would be a ship the next morning." That night of terror passed, and so did the others. At last the *Alert* rounded the Cape and once again broke into tropical waters.

Slipping through warm waters and soft air was a thing of serene beauty to Dana. Out on the end of the flying jib-boom he could look back on the ship as a separate vessel "and there rose up from the water, supported only by the small black hull, a pyramid of canvas, spreading out far beyond the hull, and towering up almost, as it seemed in the indistinct night air, to the clouds. The sea was as gentle as an inland lake; the light trade wind was gently and steadily breathing from astern; the dark blue sky was studded with the tropical stars, there was no sound but the rippling of the water under the stem; and the sails were spread out wide and high . . . " An old withered seaman, who had gone out on the flying jib-boom with him, and whom Dana had almost forgotten was there, looked at the marble sails and said almost to himself, "How quietly they do their work."

The sea has meant so much to San Diego throughout the centuries, and across its vast emptiness have come the men of history, the Cabrillos, the Vizcaínos, the Vilas, the Vancouvers, the Winships, the Shalers, the Bradshaws, the Robinsons and the Danas. And the ships that came and went shaped the destiny of a city.

CHAPTER FIFTEEN

THE TOLL OF TIME

The missionary story on the Pacific Coast was over. The era that began with the Jesuits in Lower California and closed with the Franciscans in Upper California, had lasted 150 years. The missions themselves were not yet dead, but their day was over. Some of the Indians who had fled, slowly returned to the security they had learned to need.

Five years after secularization of the missions, M. Duflot de Mofras, an attaché of the French Legation to Mexico, visited both Californias, at the order of his government. He followed the route of the padres, from Tepic to San Blas, and wrote that "the ancient Spanish route, known as El Camino Real — the King's Highway — which traverses the lowlands, has almost entirely disappeared." At San Blas, the port city that had been built to supply San Diego and Monterey, and to help secure California for the Spaniards, he found that, "the supply shop, the hospital, the docks, and the arsenal are in ruins. Only the debris of the fine buildings erected during the Spanish regime remain. Not a battery, not a soldier, not a piece of wood, not a work at the port where the Spanish employed 3000 men, and where her frigates were constructed, is visible."

Across the Gulf of California, or the Sea of Cortés, he visited Loreto and its mission, from where Fr. Junípero Serra had started

GAUNT, BROKEN WALLS are all that are left of Mission San Miguel, 55 miles below San Diego just off the highway to Ensenada. For many years it was under protection of the San Diego Presidio but in time abandoned.

on the long march to San Diego more than 70 years before. He found 200 inhabitants.

"At one time this mission was the capital of Lower California but it has fallen into decay, and its prestige transferred to the Real de San Antonio." (This was a settlement below La Paz.) "The presidio, mission and the church are now slowly crumbling away, although the buildings were . . . designed by the Jesuit Fathers to afford shelter, in face of attack to the colonists. The presidio has a small esplanade defended by two bronze swivel guns; guns whose breeches are now wide open and whose gun carriages are missing."

The church, he wrote, still had its paintings and silver cases, and the doors were never closed.

"During the Spanish regime a messenger left Guaymas once a month, crossed the gulf in a small boat and landed at Loreto. From there the letters were carried overland to Monterey. This service has been discontinued for some-time and frequently an entire year passes without news from California."

At La Paz, where once 800 divers were employed in the pearl fishing industry, he said it was now difficult to find Indians for the task "since each season several of the poor creatures are devoured by sharks and manta rays, a kind of a giant skate."

De Mofras spent a week or 10 days in San Diego in January of 1842, and surveyed conditions on Presidio Hill and in the village below it.

"At San Diego the fort and the presidio are uninhabited: on one side of the fort under the crumbling walls a few pieces of bronze cannon lie partially buried; at the pueblo, a few soldiers in charge of an officer reside. Only ships of 400 tons drawing less than 20 feet of water are allowed to enter the port of San Diego. Certain areas are shallow, and some parts are so covered with sand

THIS PICTURE BY VISCHER of 1874 from the entrance of Mission Valley shows ruins of presidio. The hill was cut away to dike river. Officials had warned the presidio was exposed to weather and could not last.

banks that ships can easily run aground on the silt that the tiny San Diego River brings down from the mountains in the rainy season.

"Within the last few years the river, through the negligence of the inhabitants, has returned to its former channel and now empties into the waters of San Diego Harbor. The fort (Fort Guijarros) and neighboring buildings are deserted and in ruins; fragments of six or eight bronze cannon may be seen embedded in the sand."

The temperamental San Diego River had changed its course a number of times. In the Autumn of 1821 a flood caused some damage to homes and gardens of Old Town and banked up sand along the old channel into San Diego Bay and the waters were turned into False or Mission Bay. Juan Bandini records that the forces of nature swung the river back into San Diego Bay in 1825. Pío Pico wrote that this occurred in 1828. Duhaut-Cilly found the river flowing into False Bay in 1827. Over the centuries the river wandered back and forth over the bed of silt it had built between San Diego and Point Loma, and no attempts to control it were made until after the American occupation.

The bells of San Blas are silent in this old church by the sea.

A dozen English and American sailors from hide ships trading along the coast comprised the population at La Playa while the village of San Diego itself, de Mofras wrote, had only about 20 houses. In the hands of another power, he concluded, "the port of San Diego would have acquired an importance very quickly; it would have joined the two Californias and Sonora, and could have become the center of a numerous population and of an extensive commerce."

The mission, which like all of them, was supposed to have become a thriving Indian pueblo, and former mission properties presented the grim picture that had been foreseen by those who were opposed to a premature secularization. In turn, these people perhaps could not envision the new California that soon was to arise from the disorder and neglect.

"Today the buildings and church are in ruins . . . in front of the buildings stands a superb grove of olives; nearby stretch flourishing vineyards that are capable of furnishing the best wine in California. Because of its favorable climate, at San Diego all European fruit trees even palms and oranges, attain extraordinary size. In its prime this mission supported 2500 Indians, 14,000 cattle, 1500 horses and 3200 sheep.

"These ranchos now belong to private individuals who have appropriated them, and even all cattle owned by the mission have disappeared. The mission buildings are occupied by a few Indians, a white family, and Rev. Fr. Vicente Oliva, a Spaniard from Aragón who is already well-advanced in years. This father was able to save from pillage only the rancho called Santa Isabel that lies . . . toward the mountains and here 500 Indians have congregated under the direction of their alcaldes and a majordomo. These poor wretches own a few pair of work oxen, and harvest barely enough grain for their own support."

At San Luis Rey, de Mofras found conditions a little better, though he accepted as fact some of the extravagant figures as to livestock the mission possessed at its height, as stories about the "King of the Missions" and its wealth were growing with the years. He wrote that there were still about 600 Indians, about 2000 cattle, 400 horses and 4000 sheep.

"Many of the fine vineyards have recently been abandoned. The parish of San Luis Rey is in charge of the Rev. A. Francisco González de Ibarra, a Spaniard no longer in his prime, who was able to save something from the wreckage of the mission and assemble 400 Indians at Rancho Las Flores, where they live with a white family. The fathers at Mission San Luis Rey are daily subjected to the most humiliating situations. Fr. González, for example, is obliged to sit at the administrator's table and to listen to insults of the same cowboys and majordomos who, a few years ago, would have deemed it an honor to serve the fathers in the capacity of servants."

The leading ranchos of the mission, Las Flores, San Antonio de Pala, San Jacinto, Santa Margarita, Agua Caliente, San Onofre, San José and Temécula, had nearly all been plundered.

"At San Luis Rey a tablet was seen that represented Fr. Peyri surrounded by several Indian children. When the Indians stop before this portrait they offer up the same prayers that are said before the images of saints that

THE KING OF THE MISSIONS, San Luis Rey, fared better than the San Diego Mission. It had thick walls, tile pilars, and its height thwarted theft of its roof tiles and saved the church interior from the ravages of the weather.

adorn the church. They have not abandoned the hope of having the good father return to this mission."

After a decade or more of mismanagement by majordomos and administrators, the official end of Mission San Diego de Alcalá came on June 8, 1846. Unable even to support a parish priest, the mission and more than 58,000 acres of land embracing much of San Diego, lying just east of the old Pueblo lands, and downtown area, and extending from National City to Clairemont, and inland to the edge of the El Cajon Valley, were granted to Don Santiago Argüello by Gov. Pío Pico. The deed of sale reads as follows:

"Being previously authorized by the Departmental Assembly to alleviate the missions, in order to pay their debts and to avoid their total ruin: and knowing that Don Santiago Argüello has rendered the government important services at all times, and has also given aid when asked, for the preservation of the legitimate government and the security of the Department, without having received any indemnification: and whereas, this gentleman, has, for his own personal benefit and that of his numerous family, asked to purchase the Mission of San Diego, with all the lands and property belonging to it, both in town and country, he paying fully and religiously the debts of said mission, which may be established by the reports of the Committee of Missions, binding himself to provide for the support of the priests located at said mission, and of Divine Worship. In view of all which I have made real sale and perpetual alienation of it forever, to Don Santiago Argüello, according to, and in conformance with, what has been agreed upon, with all the appurtenances found and known at the time as belonging to it, whether consisting of lands, buildings, improved real estate, or cattle."

It didn't cost him anything.

Another three years passed and we have a report this time from an American, John Russell Bartlett, a governmental representative, who wrote a "Personal Narrative of Explorations and Incidents," and visited San Luis Rey Mission in 1852:

"An old man presented himself in the dress of a Mexican officer — a blue coat with red facings trimmed with gold lace, and a high military cap with a feather.

"On enquiring as to the state of things when the padres were here, the old man heaved a deep sigh. He said his tribe was large and his people all happy, when the good fathers were here to protect them. That they cultivated the soil, assisted in rearing large herds of cattle; were taught to be blacksmiths and carpenters, as well as other trades, that they had plenty to eat and were happy. He remembered when 3000 of his tribe were settled in the valley, dependent on or connected with the mission. Now he said they were scattered about, he knew not where, without a home or protectors, and were in a miserable, starving condition. A few hundred alone remained in some villages up the valley, a few miles from the mission."

Events had overwhelmed the mission Indians, but the story was not peculiar to California. It had been written many times when continents had been conquered and settled by more advanced peoples. In San Diego County the majority of Indians, for whom

After San Diego Mission died, Ramona in famed novel found bells hanging in open to call last of faithful to worship in Old Town.

Graveyard at San Luis Rey has memories of men who made history.

Christianity had been a tenuous attachment, or who had held themselves aloof in the mountains and deserts, quickly reverted to a savage state, joining in pagan bands and for a time engaging in sporadic raiding and killing. Many whites were to lose their lives in final Indian uprisings.

Twenty-four years after Richard Henry Dana, Jr. had cured hides at La Playa, he returned to San Diego as a passenger on the ship *Golden Gate*. When she had dropped anchor, Dana avoided the other passengers and was quietly pulled ashore in a boat and left to himself.

"The past was real. The present, all about me, was unreal, unnatural, repellent. I saw the big ships lying in the stream, the *Alert*, *California*, *Rosa*, with her Italians; then the handsome *Ayacucho*, my favorite; the poor dear old *Pilgrim*, the home of hardship and helplessness; the boats passing to and fro; the cries of the sailors at the capstan or falls; the peopled beach; the large hide-houses, with their gangs of men; and the Kanakas interspersed everywhere. All, all were gone! not a vestige to mark where one hide-house stood. The oven, too, was gone, I searched for its site, and found, where I thought it should be, a few broken bricks and bits of mortar. I alone was left of all, and how strangely was I here! What changes to me! Where were they all? Why should I care for them—poor Kanakas and sailors, the refuse of civilization, the outlaws and beachcombers of the Pacific? Time and death seemed to transfigure them. Doubtless nearly all were dead; but how had they died, and where! In hospitals, in fever climes, in dens of vice, or falling from the mast, or dropping exhausted from the wreck . . ."

He went up to Old Town, where he so long before had first tested his competence in the hazards of a seaman's life ashore in a strange land.

"The little town of San Diego has undergone no change whatever that I can see. It certainly has not grown. It is still, like Santa Barbara, a Mexican town. The four principal houses of the *gente de razón* — of the Bandinis, Estudillos, Argüellos, and Picos — are the chief houses now; but all the gentlemen — and their families, too, I believe are gone. The big vulgar shop-keeper and trader, Fitch, is long since dead; Tom Wrightington, who kept the rival *pulpería*, fell from his horse when drunk, and was found nearly eaten up by coyotes; and I can scarce find a person whom I remember. I went into a familiar one-story adobe house, with its piazza and earthen floor, inhabited by a respectable lower-class family by the name of Machado, and inquired if any of the family remained, when a bright-eyed middle-aged woman recognized me, for she had heard I was on board the steamer, and told me she had married a shipmate of mine, Jack Stuart, who went out as second mate the next voyage, but left the ship and married and settled here. She said he wished very much to see me. In a few minutes he came in, and his sincere pleasure in meeting me was extremely grateful. We talked over old times as long as I could afford to. I was glad to hear that he was sober and doing well. Doña Tomasa Pico I found and talked with. She was the only person of the old upper class that remained on the spot, if I rightly recollect.

"I must complete my acts of pious remembrance, so I take a horse and make a run out to the old mission, where Ben Stimson and I went the first liberty-day we had after we left Boston. All has gone to decay. The buildings are un-

TIME AND WEATHER virtually destroyed the San Diego Mission. Hardly anything is left of the original structures. The old face of the church lasted longest. No kind hands were left to stay the inexorable progress of sad decay.

used and ruinous, and the large gardens show now only wild cactuses, willows, and a few olive trees. A fast run brings me back in time to take leave of the few I knew and who knew me, and to reach the steamer before she sails. A last look — yes, last for life — to the beach, the hills, the low point, the distant town, as we round Point Loma, and the first beams of the lighthouse strike out towards the setting sun."

At San Luis Rey, San Juan Capistrano and San Gabriel Missions, where restoration work has been extensive, much of the original buildings remain. The churches, the living quarters, the work shops, wine rooms and kitchens — all are quiet and cool and suggestive of an era when the only pressure of life were those of the bell and the sundial. In the yards can be seen the old kilns, the vats and the paved areas used in curing and tanning hides and making tallow for soap and candles.

Humps of adobe are all that remain of little Las Flores Mission.

At Pala, Mission San Antonio de Pala, almost completely restored, serves the Indians as it has done continuously since its founding in 1816. The Las Flores *asistencia* of Mission San Luis Rey, deep in what is now Camp Pendleton, and Mission San Miguel, below the border, are washing back into the ground. A chapel at Santa Ysabel on the site of the old *asistencia* of Mission San Diego, still brings the word to the Indians who come from nearby reservations.

Gone, too, is any trace of a new presidio that had been started on Point Loma and which Alfred Robinson had noted while riding from La Playa to Old Town. The site has never been found but it probably was in the Loma Portal area, on the lee of the point for protection from wind and rain and above an old channel of the San Diego River. The river never came back that way, and the presidio, with no nearby source of water, was abandoned while still in an unfinished state.

Very little is left at the San Diego Mission. The church has been rebuilt and serves as a parish church. Only one original building still stands, just east of the church. Its floor sits a few feet below the surface of the ground. It is narrow and has a fireplace. It may have been the fathers' dining room. To the north across a small gully and near the top of the hillside overlooking the San Diego River, are evidences of four kilns, now almost completely filled with dirt and rubbish. The past lives mostly in the bell tower. There are five bells. In the middle row is one enscribed *"Santa Maria Amadalena año de* 1738 X." This is believed to be one of the original bells brought to California by Fr. Junípero Serra. It weighs 63 pounds. Another bell is the *"Mater Dolorosa,"* or Mother of Sorrows. It was cast in New Spain in 1796. The bells again call the faithful to worship in Mission Valley.

In the historic gardens of the mission at San Gabriel there is an old sundial made of heavy bronze set on a pillar of tile. Its Latin motto reads: "Every Hour Wounds — the Last One Kills."

1769 Founding of San Diego Mission and beginning of Western civilization on West Coast.

1769 Indian uprising against San Diego Mission.

1770 Founding of Presidio and Mission at Monterey.

1773 Fr. Junípero Serra arrives in Mexico to obtain permission to run missionary activities without interference of presidio.

1773 The Boston "Tea Party."

1774 San Diego military camp raised to Royal Presidio.

1774 San Diego Mission removed from presidio to present site.

1774 Juan Bautista de Anza leads overland expedition from Mexico to California.

1775 Indian uprising at San Diego Mission. Martyrdom of Fr. Luis Jayme; mission destroyed.

1776 Yuma Indians massacre Spanish settlers along the Colorado River.

1776 Juan Bautista de Anza leads a colonizing expedition to San Francisco.

1776 The Thirteen Colonies declare their independence of Great Britain.

1776 San Diego Mission re-established.

1777 Founding of California's first pueblo, San José de Guadalupe.

1778 James Cook, an English navigator, discovers the Hawaiian Islands; visits the northern California Coast.

1779 Gov. Felipe de Neve issues Reglamento on governing and colonizing of California.

1781 Founding of the Pueblo de Nuestra Señora la Reina de los Angeles.

1782 Pedro Fages opens new route from Sonora directly to San Diego over Cuyamaca Mountains.

1783 Fr. Junípero Serra visits San Diego Mission for the last time.

1784 Death of Fr. Junípero Serra, at Mission San Carlos. Fr. Francisco Palóu becomes Father President of the California missions.

1784 Granting of first private ranchos in California by Gov. Pedro Fages.

1785 Fr. Fermín de Lasuén becomes Father President of the California missions.

1786 The French navigator, La Pérouse, visits California.

1787 Adoption of the Constitution of the United States of America.

1792 Capt. Robert Gray, an American ship captain, discovers the Columbia River.

1793 George Vancouver arrives on *Discovery* at San Diego Harbor.

1795 Fort projected on Ballast Point (Point Guijarros).

1796 Fortifications completed at San Diego Presidio.

1796 Arrival of the *Otter* at Monterey marks the opening of the historic New England–California trade.

1798 Founding of the San Luis Rey Mission.

1799 English sloop-of-war, *Mercedes,* arrives at San Diego.

1800 First American ship, *Betsy,* arrives at San Diego.

1803 The Louisiana Purchase.

1803 The Spanish battery on Fort Guijarros fires on American ship, the *Lelia Byrd.*

1805 The Lewis and Clark Expedition reaches the mouth of the Columbia River.

1806 Zebulon R. Pike's Expedition to the Rocky Mountains.

1806 Capt. O'Cain on the *Eclipse* threatens to attack San Diego.

1808 Construction of new San Diego Mission church structure begins.

1810 Mexican War of Independence.

1812 Opening of the War of 1812 between the United States and Great Britain.

1812 Founding of the Russian colony at Fort Ross, Bodega Bay.

1813 San Diego Mission church completed; aqueduct system under construction.

1813 Soldiers arrested in plot to revolt and seize post at San Diego.

1818 Hippolyte de Bouchard raids the California Coast.

1821 Mexico wins independence from Spain and establishes a short-lived empire under Agustín de Iturbide.

1822 The *Sachem* begins hide trade between Boston and San Diego.

1822 San Diego officially under Mexican rule.

1823 William P. Hartnell arrives in San Diego aboard the *John Begg.*

1823 Founding of the last of the California missions, San Francisco de Solano, at Sonoma.

1823 First of private ranchos granted in San Diego County.

1824 Colonization Law passed by Mexican Congress.

1825 Gov. José María Echeandía establishes rule at San Diego.

1825 Population begins to move downhill from San Diego Presidio to Old Town.

1826 Jedediah S. Smith arrives in San Diego, opening a route from Salt Lake to Southern California.

1826 Death of Thomas Jefferson and John Adams.

1826 San Diego Presidio soldiers skirmish with Indians, killing 28.

1827 French Capt. Duhaut-Cilly visits San Diego.

1827 Deputies meet in San Diego to organize territorial assembly.

1828 American ship, *Franklin,* forced to flee San Diego under fire.

1828 Trapper James O. Pattie imprisoned in San Diego.

1829 Alfred Robinson arrives at San Diego, on *Brookline.*

1829 First hide house built in San Diego by carpenters of trading ship, *Brookline.*

1829 Series of revolutions begin in California.

1829 Capt. Henry D. Fitch elopes with Spanish girl from San Diego

1832 Fr. Antonio Peyri flees from California via San Diego.

1833 Secularization Act passed by Mexican Congress. Beginning of end of the mission system and opening of the era of the ranchos.

1835 Joaquín Ortega becomes administrator of San Diego Mission; San Diego made a Pueblo.

1835 Richard Henry Dana, Jr., arrives at San Diego aboard the *Pilgrim.*

LIST OF SPANISH AND MEXICAN MILITARY COMMANDANTS AT SAN DIEGO, 1769-1840

Lt. Pedro Fages
Military commandant of California; July, 1770, to May, 1774.

Lt. José Francisco Ortega
From July, 1771; made lieutenant and put in formal charge, 1773; continued until 1781.

Lt. José de Zúñiga
September 8, 1781, to October 19, 1793.

Lt. Antonio Grajera
October 19, 1793, to August 23, 1799.

Lt. José Font
Temporary commandant of military post, ranking Rodríguez, August 23, 1799, to 1803.

Lt. Manuel Rodríguez
Acting commandant of the company from August 23, 1799, until 1803, when he became commandant of the post and so continued until late in 1806.

Lt. Francisco María Ruiz
Acting commandant from late in 1806 until 1807.

Lt. José de la Guerra y Noriega
For a short time in 1806-1807.

Capt. José Raimundo Carrillo
From late in 1807 until 1809.

Lt. Francisco María Ruiz
Lieutenant and acting commandant from 1809 until 1820.

Capt. Ignacio del Corral
Nominally commandant from 1810 to 1820, but never came to California.

Lt. José María Estudillo
October 23, 1820, to September, 1821.

Capt. Francisco María Ruiz
September, 1821, to 1827, when he retired at age of 73.

Lt. José María Estudillo
From early in 1827 to April 8, 1830.

Lt. Santiago Argüello
From April 8, 1830, to 1835.

Capt. Agustín V. Zamorano
From 1835 to 1840; was in San Diego only during 1837-1838 and never assumed command of the company.

Capt. Pablo de la Portilla *was nominally commandant of the post by seniority of rank, whenever present, from 1835 until he left California in 1838.*

LIST OF RESIDENT FATHERS WHO OFFICIATED
AT SAN DIEGO MISSION

Fr. Junípero Serra
July 1, 1769–April 16, 1770

Fr. Fernando Parrón
April 29, 1769–April, 1771

Fr. Juan Vizcaíno
April 11, 1769–Feb. 11, 1770

Fr. Francisco Gómez
April 11, 1769–March, 1771

Fr. Juan Crespí
May 14, 1769–July 14, 1769;
Jan. 24, 1770–left few
months later

Fr. Francisco Dumetz
March 12, 1771–Sept., 1772

Fr. Luis Jayme
July, 1771–Nov. 4, 1775

Fr. Juan Crespí
May, 1772–Sept., 1772

Fr. Tomás de la Peña
May, 1772–Sept., 1773

Fr. Gregorio Amurrió
Aug. 30, 1773–May, 1774

Fr. Vicente Fuster
Aug. 30, 1773–July 27, 1777

Fr. Pablo Mugártegui
March 13, 1774–Sept., 1774

Fr. Fermín Francisco de Lasuén
Nov. 10, 1775–Sept. 5, 1785

Fr. Juan Figuer
Aug. 31, 1777–Dec. 18, 1784

Fr. Juan Antonio García Riobó
Sept. 28, 1785–Nov. 7, 1786

Fr. Juan Mariner
Dec. 5, 1785–Jan. 29, 1800

Fr. Hilario Torrent
Nov. 11, 1786–Sept. 27, 1798

Fr. Pedro Esteban
Nov. 14, 1795–July 1, 1797

Fr. José Panella
June 2, 1797–Jan. 20, 1803

Fr. José Barona
Aug. 4, 1798–Jan. 24, 1811

Fr. Mariano Payeras
Dec. 11, 1803–Sept. 30, 1804

Fr. José Bernardo Sánchez
Oct., 1804–May 16, 1820

Fr. Pedro Panto
Jan., 1811–July 1, 1812

Fr. Fernando Martín
July 6, 1812–Oct. 19, 1838

Fr. Vicente Pascual Oliva
June 28, 1820–Jan., 1832

Fr. Antonio Menéndez (at Presidio)
March 31, 1824–Oct. 16, 1829

Fr. Buenaventura Fortuni
Sept. 22, 1833–July 27, 1834

Fr. Vicente Pascual Oliva
Aug. 1834–June 14, 1846

Fr. J. Chrisostom Holbein
July, 1849–Sept., 1854

Fr. Pedro Bagaria
1855–1857

Fr. John Molinier
1858–1863

Fr. Antonio Ubach
1866–April 27, 1907

LOCAL OFFICIALS

The following, prominent in San Diego history, served in the federal congress or the provisional legislature, or *diputación,* between 1822 and 1834:

Diputados to Congress

1827 – Pablo de Solá.

1827 – Capt. José de la Guerra y Noriega; Gervasio Argüello, substitute.

1828 – Gervasio Argüello.

1829 – Lt. José Joaquín Maitorena; Santiago Argüello, substitute.

1830 – Carlos A. Carrillo; Juan Bandini, substitute.

1833 – Juan Bandini; José Antonio Carrillo, substitute.

1833 – Juan Bandini (re-elected).

1834 – José Antonio Carrillo; Mariano G. Vallejo, substitute.

Partido Electores

1822 – Ignacio López.

1827 – Agustín Zamorano.

Vocales, Diputacion

1822 – Francisco Castro.

1827 – Juan Bandini.

1830 – Juan María Osuna; Santiago Argüello, substitute.

1833 – José Antonio Carrillo, José Antonio Estudillo, Pío Pico.

1834 – José Antonio Carrillo, José María Estudillo.

Comisario Subalterno

1825 – Domingo Carrillo
1828 – Juan Bandini

Receptor of Customs

1833 – Santiago Argüello
1834 – Martín S. Cabello; Juan Bandini

CALIFORNIA MISSIONS AND DATES OF FOUNDINGS

San Diego de Alcalá	July 16, 1769	La Purísima Concepción	Dec. 8, 1787
San Carlos Borromeo de Carmelo (Carmel)	June 3, 1770	Santa Cruz	Aug. 28, 1791
		Nuestra Señora de la Soledad	Oct. 9, 1791
San Antonio de Padua	July 14, 1771	San José de Guadalupe	June 11, 1797
San Gabriel Arcángel	Sept. 8, 1771	San Juan Bautista	June 24, 1797
San Luis Obispo de Tolosa	Sept.1, 1772	San Miguel Arcángel	July 25, 1797
San Francisco de Asís (Dolores)	Oct. 9, 1776	San Fernando Rey de España	Sept. 8, 1797
San Juan Capistrano	Nov. 1, 1776	San Luis Rey de Francia	June 13, 1798
Santa Clara de Asís	Jan. 12, 1777	Santa Inés	Sept. 17, 1804
San Buenaventura (Ventura)	Mar. 31, 1782	San Rafael Arcángel	Dec. 14, 1817
Santa Bárbara	Dec. 4, 1786	San Francisco de Solano (Sonoma)	July 4, 1823

CIVIL AND MILITARY GOVERNORS OF CALIFORNIA 1769-1835

SPANISH RULE

1769-1770
Gaspar de Portolá, Military Commander

1770-1774
Pedro Fages, Military Commander

1774-1777
Fernando Rivera y Moncada, Military Commander

1777-1782
Felipe de Neve, First Civil Governor

1782-1791
Pedro Fages

1791-1792
José Antonio Roméu

1792-1794
José Joaquín de Arrillaga, ad interim

1794-1800
Diego de Borica

1800-1814
José Joaquín de Arrillaga (ad interim 1800-1804)

1814-1815
José Darío Argüello, ad interim

1815-1822
Pablo Vicente de Solá

MEXICAN RULE

1822-1825
Luis Antonio Argüello, ad interim

1825-1830
José María de Echeandía

1830-1831
Manuel Victoria

1831-1833
Interregnum
    Pío Pico, January to February, 1832
    J. M. de Echeandía, south of San Fernando, to 1833
    Agustín V. Zamorano, north of San Fernando, to 1833

1833-1835
José Figueroa

1835-1836
José Castro, ad interim to January, 1836

STATE OF THE MISSIONS ON DECEMBER 31, 1832

SAN DIEGO

Baptisms, 6552; marriages, 1794; deaths, 4322; neophytes, 1455; cattle, 4500; sheep, 13,250; horses, 220.

SAN LUIS REY

Baptisms, 5399; marriages, 1335; deaths, 2718 neophytes, 2788; cattle, 27,500; sheep, 26,100; horses, 1950.

SAN JUAN CAPISTRANO

Baptisms, 4340; marriages, 1153; deaths, 3126; neophytes, 900; cattle, 10,900; sheep, 4800; horses, 450.

SAN GABRIEL

Baptisms, 7825; marriages, 1916; deaths, 5670; neophytes, 1320; cattle, 16,500; sheep, 8500; horses, 1200.

SAN FERNANDO

Baptisms, 2784; marriages, 827; deaths, 1983; neophytes, 782; cattle, 7000; sheep, 1000; horses, 1000.

SAN BUENAVENTURA

Baptisms, 3875; marriages,1097; deaths, 3150; neophytes, 668; cattle, 4050; sheep, 3000; horses, 200.

SANTA BARBARA

Baptisms, 5556; marriages, 1486; deaths, 3936; neophytes, 628; cattle, 1800; sheep, 3200; horses, 480.

SANTA INES

Baptisms, 1348; marriages, 400; deaths, 1227; neophytes, 360; cattle, 7200; sheep, 2100; horses, 390.

PURISIMA CONCEPCION

Baptisms, 3255; marriages, 1029; deaths, 2609; neophytes, 372; cattle, 9200; sheep, 3500; horses, 1000.

SAN LUIS OBISPO

Baptisms, 2644; marriages, 763; deaths, 2268; neophytes, 231; cattle, 2500; sheep, 5422; horses, 700

SAN MIGUEL

Baptisms, 2471; marriages, 764; deaths, 1868; neophytes, 658; cattle, 3710; sheep, 8282; horses, 700.

SAN ANTONIO

Baptisms, 4419; marriages, 1142; deaths, 3617; neophytes, 640; cattle, 6000; sheep, 10,500; horses,774.

N. SRA DE LA SOLEDAD

Baptisms, 2131; marriages, 648; deaths, 1705; neophytes, 339; cattle, 6000; sheep, 6200; horses, 252.

SAN CARLOS

Baptisms, 3827; marriages, 1032; deaths, 2837; neophytes, 185; cattle, 2100; sheep, 3300; horses, 410.

SAN JUAN BAUTISTA

Baptisms, 4016; marriages, 1003; deaths, 2854; neophytes, 916; cattle, 6000; sheep, 6004; horses, 296.

SANTA CRUZ

Baptisms, 2439; marriages, 827; deaths, 1972; neophytes, 284; cattle, 3600; sheep, 5211; horses, 400.

SANTA CLARA

Baptisms, 8536; marriages, 2498; deaths, 6809; neophytes, 1125; cattle, 10,000; sheep, 9500; horses, 730.

SAN JOSE

Baptisms, 6673; marriages, 1990; deaths, 4800; neophytes, 1800; cattle, 12,000; sheep, 11,000; horses, 1100.

SAN FRANCISCO DE ASIS

Baptisms, 6898; marriages, 2043; deaths, 5166; neophytes, 204; cattle, 5000; sheep, 3500; horses, 1000.

SAN RAFAEL

Baptisms, 1821; marriages, 519; deaths, 652; neophytes, 300; cattle, 2120; sheep, 3000; horses, 370.

SAN FRANCISCO SOLANO

Baptisms, 1008; marriages, 263; deaths, 500; neophytes, 996; cattle, 3500; sheep, 600; horses, 900.

TOTAL BAPTISMS, 87,787; MARRIAGES, 24,529; DEATHS, 63,789; NEOPHYTES, 16,951; CATTLE, 151,180; SHEEP, 137,971; HORSES, 14,522.

VESSELS TOUCHING AT SAN DIEGO FROM 1769-1835

The following ships are ones which are known to have visited the coast, from information in ships' logs, in ship registers, or Spanish and Mexican customs' reports. Many other "phantom" ships plied the coast in illegal trading and left no records of their operations.

1769-1799
San Antonio (El Príncipe), and *San Carlos,* packet-boats; *Princesa, Favorita, Aranzazú, Concepción,* frigates; *Activa,* schooner, Spanish Government ships, San Blas. *Discovery* and *Mercedes,* sloops, Great Britain.

1800
Betsy, American brig, Boston.

1801
Enterprise, American ship, New York.

1803
Lelia Byrd, American brig, Hamburg, Germany; *Alexander* and *O'Cain,* American ships, Boston; *Hazard,* American ship, Providence, R. I.

1804
Hazard, American ship, Providence, R. I.

1805
Lelia Byrd, American brig, Hamburg, Germany.

1806
Eclipse, American ship, Boston; *Peacock,* American brig, Boston.

1807
Activa, Spanish brig, San Blas; *Princesa,* Spanish frigate, San Blas; *Peacook,* American brig, Boston.

1809
Mercury, American ship, Boston.

1815
Forester, American brig, New York.

1817
Traveller, American schooner, Canton.

1818
Clarion, American brig, Boston.

1820
Discovery, British whaler.

1821
Eagle, American schooner, Boston.

1822
Sachem, American ship, Boston.

1823
John Begg, English brig, Liverpool; *Sachem,* American ship, Boston; *San Carlos,* Imperial Mexican man-of-war, Mexico; *Thomas Nowland,* English ship.

1824
Arab, American brig; *Mentor,* American ship, Boston; *Washington,* American schooner, Boston.

1825
Young Tartar, British coastal schooner; *Baikal,* Russian brig, Ft. Ross.

1826
Baikal, Russian brig, Ft. Ross; *Harbinger,* American brig, Honolulu; *Owhyhee,* American brig, Boston; *Rover,* California schooner, Monterey; *Waverly,* Hawaiian brig, Honolulu.

1827
Okhotsk and *Baikal,* Russian brigs, Ft. Ross; *Harbinger,* American brig, Honolulu; *Waverly,* Hawaiian brig, Honolulu; *Courier,* American ship; *Le Heros,* French ship, Le Havre.

1828
Franklin, American ship, Boston; *Courier,* American ship; *Clio* and *Andes,* American brigs; *Okhotsk* and *Baikal,* Russian brigs, Ft. Ross; *Waverly* and *Karimoku,* Hawaiian brigs, Honolulu.

1829
Brookline, American ship, Boston; *Washington,* American schooner, Boston; *Okhotsk* and *Baikal,* Russian brigs, Ft. Ross; *Vulture,* English brig, Callao.

1830
Leonor, Mexican ship, Acapulco; *Baikal,* Russian brig, Ft. Ross.

1831
Convoy, American brig, Honolulu; *Louisa,* American bark, Honolulu.

1832
Pocahontas, American ship.

1833
Volunteer, American bark, Honolulu; *Harriet Blanchard,* American schooner, Honolulu.

1834
Don Quixote, American bark, Honolulu; *Natalia,* Mexican ship, Acapulco.

1835
Pilgrim, Alert, Lagoda and *California,* American ships, Boston; *Ayacucho,* English brig, Callao; *Loriot,* American schooner, Honolulu; *La Rosa,* Italian ship, Sardinia; *Facio,* Mexican brig, Guaymas; *Catalina,* American brig under Mexican flag, La Paz.

Diary of Pedro Fages (Page 57)

Diary of the journey made by land to the Colorado River by order of Don Theodoro de Croix, caballero de Croix, field-marshal of the royal armies, and commandant-general of the Provincias Internas, etc., by the troops of His Majesty detailed for the purpose under the command of Lieutenant-Colonel Don Pedro Fages, captain of one of the free companies of volunteers of Catalonia, and his second in command, Don Pedro Tueros, captain of cavalry, commandant of the Royal Presidio of Altar.

Sunday, September 16, 1781 — After mass we set out from the presidio of Pitic, and, after travelling three leagues, stopped at Lomas Blancas, on account of the storm of rain and hail that came up in the afternoon, obliging us to sleep in that place.

From Pitic to Lomas Blancas, 3 leagues. Distance from Pitic, 3 leagues.

Monday, September 17. — We broke camp in the morning at this place, and arrived at the Hacienda del Torreón, where we slept.

To Torreón, 9 leagues. Distance from Pitic, 12 leagues.

(Original manuscript from the "Robert E. Cowan Collection.") Translated by The Academy of Pacific Coast History, University of California, Berkeley.

Notation appearing below Velasquez map: (Page 48)

The dots indicate the summit of the sierra and hill which descend to S. Sebastian. Where I indicate an A are running streams, but very short. Pasture in abundance, all over the summit.

Velasquez (signed)

This is an exact copy taken from the original

Frontispiece or title page to Fr. Font's Diary (Page 31)

DIARY
TO
MONTEREY BY WAY OF
THE COLORADO RIVER

AUTOGRAPHED AND UN-
EDITED MANUSCRIPT OF
FATHER FR. PEDRO FONT.

1777

List of padres assigned to Upper California Missions: (Page 16)

Departing by land to the Missions of San Diego and Monterey:

Rev. Fr. President Fray Francisco Palou
Rev. Fr. Fray Juan Prestamero
Rev. Fr. Fray Josef Murguía
Rev. Fr. Fray Pedro Cambon
Rev. Fr. Fray Fermín Lasuen
Fev. Fr. Fray Juan Fíguer
Rev. Fr. Fray Ramon Usson . . . left ahead
Rev. Fr. Fray Vicente Fuster . . . left ahead

Remaining to follow by land to their destination:

Rev. Fr. Fray Miguel de la Campa
Rev. Fr. Fray Miguel Sanchez

At Presidio of Loreto, June 19, 1773 —
(signed) Don Felipe Barri

List of leatherjacket soldiers stationed at the ports of San Diego and Monterey: (Page 20)

AT SAN CARLOS OF MONTEREY

Corporal Mariano Carrillo
Jph. Maria Congora
Anastasio Xavier Berdurco
Alexandro de Soto
Carlos Ruvio . . . Married
Antonio Cota
Francisco Xavier Aguilar . . . Married

AT THE PORT OF SAN DIEGO

1	Capt. Don Fernando de Rivera y Moncada . . . Married
1	Corporal Guillermo Carrillo
1	Juan Jph. Robles
1	Bernardo Ruvio . . . Married, touched with (illness)
1	Matheo Ignacio de Soto
1	Juan Maria Miranda . . . Married
1	Francisco de Abila
1	Raphael Hernandez
1	Marcelo Brabo
1	Nicolas Antonio Sambrano . . . Married
1	Jph. Ignacio Olivera
1	Mariano de la Lus Berdugo
1	Alejandro Antonio Gonzales
1	Juan de Osuna . . . Married, remained with temperature
1	Sebastian Albitre
1	Andres Cota . . . Married
1	Jph. Joachin Espinosa . . . Married
1	Augustin Canelo
18	Total

Estimated payroll of San Diego Presidio: (Page 127)

ROYAL PRESIDIO OF SAN DIEGO

PROJECTION OF THE PAYROLL WHICH WILL BE OWED THIS COMPANY NEXT YEAR, 1800:

		PESOS RS.
One Lieutenant	....	550. 0
One Ensign *(Alférez)*	....	400. 0
One Sergeant	....	262. 4
Five Corporals @ 225 ps. each	......	1,125. 0
Fifty-one soldiers @ 217 ps. 4 rs. each.		11,092. 4
The 10 peso-gratuity for simple-office. .		510. 0
COMPANY TOTAL		13,940. 0

INVALIDS

One Ensign	200. 0	
Four Sergeants, with 90 rs. monthly	540. 0	
Two Corporals and 5 soldiers @ 96 ps. per year	672. 0	1,472. 0
One retired Carpenter	60. 0	

DISCOUNTS

For the Invalids' Fund	410. 0	
For the Military Loan Fund .	27. 2	437. 2

NET CREDIT 14,974. 6

Note: The positions of professional carpenter and blacksmith are vacant at 180 pesos each.
San Diego, Feb. 23, 1799
(signed) MANUEL RODRIGUEZ

Frontispiece to Duhaut-Cilly's narrative "Voyage Around the World..." (Page 137)

VOYAGE

AROUND THE WORLD

PRINCIPALLY

To California and the Sandwich Islands, During the Years, 1826, 1827, 1828, and 1829:

By A. DUHAUT-CILLY,

Captain of the Long-Course, Chevalier of the Legion of Honor, Member of the Paris Academy of Industrial Manufacture, Agricultural and Commercial

Illi robur et aes triplex

HORACE

VOLUME ONE

PARIS,
1834.

Invoice for supplies used in the repairs to the Esplanade of Fort Guijarros by order of the Commandant of this Presidio, Don Jph. Raymundo Carrillo (Page 83)

Pesos Rs.

In the first place, the item of 24 pesos which was entered on invoice dated Feb. 24 of this year, of the Treasurer's Office of San Blas, covering 90 *(tt)* of nails which were used on the above mentioned esplanade, were prepaid by the ships of that stopping place 24. 0. 0

For 18 pesos 3 rs. paid to the carpenter of the same vessels, Pablo Bejar, in payment of his invoice No. 1, covering the days he worked on the esplanade 18. 3. 0
To satisfy Salvador Bejar in connection with the same thing in his line, per his invoice No. 2 .... 36. 0. 0

For payment made to the immediate Mission of San Diego, covering 24 days in which one of its Indians worked, at 2 rs. per day, as substantiated on Mission Administrator's invoice No. 3 .... 6. 0. 0

84. 3. 0

Which amount of eighty-four pesos three reals must be credited by the Finance Dept. to this office.
San Diego, Dec. 31, 1808
(signed) José de la Guerra

The following is a translation of the first page of Jayme's letter to Serra in connection with the moving of the mission: (Page 25)

"Praised be Jesus, Mary and Joseph
   Rev. Fr. President Junípero Serra

"May the grace of the Holy Spirit be with Your Reverence and with me. Amen.

"On the 2nd of this month, letter arrived from Monterey in which we are advised of the happy arrival of *El Príncipe*; things appear to have adjusted themselves well. The Indians here, as more come, become humbler and the gentiles show greater desire to be baptized. In days passed all the boys from the corner rancheria came to learn the doctrine and be baptized, but since we were unable to give them *azote* each time they came because of the scarcity we have of corn (and if the boat delays in arriving, there will hardly be any left for the Indians of California) they stopped coming. If we are able to harvest some of the wheat we planted, then we may be able to baptize them. We planted here about five *fanegas* of wheat, it sprouted and kept in good shape until the month of January, but later because of the lack of water, most of it dried up; it rained in March on two occasions, and it seemed to have recovered, and now it appears..."

List of soldiers stationed at Fort Guijarros (Page 181)

ARTILLERY CORPS
DETACHMENT OF THE
SAN DIEGO PRESIDIO

Exact list of the review passed by me, Lt. Don José María Estudillo, Commandant of this Presidio, of the Veteran Artillerymen and Militiamen who are of the Fort of Point Guijarros garrison, of this Port, as of today, Jan. 1, 18—:

VETERAN ARTILLERYMEN

2nd Corporal	Jose Meneses——————P	(present)
	Juan Mariner——————A	(absent)
Artillerymen with permit for —		At the San Luis Mission
Ditto with 6	Aniceto Zavaleta————P	of the Battery
	Jose Aguilar——————P	
(Undated)	Ramon Espindola———P	of ditto
	Manuel Candia————P	
	Jose Camarillo—————A	Ill in San Gabriel Mission

MILITIAMEN

2nd Corporal	Bartolo Tapia—————P	of the Guard
ditto	Salvador Besco————P	
Artillerymen	Teodoro Silbas————P	Ill
	Jose Berdujo—————A	At San Gabriel
	Juan Peralta—————A	ditto
	Justo Morillo—————A	ditto
	Antonio Maria Nieto——————A	ditto
	Yrineo Perez—————P	
	Luis Rosas——————P	
	Rafael Cañedo————P	of the Battery
	Domingo Barreras———	
	Silvestre Cañedo———P	
	Juan Albirre—————P	
	Juan Ontiveros————P	
	Jose Bermudez————A	At San Gabriel
	Guadalupe Careaga——P	

TOTAL SUMMARY

2nd Corporals	P.	3
Artillerymen	P.	13
ditto	A.	7
Total		23

This is in conformance with review passed by me as of this date to which I certify.

First page of George Vancouver's letter to Viceroy Revilla Gigedo from his ship "Discovery" dated Monterey, Jan. 13, 1793. (Page 82)

My Lord,

Being on the eve of taking my departure from this country under the government of your excellency, I should be guilty of a point of the highest ingratitude were I to omit returning my most sincere and grateful thanks for the refreshments we have received, and the civil and hospitable reception we have experienced; yet, however well inclined we have found the whole of His Catholic Majesty's subjects to relieve our wants and add all in their power to our happiness, I cannot avoid attributing that conduct in a great measure to the advice, direction, and example, of my much esteemed and brotherly friend Sr. Quadra, whose unremitting attention to our welfare, as likewise that of the service of the King my master entrusted to my charge, has stamped such an impression of . . .

From R. H. Dana's ship's log — Journal of a voyage from Boston to the coast of California. (Page 210)

Thursday, Aug. 14th, 1834. Went on board brig *"Pilgrim"* lying at central Wharf. Towards night, being nearly ready for sea, the vessel hauled out into the stream, & came to anchor.

Friday, Aug. 15th — 34. Took on board gunpowder, had a fine breeze but did not set sail.

Saturday, Aug. 16th — 34. At 10. A.M. Wind E.N.E. took a pilot on board, weighed anchor, & set sail; but the wind coming round dead East, came to anchor in the Roads. At 10. P.M. a light breeze springing up from the Southward & Westward, got under weigh, & stood out to sea.

Sunday, Aug. 17th — 34. Here out of sight of the land. At night all hands called aft, & the sea watch set. The Crew consists of Fr. A. Thompson, Captain; Andrew B. Amerzene, chief mate; Geo. Forster, 2nd Mate; 5 able seamen, 4 greenhands, Steward, Cook, & Carpenter. This vessel is about two hundred tons burthen & owned by Messrs. Bryant, Sturgis & Co., Boston.

Tuesday, Aug. 19. Came into the Gulf Stream. In the evening wind, rain, and a heavy sea. Double reefed the topsails.

Wednesday, Aug. 20. Fine weather returned with the morning. About two o'clock P.M. two sails hove in sight; they passed to leeward, out of . . .

Log from Journal On The Coast of California, by Alfred Robinson, on ship Brookline — *Year 1829. (Page 192)*

. . . made the Islands of St. Clements. Set the main top G Sail — At 2 AM St. Clements bore N.E. by E by compass. At meridian it bore the S.E. point NW/N distance 12 or 14 miles.
Lat. Obsn. 32.41. north

March 25th, Wednesday — Commenced with light airs and pleasant weather. Midnight modirate the Islands in Sight — At meridian the Coronados bore S.E. by S. per compass — Point Loma East by N per compass.
Lat. Obsn. 32.40. north

Thursday, 26th — Commenced with good Breezes and Cloudy. At 2 PM. hove too off Point Loma (St. Diego). Mr. Gale went up in the boat to the Precidio. Directly wore Ship and stood out for Sea — during the night we lay off, on towards the sand — Meridian Point Loma bore N. per compass. At 1 P.M. the boat returned with orders from Mr. Gale to Capt. Locke for to run the Ship into proper anchorage and then to wait further orders.

Therefore every thing was prepared — the cables were ranged the deck — the decks clearid and ship directid for the harbour — at 2 P.M. came to anchor in 3½ fathoms — during the night came in and anchored close along side the Brig *Maria Esther* Capt. A. Holmes.

Friday, 27th — At 10 AM with the directions of Mr. Gale the Ship proceeded for the usual place of anchorage above the Fort — to be as handy as possible for discharging cargo and came too in 9½ Fathoms. Hoisted out the Launch clearid the decks and landed all our Spars.

Saturday until Sunday, April 26 — The carpenter employed erecting a house for the acomodation of Hides & c — the crew discharging lumber & c — Employed settling with the Government for duties — April the 2nd, we were visited by the Rev. Padre Antonio (Peyri) of the Mission of St. Luis Rey — Fired a Salute of Guns and hoisted the colours. At dinner we were accompanied by Mr. Vermond owner of the *Maria Esther* and Mr. Anderson of the Ship *Thomas Nowlan* (trading on the coast) with Captains Holmes & Barry & several others. The following day made shift to trade with the Padre Antonio to the amt of about $4,000.

Aller, Paul and Doris
Build Your Own Adobe (Stanford University Press, 1946).

Atherton, Lucien C.
The Early History of the San Diego Presidial District, 1542-1782 (Master's thesis, Graduate Division, University of California).

Bancroft, Hubert Howe
History of California, Vols. I, II and III (San Francisco, The History Company, Publishers, 1886).

Bandini, José
A Description of California in 1828 trans. by Doris Marion Wright (Berkeley, Friends of the Bancroft Library, University of California, 1951).

Bandini, Juan
History of Upper California, manuscript (The Bancroft Library, University of California).

Bartlett, John Russell
Personal Narrative of Explorations and Incidents in California During the Years 1850-1853 (New York, D. Appleton & Company, 1854).

Beechey, Frederick William
Narrative of A Voyage to the Pacific and Bering Strait in the Years 1825-1828 (London, Henry Colburn and Richard Bentley, 1831).

Belcher, Edward
Narrative of A Voyage Round the World Performed in Her Majesty's Ship Sulphur, During the Years 1836-1842 (London, Henry Colburn, 1843).

Bolton, Herbert Eugene, ed.
Anza's California Expeditions Vols. II-V (University of California Press, 1930).
Spanish Explorations in the Southwest, 1542-1706 (New York, Barnes and Noble, 1959).

Bolton, Herbert Eugene, and
Marshall, Thomas Maitland
The Colonization of North America, 1492-1783 (New York, The Macmillan Company, 1920).

Carter, Charles Franklin, trans.
Duhaut-Cilly's Account of California in the Years 1827-1828 in *California Historical Society Quarterly,* Vol. VIII No. 2 (1929) 130-166; No. 3 (1929) 214-250; No. 4; (1929) 306-336.

Chapman, Charles E.
A History of California: The Spanish Period (New York, The Macmillan Company, 1921).

Cleland, Robert Glass
California Pageant: The Story of Four Centuries (New York, Alfred A. Knopf, 1955).
From Wilderness to Empire: A History of California, 1542-1900 (New York, Alfred A. Knopf, 1944).

Cleveland, Horace William Shaler
Journal and Records of the Late Richard J. Cleveland (New York, Harper Brothers, 1886).

Cleveland, Richard J.
Narrative of Voyages and Commercial Enterprises (Cambridge, 1842; reprinted in Sacramento Union, March 4, 1861).

Clyman, James
James Clyman — Frontiersman: The Adventures of a Trapper, 1792-1881 ed. by Charles A. Camp (Portland, Champoeg Press, 1960).

Corney, Peter
Voyages in the Northern Pacific (Honolulu, Thos. G. Thrum, 1896).

Cowan, Robert Ernest
Bibliography of the History of California and the Pacific West, 1510-1930 3 vols, (San Francisco, The Book Club of America, 1914).

Cunningham, William H.
Log of the Courier (1826-1827-1828) Early California Travel Series, Vol. 44 (Los Angeles, Glen Dawson, 1958).

Cutter, Donald C.
Malaspina in California (San Francisco, John Howell-Books, 1960).

Dana, Richard Henry, Jr.
Two Years Before the Mast (New York, Harper & Brothers, 1869).
An Autobiographical Sketch ed. by Robert F. Metzdorf (Hamden, Connecticut, The Shoe String Press, 1949).

Dakin, Susanna Bryant
The Lives of William Hartnell (Stanford University Press, 1949).

Daniel, Hawthorne
Ships of the Seven Seas (New York, Dodd, Mead and Company, 1930).

Davidson, Winifred
Where California Began (San Diego, McIntyre Publishing Company, 1929).

Davis, William Heath
Seventy-five Years in California — A History of Events and Life in California: Personal, Political and Military. (San Francisco, John Howell, 1929).

DeVoto, Bernard
Course of Empire (Boston, Houghton Mifflin Company, 1952).
The Year of Decision 1846 (Boston, Little, Brown & Company, 1943).

Dwinelle, John W.
The Colonial History of the City of San Francisco (San Francisco, Towne & Bacon, 1866).

Eastwood, Alice
Archibald Menzies' California Journal in *California Historical Society Quarterly* Vol. II No. 4 (1924) 267-340.

Engelhardt, Fr. Zephyrin, O.F.M.
Missions and Missionaries of California Vols. I and II, 2nd edit. (Santa Barbara Mission, 1929 and 1930 respectively). Vols. III and IV (San Francisco, The James H. Barry Company, 1913 and 1915 respectively).
San Diego Mission (San Francisco, The James H. Barry Company, 1920).
San Luis Rey Mission (San Francisco, The James H. Barry Company, 1921).

Evarts, Hal G.
Jedediah Smith — Trail Blazer of the West (New York, G. P. Putnam's Sons, 1958).

Forbes, Alexander
California: A History of Upper and Lower California (London, Smith Elder & Company, 1839).

Geiger, Maynard J., O.F.M.
The Life and Times of Fray Junípero Serra or The Man Who Never Turned Back, 1713-1784 2 vols. (Washington, D.C., Academy of American Franciscan History, 1959).
Palóu's Life of Fray Junípero Serra (Washington, D.C., Academy of American Franciscan History, 1955).

Gerhard, Peter and Bulick, Howard E.
Lower California Guidebook (Glendale, California, The Arthur Clark Company, 1958).

Gleason, Duncan
Islands and Ports of California (New York, The Devin-Adair Company, 1958).

Green, F. E.
San Diego Old Mission Dam and Irrigation System (San Diego Public Library, 1933).

Guillén y Tato, José Fernando de
Publicaciones del Museo Naval (Madrid, Naval Museum, 1932).

Halleck, Henry W.
Halleck's Report — Executive Document No. 17 (Thirty-First Congress, House of Representatives, Washington, 1850).

Hardy, R. W. H.
Travels in the Interior of Mexico in 1825, 1826, 1827 and 1828 (London, for London Fishery Association, 1829).

Haring, C. H.
The Spanish Empire in America (New York, Oxford University Press, 1947).

Harrington, M. R.
How to Build a California Adobe (Los Angeles, The Ward Ritchie Press and The Southwestern Museum, 1948).

Hayes, Benjamin
Emigrant Notes and Scrapbooks (Bancroft Library, University of California).

Heilbron, Carl H.
History of San Diego County (San Diego Press Club, 1936).

Herring, Hubert
History of Latin America From the Beginnings to the Present (New York, Alfred A. Knopf, 1955).

Hill, Joseph J.
History of Warner's Ranch and Its Environs (Los Angeles, privately printed, 1927).

Hittell, Theodore Henry
History of California Vols. I and II (San Francisco, Pacific Press Publishing House and Occidental Publishing Co., 1885).

Holmes, Brig. Gen. Maurice G., USMC, ret.
Spanish Nautical Explorations Along the Coast of the Californias (Thesis for Ph. D., University of Southern California, 1959).

Jackson, Helen Hunt
Glimpses of California and the Missions (Boston, Little Brown & Company, 1907).

Jaeger, Edmund
North American Deserts (Stanford University Press, 1957).

James, George Wharton
In and Out of the Old Missions of California (New York, Grosset & Dunlap, 1927).

King, Kenneth M.
Missions to Paradise: The Story of Junípero Serra and the Missions of California (London, Burns and Oates, 1956).

Kroeber, A. L.
Handbook of the Indians of California (Berkeley, California Book Company Ltd., 1953).

La Pérouse, Jean Francois Galaup de
A Voyage Round the World Performed in the Years 1785-1788 by the Boussole and Astrolabe (London, A. Hamilton for G. G. and J. Robinson, 1798).

Madariaga, Salvador de
The Fall of the Spanish American Empire (New York, The Macmillan Company, 1948).
The Rise of the Spanish American Empire (New York, The Macmillan Company, 1949).

Martin, Douglas D.
Yuma Crossing (Albuquerque, University of New Mexico Press, 1954).

Martínez, Pablo L.
A History of Lower California trans. by Ethel Duffy Turner (Mexico D. F., Editorial Baja California, 1960).

McCracken, Harold
Hunters of the Stormy Sea (New York, Doubleday & Company, 1957).

McKittrick, Myrtle M.
Vallejo, Son of California (Portland, Binfords & Mort, 1944).

Meigs, Peverill III
The Dominican Mission Frontier of Lower California (University of California Press, 1935).

Mofras, Eugene Duflot de
Travels on the Pacific Coast ed. and trans. by Marguerite Eyer Wilbur (Santa Ana, California, 1937).

Morison, Samuel Eliot
The Maritime History of Massachusetts (Boston, Houghton Mifflin Company, 1921, 1941).

Morrell, Benjamin
A Narrative of Four Voyages to the South Sea, 1822-1831 (The Bancroft Library, University of California).

Nasatir, Abraham P.
French Activities in California (Stanford University Press, 1945).
The French Consulate in California in *California Historical Society Quarterly*, Vol. XI (1932) 202-203.

Ogden, Adele
The California Sea Otter Trade 1784-1848 (University of California Press, 1941).
Business Letters of Alfred Robinson in *California Historical Society Quarterly* Vol. XXIII No. 4 (1944) 301-334.

Alfred Robinson, New England Merchant in Mexican California in *California Historical Society Quarterly* Vol. XXIII, No. 3 (1944) 193-202.
Hides and Tallow in *California Historical Society Quarterly* Vol. VI (1927) 254-264.
Boston Hide Droghers Along California Shores in *California Historical Society Quarterly* Vol. VIII No. 4 (1929) 289-305.

Older, Mrs. Fremont
California Missions and Their Romances (New York, Tudor Publishing Company, 1945).

Palóu, Fray Francisco, O.F.M.
Historical Memoirs of New California 4 vols. ed. by Herbert Eugene Bolton (University of California Press, 1926).
Life of Fray Junípero Serra ed. by Maynard J. Geiger, O.F.M. (Washington, D.C., Academy of American Franciscan History, 1955).

Parker, Horace
Anza-Borrego Desert Guide Book (Palm Desert, California, Desert Magazine Press, 1957).

Pattie, James Ohio
The Personal Narrative of James O. Pattie of Kentucky, 1824-1830 ed. and with notes, introductions, by Reuben Gold Thwaites, LL.D. (Cleveland, The Arthur H. Clark Company, 1905).

Phillips, James Duncan
Salem and the Indies (Boston, Houghton, Mifflin Company, 1947).

Portolá, Gaspar de
Diary of Gaspar de Portolá During the California Expedition of 1769-1770, ed. by Donald Eugene Smith and Frederick J. Teggart in *Publications of the Academy of Pacific Coast History*, Vol. III (1909) 31-89.

Pourade, Richard F.
The Explorers—The History of San Diego, Commissioned by James S. Copley (San Diego, The Union-Tribune Publishing Company, 1960).

Powell, H. M. T.
Santa Fe Trail to California 1849-1852 ed. by Douglas S. Watson (San Francisco, The Book Club of California, 1931).

Priestley, Herbert Ingram, ed.
The Colorado River Campaign 1781-1782, Diary of Pedro Fages in *Academy of Pacific Coast History* Vol. 3, No. 2 (University of California, 1913).

Reid, Joseph L.: Gunnar I. Roden
and John G. Wyllie
Studies of the California Current System (La Jolla, Scripps Institution of Oceanography, University of California, New Series, No. 998, 29-57).

Rensch, Hero Eugene
   Fages' Crossing of the Cuyamacas in *California Historical Society Quarterly* Vol. XXXIV, No. 3 (1955) 193-208.
   Cullamác, Alias El Capitán Grande in *San Diego Historical Society Quarterly,* Vol. II, No. 2 (1956).

Rensch, Eugene and
Ethel Grace
   Historic Spots in California: The Southern Counties (Stanford University Press, 1932).

Roberts, Elizabeth E.
   The Spanish Missions at Yuma, 1779-1781 (University of California, 1920).

Robinson, Alfred
   Life in California (New York, Wiley & Putnam, 1846).

Roden, Gunnar I.
   Oceanographic and Meteorological Aspects of the Gulf of California in *Pacific Science,* Vol. XII (1958) 21-45.

Rush, Philip S.
   History of the Californias (San Diego, Philip S. Rush, 1958).

Schurz, William Lytle
   The Manila Galleon (New York, E. P. Dutton and Company, 1959).

Serra, Junípero, O.F.M.
   Writings of Junípero Serra ed. by Antonine Tibesar, O.F.M. Vol. I (Washington, D.C., Academy of American Franciscan History, 1955).

Shaler, William
   Journal of A Voyage Between China and the Northwestern Coast of America Made in 1804 (Claremont, California, Saunders Studio Press, 1935).

Smythe, William E.
   History of San Diego, 1542-1908 (San Diego, The History Company, 1908).

Stephens, H. Morse and
Herbert E. Bolton, eds.
   The Pacific Ocean in History (New York, The Macmillan Company, 1917).

Sullivan, Maurice S.
   Travels of Jedediah S. Smith (Santa Ana, Fine Arts Press, 1934).

Vallejo, Mariano G.
   History of California, manuscript (The Bancroft Library, University of California).

Velásquez, Josef
   Diary of Journey Made by Pedro Fages from San Diego to the Colorado River and Return, 1785, manuscript (The Bancroft Library, University of California).

Walker, Franklin
   Literary History of Southern California (Berkeley and Los Angeles, University of California Press, 1950).

Webb, Edith Buckland
   Indian Life at the Old Missions (Los Angeles, Warren F. Lewis, 1952).

Wheat, Carl
   Mapping of the Transmississippi West, 1540-1861 Vol. I (San Francisco, Institute of Historical Cartography, 1957).

Wilbur, Marguerite Eyer, ed.
   Vancouver in California, 1792-1794 (Los Angeles, Glen Dawson, 1954).

Wolf, Eric R.
   Sons of the Shaking Earth (Chicago, University of Chicago Press, 1959).

Color photograph from miniature of Don Santiago Argüello. Paintings of *San Carlos* Leaving La Paz and Mounted Soldier of Spain by Walter Francis. Photographs of title pages of Pedro Fages' *Diary of Expedition to the Colorado River,* Jose Bandini's *Description of California in 1828.* Map from Josef Velásquez Diary of Fages Journey, 1783. Photographs of San Carlos Mission, and Californian Mode of Catching Cattle sketched by Capt. Smyth. Photographs of Alfred Robinson, Benjamin Morrell and Henry Delano Fitch. Letter from George Vancouver to Viceroy Revilla Gigedo. Reproductions of Spanish and Mexican documents. The Bancroft Library, University of California, Berkeley.

Photograph of José Bandini, the Luther A. Ingersoll Collection. Los Angeles Public Library.

Painting of the Brig *Pilgrim.* The Santa Barbara Historical Society, Santa Barbara.

Jedediah Smith's Bible Birth Record. Security First National Bank, Los Angeles.

Letter from Fr. Jayme to Fr. Serra, dated Apr. 3, 1773. The Academy of American Franciscan History, Washington, D.C.

French maps of San Diego and San Blas Bays. Louis H. Hunte, RAdm. USN (Ret.), La Jolla.

Photographs of ship *Alexander;* Canton Factories Around 1800; View of the Island of Woahoo; Crowninshield's Wharf, Salem. Silhouettes of sailing ships. The Peabody Museum, Salem, Mass.

Painting of Ruins of San Diego Presidio, 1874, by Vischer. Originally of the Pierce Collection.

Drawing of View of Boston from the South Boston Bridge by Jacques Milbert The New York Historical Society, New York.

Church interior at Carmel Mission, photographed by Lewis Josselyn.

Drawing of Rodeo at San Gabriel Mission, by E. Wyttenbach. California State Library, Sacramento.

Photograph of San Fernando Church. Rómulo O'Farrill, of *Novedades,* Mexico.

Painting of Mission San Gabriel Arcángel. M. H. De Young Memorial Museum, San Francisco.

Photographs of San Blas. Roy Jasper, San Diego.

Drawing of Spanish Colonial Ball, by William H. Meyers, from Meyers' Journals. The New York Public Library, New York.

Drawings of Soldier of Monterey, Wife of Soldier of Monterey; California Method of Fighting Indians, from *Malaspina in California,* by Donald C. Cutter. Howell Books, San Francisco.

Pantoja's Map of the Port of San Diego; Dunn's map of North America, 1789; Nolin's Mappe Monde (World Map), 1779. Maps from George Vancouver's *Voyage to North Pacific:* Entrance to the Port of San Diego, Port of San Diego, and San Diego and the Northern Coast of Baja California. Hunting Grizzly Bears and Sailors' Romances, and drawings of Rendering Tallow and Drying Hides, by William R. Hutton. H. M. T. Powell Sketch of San Diego Mission 1849. The Huntington Library, San Marino, Calif.

Photographs of title and first page of Pedro Font's Diary. John Carter Brown Library, Brown University, Rhode Island.

Photographs of ship *Brookline,* page from Alfred Robinson's *Journal on the Coast of California, 1829;* title page and sketch of San Luis Rey Mission, sketches of Monterey, from Duhaut-Cilly's *Account of California.* Fort Ross. California Historical Society, San Francisco.

Engravings of San Diego and Colorado River Indians by Arthur Schott, from *Report on the United States and Mexican Boundary Survey,* Vol. I, by William H. Emory.

Etching of Richard Henry Dana, Jr., from a daguerreotype by Alonzo Schoff.

Photograph of model of the *Pilgrim.* The Maritime Museum of San Francisco.

Logs from Richard Henry Dana's Journal of *A Voyage from Boston to the Coast of California.* Massachusetts Historical Society, Boston.

Photograph of statue of Father Francisco Garcés. Yuma Chamber of Commerce.

Sketch of Presidio of Monterey. Naval Museum, Madrid, Spain.

Photographs of San Diego Mission and Mission Bells; Casa de Estudillo and Casa de Bandini; Santa Ysabel Mission Church and Bells, 1887; Don Juan Bandini and Pío Pico; San Luis Rey Mission; San Diego Padre Dam and Aqueduct. Photograph of Presidio Record. Historical Collection, Union Title Insurance Co., San Diego.

Drawings of Messrs. Pattie and Slover Rescued from Famish and Burial of Sylvester Pattie at Presidio, from *Pattie's Personal Narrative*.

Photograph of Old Mission at Loreto. Rivera Cambas' *Mexico Pintoresco*.

Map of Californias: Old and New, from Palou's *Historical Memoirs of New California*.

Photograph of Palacio Nacional, Mexico, in the 18th Century. La Ilustración Mexicana, Mexico.

Color photograph of San Luis Rey Church interior by Ed Neil.

Color photograph of San Miguel Mission by Phil McMahan.

The paintings commissioned for this book were done by D. Wayne Millsap, illustrator for Image, the Art Division of Frye & Smith, Ltd. The paintings are: Martyrdom of Fr. Luis Jayme, page 22; Fort Fires on the Lelia Byrd, page 98; San Diego Mission, Golden Age, page 112; Presidio as it looked in 1823, page 128; The Fitch-Carrillo Elopement, page 188.

Typesetting of the Historical Statistics (pages 238-254) by John F. Mawson Company, San Diego.

PERMISSION CREDITS

Quotations from Zephyrin Engelhardt, OFM. From MISSIONS AND MISSIONARIES OF CALIFORNIA and SAN DIEGO MISSION. Used by permission of the publisher, Academy of American Franciscan History.

Quotations from Edith Buckland Webb. From INDIAN LIFE AT THE OLD MISSIONS. Used by permission of the publisher, Warren F. Lewis.

Quotations from Antonine Tibesar, OFM. From WRITINGS OF JUNIPERO SERRA. Used by permission of the publisher, Academy of American Franciscan History.

Quotations from José Bandini. From A DESCRIPTION OF CALIFORNIA IN 1828, translated by Doris Marion Wright. Used by permission of Friends of the Bancroft Library, University of California.

Excerpts from Duhaut-Cilly's account of California; excerpts from Archibald Menzies' California journal; excerpts re Alfred Robinson and hides and tallow by Adele Ogden; excerpts re Fages and the Cuyamacs by Hero Eugene Rensch. Used by permission of the publisher, the California Historical Society.

Excerpts re San Diego. From MALASPINA IN CALIFORNIA by Donald C. Cutter. Used by permission of the publisher, Warren R. Howell.

Quotations from Maynard J. Geiger, OFM. From THE LIFE AND TIMES OF JUNIPERO SERRA and PALOU'S LIFE OF FRAY JUNIPERO SERRA. Used by permission of the author and published by Academy of American Franciscan History.

Quotations from Pablo L. Martínez. From A HISTORY OF LOWER CALIFORNIA, translated by Ethel Duffy Turner. Used by permission of the author and published by Editorial Baja California, Mexico.

Excerpts from diaries of Pedro Fages and Gaspar de Portolá. Published by the Academy of Pacific Coast History. Used by permission of The Bancroft Library, University of California.

Excerpts from Josef Velásquez. From DIARY OF JOURNEY MADE BY PEDRO FAGES FROM SAN DIEGO TO THE COLORADO RIVER AND RETURN. Used by permission of The Bancroft Library, University of California.

This second volume of the History of San Diego was designed by Rene Sheret, Art Director of Image, the Art Division of Frye & Smith. Lithography by Frye & Smith, Ltd., on Hamilton Louvain 80 pound text. Typography by Central Typesetting, Inc. using American Typefounders' and Intertype's Century Schoolbook, and binding by Cardoza Bookbinding Company.